WELSH RUGBY: THE CROWNING YEARS 1968–80

Clem Thomas
and Geoffrey Nicholson

WELSH RUGBY:
THE CROWNING YEARS
1968–80

COLLINS
St James's Place, London
1980

William Collins Sons and Co Ltd
London · Glasgow · Sydney · Auckland
Toronto · Johannesburg

We gratefully acknowledge the help of Paul Gunnion when this book was at its earliest stages.

First published 1980

ISBN 0 00 211641 3

Set in 11 pt Baskerville
Made and Printed in Great Britain by
Wm Collins Sons & Co Ltd, Glasgow

Contents

Illustrations

Introduction

This book celebrates the most successful period in Welsh rugby, the twelve years from 1968 to the present day which happily brought up the century for the Welsh Rugby Union. It's an awesome thought that there are men of thirty who began watching Wales at Cardiff Arms Park in their late teens *and have never seen their country beaten in an international championship match.* Wales have certainly not been invincible during this time, but ever since the winter of 1968, when France won 14-9 at Cardiff, they have lost championship games only (and pretty infrequently) away from home and lost at their national stadium only to the All Blacks of New Zealand.

What makes this run of success all the more remarkable is that the championship is the most open of international competitions. During its annual round of ten matches, no victory can ever be taken for granted, no opponent can ever be written off. In their time all five nations involved have made the grand slam, and while it's true that over the past 25 years Ireland have only once taken the title and Scotland only once shared it, both have jealously preserved their casting vote over the fate of the other three countries. Regularly favourite sons of England, France and Wales have arrived at Murrayfield and Lansdowne Road full of brave ideas only to get the thumbs-down. Uncertainty is the beauty of the tournament. Whatever has happened the previous season, when January comes round again everyone starts equal.

Yet from time to time there are spells when one nation appears – especially in retrospect – to have become more equal than the others, and Wales first entered one of these periods at the turn of the century. They took over as the innovators, developing a game in which the forwards stuck to hard scrummaging and left the backs to move with a freedom and ingenuity never seen before on the rugby field. Whether or not events created the men, or men the events, the Welsh discovered a new pantheon of heroes in Rhys Gabe, Billy Trew, Dick Jones, Dicky Owen and the Bancroft brothers. And helped by the fact that England, the traditional strong men of the championship, were still weakened by the split between Union and League, in the twelve years up to 1911 Wales won six championship titles (sharing another with Scotland), six triple crowns and three grand slams.

As it receded in time this period came to be known as the Golden Era, but the memory of it had to nourish Welsh self-esteem for many decades. Before World War I England had opened their Twickenham stadium and started to rebuild their game on the principles of a brilliant generation of Harlequins, among them Adrian Stoop, Poulton-Palmer and Wavell-Wakefield. Then came the Depression, which hit Wales far harder than the other home countries who tended to draw their rugby players from the protected middle class. It became an aching temptation for talented Welshmen to accept a professional contract with the Rugby League. Wales continued to enjoy occasional good years, but thirty-nine seasons passed before they won another triple crown.

So when Wales took the title in 1969 they were just the first among equals once again. There was nothing so auspicious about the event as to suggest that they were on the brink of a second Golden Era. Yet within 11 seasons they had precisely equalled the record of the first: six championships and another shared, six triple crowns and three grand slams. And in at least two respects this was an even greater achievement. They had won four triple crowns in succession, which was unprecedented. And they had carried off their grand slams against French sides of greater substance than their forerunners had ever known. France only entered the championship, making it a five nations' tournament, in 1908. And at that time they were so inexperienced that when Wales won triple crowns in that year, in 1909 and 1911 it was little more than a formality to add grand slam to their honours. But the French teams of the seventies were another matter; throughout the whole of this period they were Wales's closest rivals for the title.

Far more important than the figures on the page, of course, were the figures on the field, and it is around latter-day folk heroes like Gareth Edwards, Barry John, Phil Bennett, J. P. R. Williams, Gerald Davies, Mervyn Davies and the Pontypool front row that our narrative revolves. But it isn't our business just to praise famous men; we hope to explain why they became famous. And an abundance of natural talent is not the only answer.

We believe, for instance, that these players owed more than perhaps they knew to the democratic pressure from the clubs which led to the national coaching scheme and the squad training system. The one raised and unified the standard of Welsh club rugby; the other shaped a group of gifted individuals into a national side with a coherent aim and the single-minded purpose to achieve it. Indeed we would argue that the work of Ray Williams, the national coaching organizer, behind the scenes made as important a contribution to success as the play of the stars who were attracting applause at the centre of the scene.

Not that it was all roses anyway. Although for most of this period Wales could claim to be the champions of Europe, they consistently failed to get the better of the South Africans, New Zealanders and, away from home, the Australians. In fact despite the vital part played by the Welsh in the British Lions' triumphs in New Zealand in 1971 and – on a slightly diminished scale – in South Africa three years later, their own national tours abroad have generally been abysmal disasters. We will try to account for this, and also to answer some of the other questions raised by the critics during the seventies. Is the hostility towards Wales in the other home countries as real as it is apparent? Are the Welsh sides and their supporters obsessed with the need for success? Are they bad losers and, perhaps worse, ungracious winners? Have the leading players a right to complain about the pressures put upon them? And why did growing indiscipline lead to the outbreak of violence at Twickenham in 1980?

This has been an enormously stimulating twelve years, and the Welsh have amply repaid their winnings with the entertainment, the excitement and the creative ideas they have contributed to the game. They have had an influence far beyond their borders. Would the other home countries have devised the squad system if Wales hadn't taken the lead? And would England now be planning to introduce leagues for their leading clubs if Wales had not shown that success in the championship is bred by intense club competition on all the other Saturdays of the season?

Finally, a word to explain how we collaborated on this book. Clem Thomas wrote the first half, the sections dealing with the broader themes; Geoffrey Nicholson chronicled the period season-by-season in the second. But of course after checking, discussing and criticizing each other's contributions we take joint responsibility for the whole.

Part One

I

Obsessed with Success?

If you are a Welshman, once you cross the Severn Bridge and head west from Offa's Dyke you are in the Holy Land of rugby. The game was carried there by young missionaries coming home from the grand universities of England and the great teaching hospitals of London. Its arrival coincided with the time when the rural population began to congregate at the summons of the coal and iron masters, in the coastal towns and valleys that were to become ravaged by industries which would brutally scar both the landscape and the populace.

Such conditions demanded a huge release from both spiritual and physical tensions, and the panaceas came in the form of evangelical and nonconformist socialism, religion and rugby. A small, historically subjected nation (but never permanently) had suddenly found eloquent ways to express its exploding restless virility, and in rugby football had found the means to establish and prove an identity. It began building a new grand dynasty which was to become more famous than that of its ancient warrior princes and which needed no political or financial investment, only a patch of level ground, inflated leather, unusual skills and a fair amount of courage.

Strangely, the immigration into the eastern and western valleys in search of work in the new industries was cosmopolitan and, if you examine the programme when valley or seaport clubs play each other often more than half the players are of largely English origin. They have surnames which sound Saxon and Norman – Cobner, Squire, Butler, Gregory, Perkins, Leleu, Alexander, Cooksley and Swain – and these are interspersed with the inevitable Irishmen like O'Sullivan,

O'Connor or Reilly. In recent Welsh teams names such as Blyth, Fenwick, Keen, Holmes, Wheel, Ringer, Martin and Squire could in no way be Welsh. This was one reason why the language almost died, but within a generation the intruders were absorbed and became Welsh by adoption and in spirit as the new communities, built on hard graft, suckled and nurtured them to become a new mongrel nation, integrated through hardship, fellowship and the new nonconformist culture.

There is, therefore, no ethnic reason why the Welsh should be better at rugby football than any of the other nations which make up the four Home Unions. The explanation is more likely to be found in the fact that, unlike the working class population of industrial England or Scotland, the Welsh working man, particularly in the smaller communities, chose to embrace rugby. Perhaps a hard life ripping out coal, or cooking steel, needed just such a hard physical game, with its strange ethics and intellectualism. Villages and towns were like separate tribes: they tended to be of different religious denominations or sects; they worked in different collieries and steelworks; and therefore the rivalry of the Eisteddfod and of industrial output was a way of life. Rugby was their means of warring with one another, and the tradition survives to this day. Welsh local derbys can still be a terrifying experience for those who do not understand the undercurrent and/or realize that there is no personal malice.

With the rise of the great industrial centres at the ports of the South Wales seaboard, Cardiff and Newport in the east, Llanelli and Swansea in the west, with Aberavon and Neath in between, soon became major clubs and they were rapidly reinforced by clubs in the new hinterland, such as Ebbw Vale, Maesteg, Pontypool and Pontypridd. Inevitably the Welsh established their major shrine in the capital city, for although St Helen's, Swansea, had its followers until the last international was played there in 1954, the great cathedral of the game became Cardiff Arms Park. I still prefer to call it that, not the National Stadium, which seems impersonal and sounds like a nationalized industry, which is almost what it is or would be if only they prevented the rich from buying all the seats.

Here in the nave the congregation produces the ultimate sound of their personal expression of nationhood, a combination of the lively fortissimo of grand opera and of the doleful hymns of Welsh Tabernacles, Ebenezers, Siloams and Gibeas. The more lachrymose hymns draw out the best descants and harmonies from what is the largest and most skilful choir of its kind in the world, so funereal at times that they have buried the expectations of many a fine foreign team before the kick-off. I remember it well, for although it is almost twenty-two years since I last appeared as a Welsh gladiator waiting to be unleashed at English, Irish, French, Scottish, Australian or New Zealand Christians, I can still recall the feeling of the hair rising at the nape of the neck, bristling like a wolf waiting to lunge at his prey, and, for the first fifteen minutes of an international, no Saxon, French or Celtic boot or bone seemed capable of penetrating a mystic armour.

With all their urge to excel at rugby, and their record of success against the rest of Europe, why have the Welsh failed so miserably against the countries of the southern hemisphere, both at home and away? Their four tours since 1964 to South Africa, Argentina, New Zealand and Australia were unmitigated disasters. Apologists say that, like some good wines, the Welsh simply do not travel because they are inclined to misery away from home. The facts are that in 1964, after sharing the championship with Scotland, Wales went to South Africa and lost the test match by the biggest margin between the two countries, of 24–3. Wales, in fact, have still to beat South Africa. In 1968 they made an unsuccessful and unhappy visit to Argentina, and the following year they were crushed in two test matches in New Zealand 19–0 and 33–12. The final straw in the disastrous Welsh crusades overseas came with the debacle in Australia in 1978 when, after winning the triple crown in three successive years and also the grand slam in 1976 and 1978, they miserably and incredibly lost the two test matches 18–8 and 19–17. Even worse, they were involved in a round of bitter acrimony with the Australian administrators and players.

Therefore Wales, so often champions of Europe in recent years, have still not proved themselves in a world context, and have never been able to style themselves world champions. Only South Africa and New Zealand can claim this distinction, as could the British Lions in 1971 and 1974.

Are the Welsh obsessed with success, and has this bred such arrogance that their supporters are only satisfied when they win by a large margin? Gareth Edwards once said, 'Losing an international when you are playing for Wales is more than just coming second in a rugby match. It is a national disaster.' There are other attitudes, and surely Gareth would have enjoyed an account, by Christopher Wordsworth in *The Observer*, of an English cup match a few years ago between London Welsh and Bristol. Having recounted a tough, hard, slogging match in mud and rain, Christopher reflected in the last paragraph not on who had won or lost, or why, but instead delightfully wrote, 'And as they trooped off the field, towards the pavilion, one felt that they had deserved their perfumed baths and fluted nymphs.'

Ray Williams, the Welsh coaching organizer appointed in 1968 after the traumas of the early and middle sixties and more responsible than anybody for laying the foundations of the superb seventies, once wrote: 'Let us remember that there is no disgrace in wanting to be successful; there is no dishonour in wanting to win. Defeat must be accepted with good grace, and victory with humility.' It is only on the latter count of humility that the Welsh rugby public can possibly be indicted. There are those unkind people who say of the Welsh that they make an enormous fuss about rugby football because it is the only thing at which they excel. This is not only unkind and unjust but inaccurate, as the nation has always made contributions of the highest quality to the public and professional life of the United Kingdom. The bar and the judiciary have always been heavily weighted with Welshmen, as have medicine and the more influential world of politics. In the field of arts Wales possesses superb classical singers in Sir

Geraint Evans, Stuart Burrows and Delme Bryn Jones. There are bright stars in theatre and films such as Richard Burton, Anthony Hopkins, Sian Phillips and the Houstons. In light entertainment there is the irrepressible Harry Secombe and the rich, more parochial talent of Max Boyce (unhappily in recent years we lost one of our greatest talents in Ryan Davies). For all their great stature I have observed many of these fine entertainers basking in the success of the Welsh rugby side and enjoying it as a personal triumph. Many have told me how they would have loved to play for Wales at Cardiff Arms Park for, being artists and performers, they recognized the great theatre of international rugby at Cardiff and this, allied perhaps to a whiff of physical danger, always presented a terrifying seduction of the senses, with which they identified only too well. Many modern players, and the public too, occasionally become enticed by the vanity of it all, and ordinary people and players become difficult and temperamental; sometimes views become irrational and all because we fell too hard for the allure of that bitch goddess – success!

It is said that the first thing a Welshman will do on meeting a stranger is to establish a relationship, however tenuous, for it is a part of his ancient and instinctive tribalism. A Welshman will always ask where you come from and what you do; and if you can discover the most distant blood relationship then you are made. But if that fails even mutual knowledge of an obscure acquaintance will do, for the Welsh, although regarding other nations as dear enemies in the rugby sense, are always the friendliest of people off the field. Any Welsh international rugby player immediately qualifies as part of the family, and so too would the likes of Billy Beaumont, Andy Irvine and Mike Gibson, for the qualification is merit or excellence. No well-established rugby star can walk in Cardiff, Swansea or Llanelli without total strangers greeting him with a knowing, 'Hello Barry, Bleddyn, Gareth or Phil'. No rugby player in Wales needs to be a Freemason when he belongs to the far greater rugby fraternity, which is a brotherhood of friendship so embracing that at times it threatens to smother you and kill you with kindness.

It has certainly been the story of my life, and I well remember as a young man when, after a holiday in Cornwall, I arrived on the pierhead at Ilfracombe to catch the paddle-steamer back to Swansea. It was pouring with rain; a friend and I took refuge in the refreshment-room and with our last half-crown quaffed a final pint. To our horror, the steamer suddenly began to move from the pierhead and, racing to the departure point, we found thirty feet of the Bristol Channel between ourselves and the rest of our party on the steamer. Ignoring the suicidal advice of our friends exhorting us to jump, which would have entailed smashing the world long-jump record, not to mention our limbs, we turned, penniless, and examined our situation. Unconcerned, we proceeded to the steamer offices and demanded help, but to no avail. We then tried the police, the local vicar and a nearby hotel, waving promissory notes, but again with no luck, for it seemed they had all been caught before. Finally, in desperation now, we turned to the local rugby pub and asked the landlord if any of the rugby club officials were present. He pointed to a gentleman in the corner, who was the secretary of the Ilfracombe Rugby Club. Inevitably he was a Welshman and, when we revealed the problem, he instantly drew out his wallet and said, 'Will a couple of fivers do?' More recently, last year I was doubling around the back of Twickenham to get to the press car park behind the east stand, only to find a one-way system operating and a barrier closing the way; but, of course, the metropolitan policeman guarding the way was from Swansea, and after a two-minute chat he moved the barrier and waved me through. All of which illustrates that being a Welsh international is not only a great ego trip and a huge satisfaction, but also an enormous advantage in making life that much more easy and worthwhile.

If there have been faults in the Welsh personality and image during these Crowning Years, surely they have been outweighed and transcended by the massive commitment and artistry of the players, by their great sense of pride and purpose, and above all by their achievements.

2

Getting the Coach on the Road

After 1911 Wales didn't win a triple crown or a grand slam until 1950. Then from 1952 they had to wait thirteen years for their next triple crown in 1965. For a nation so committed to the game this was unacceptable, and the first rumblings of discontent came in 1964 when, after sharing the championship with Scotland, Wales went on a four-match tour to South Africa. There they won two provincial games, but were annihilated in the test match 24–3. The effect was shattering. In the touring party, however, were three men who were to have a considerable influence on subsequent events: Alun Thomas, the assistant manager, Clive Rowlands, the captain, and John Dawes. There were also other forceful personalities like Dai Hayward of Cardiff, Brian Price of Newport and Alan Pask of Abertillery, who were to question the state of Welsh rugby and to add their weight with constructive suggestions for the future.

The crunch came later that summer at the annual general meeting of the Welsh Rugby Union. Mr Vernon Parfiff, who was chairman of the Welsh coaching sub-committee, presented his report which, in the opinion of representatives of the club, did not go far enough either in examining the situation or in proposing changes. Their misgivings were voiced by Mr Elvet Jones, then chairman, now president, of Llanelli RFC, a charming, popular man who had toured South Africa with the Lions in 1938, and though an uncapped player had been picked for two tests. Elvet Jones impassionedly and savagely expressed the temper of the clubs, warning the WRU that unless there was a far more radical approach the AGM would degenerate into a gathering of social not rugby clubs. 'Why,' he demanded, 'cannot Wales have a coaching supremo like Danie Craven of South Africa?' Subsequently the meeting forced the WRU general committee to carry out the task the clubs had charged them with: to examine the state of Welsh rugby and make recommendations for the future.

As a result of this pressure from the clubs, a working party was convened on 16 July 1964 with Cliff Jones as chairman. His appointment was highly significant. A celebrated outside-half of the thirties – still described as a genius by contemporaries like Wilf Wooller – Cliff Jones had gone on to spend twenty-two years on the Welsh selection committee of which he was five times chairman. Fittingly he has now been appointed president of the WRU for its centenary season.

It was of more immediate importance, however, that Cliff Jones had a long record of support for coaching. To some it may come as a surprise that there had been any coaching in Wales to support. In fact it had been started soon after the last war by a small band of dedicated people who believed implicitly in its value. In those early days the WRU gave only tacit support by setting up a coaching supervisory sub-committee run, by and large, by people from outside the Union. It had J. J. Westlake-Hall of Penarth as its chairman, and included enthusiasts like Fred Coster, Harold Phillips and Bill Heard, all of whom were highly respected referees. The operation was serviced by the Central Council of Physical Recreation, and no praise is too high for the enormous support and impact that this organization has provided for rugby football, not only in Wales, but throughout the British Isles. The committee made a strenuous attempt to spread the coaching gospel by appointing graded coaches and by breaking Wales down into areas – North Wales, the Amman Valley, Pembrokeshire and so on. From 1948 to 1967, they were magnificently served by Ted Grater, Reg Humphries and especially Cadfan Davies of the CCPR. However, they laboured in a climate of apathy and some members of the Union were even hostile to the scheme. At this point the WRU were not backing the idea of coaching, they were only playing with it. It was left to Cliff Jones to encourage the pioneers with the weight of his experience and prestige.

The new working party gave Cliff Jones the chance to advance his ideas, and he gathered a group of like-minded people around him. One of them was Alun Thomas, who had learned a great deal from his South African tour. According to his terms of reference, as assistant manager of the Welsh side he had been jointly responsible for coaching with the manager, David Phillips, and the captain, Clive Rowlands. He recognized that this dilution of authority made a nonsense of the job. Alun was obsessed not only with changing the whole Welsh approach to coaching, but also determined to create a situation in which men could be brought in from outside the Union, both as selectors and coaching administrators. Previously unless you were a member of the WRU committee you had no chance of becoming a selector. Alas, the situation is still little changed, even though the precedents have now been set and there have been a few appointments from outside.

For the working party at last brought in a refreshing injection of new blood. Young men in their prime were recruited, including ex-players who really knew their rugby: Clive Rowlands, Carwyn James, David Nash, Ieuan Evans, Alan Pask, Brian Price, Dai Hayward, Roy Bish, Geoff Whiston, David Harries, John Rees – and Derek Morgan who, oddly enough, became an England selector.

They decided to create three sub-committees, the first to be concerned with fitness, the second with the laws, the third with tactics. The first two met infrequently, but the tactics committee, under the chairmanship of Cliff Jones, went on to meet regularly. Its first vital recommendation was that clubs should accept the principle of coaching and immediately appoint suitably qualified persons to be responsible for the fitness, the training and the tactical handling of their teams. By December, 1974, eighty per cent of the clubs in the Union had appointed a coach, and a hundred and twenty representatives had attended a coaching conference. Mercifully, the clubs had taken up the challenge, which partly explains the current supremacy of Welsh club rugby in the British Isles; a supremacy reflected not only in winning statistics but, as other home union observers have remarked, by the quality, style and the techniques by which they are achieved.

Having successfully launched the first phase, the WRU then set out to create the machinery to operate its coaching scheme. They formed an advisory committee, again under the chairmanship of Cliff Jones, to review the technical details. That committee consisted of Alun Thomas, Ieuan Evans, Clive Rowlands, David Hayward, Brian Price, Ken Gwilym, Carwyn James, Roy Bish, John Robbins and Rees Stephens. According to its chairman, this was the committee which did all the work, together with that marvellous man, Cadfan Davies of the CCPR, who filled the job of Welsh coaching organizer in a purely voluntary capacity. At this point, the WRU applied for grant aid to the Labour Minister of Sport, Dennis Howell (the Government at this time was prepared to give financial assistance for coaching and developing amateur sport) and were gratified to receive a two-thirds grant towards the salary of a national coaching organizer.

The post was then advertised, and on 1 June 1967, Ray Williams, currently the Centenary Officer and secretary elect of the WRU on the imminent retirement of Mr Bill Clement, was appointed at the bargain salary of under £2,000 per annum. The other short-listed candidates for the post were Dick Palmer, now secretary of the British Olympic Association, David Nash of Ebbw Vale and Ken Jones of Aberavon.

The appointment of Ray Williams in 1967 was the best decision made by the WRU in my lifetime and, in my view, was fundamental to the ensuing success of Welsh rugby. Admittedly, he arrived at a time when the framework and the enthusiasm had already been established, but it was now apparent that there was a need for a professional with considerable ability to guide and structure the new conceptions of coaching. In Ray Williams they had found exactly the right man. His credentials for the post were impeccable. First of all, he had an immense affection and enthusiasm for rugby football. He was a past player for Northampton, London Welsh and the East Midlands and even won a final Welsh trial where, unfortunately, he was in contention with Cliff Morgan. He was a Loughborough-trained physical educationalist and, above all, he was already well versed in the field of coaching. Ironically, all his experience had been gained in England where, as the CCPR's technical representative, he was responsible for rugby in the West Midlands region. He also became involved with R. I. Scorer, president of the North Midlands RU, who was immensely keen on coaching and one of my favourite rugby men; there was never a greater enthusiast for the game and its players.

So, Ray emerged as the CCPR's rugby expert in England. He recognized the need to involve schools and he held courses for schoolmasters which eventually came under the wing of the Rugby Football Union and were directed by the legendary Bernard Gadny, one of England's greatest referees. Included on the staff of these courses were players of the calibre of Jeff Butterfield, Ian Beer, Alan Ashcroft, Frank Sykes, Bob McEwan and Hywel Griffiths. These knowledgeable people then suggested to the RFU that a full-time national coach, a coaching advisory panel, a new coaching manual and visual aids should be adopted in the cause of progress. The concept of a coaching organizer was far too radical for a relatively hide-bound English establishment. This was still a highly emotive issue although eventually J. P. Walker was appointed schools and coaching administrator. I suppose a rose by any name is just as sweet!

By now Ray was almost permanently seconded from the CCPR to the RFU, and when the Welsh Union adopted the idea of a coaching organizer, the fattest of English-grown plums was to fall into their hands. Although Ray Williams accepted a drop in salary to take the post, he had sufficient vision to see the explosive possibilities of such a job. Here was a man totally convinced of the path which rugby was bound to follow, and of the necessity for Wales to abandon the negative style which too often had caused them to come second in spite of a seemingly bottomless reservoir of rugby talent. Together with Cliff Jones and Alun Thomas, he introduced the national squad system (of which more later) and produced that remarkable uniformity of coaching at all levels which rapidly brought a more positive approach through collective understanding, and allowed players to slot more easily into representative teams. Wales, guided by Ray and an enlightened generation of staff and senior coaches, had at last found the path to effective and successful rugby.

Ray Williams fulfilled the wide-ranging terms of reference of his post, which ranged across the structure of coaching and technical development so clearly defined in his admirable book, *Skilful Rugby*. And beyond that he brought into contemporary Welsh rugby his own philosophies on the playing of the game, both in terms of conduct and attitudes. In addition, he impressed on Welsh coaches and players his now well-known dictum of the four principles of play: Go Forward, Support, Continuity and Pressure. The most important of these is pressure for, as Ray always stated, it depends on the first three principles. If you can achieve pressure then you are denying the opposition both time and space. When you reflect on the Welsh play of the last twelve years, then surely in your mind's eye you can see that Wales applied this principle with the most telling effect. It is the same principle which for too long has been the preserve of New Zealand and South Africa.

Owing to his close involvement with coaching since around 1955, and to the fact that for much of that period it had been his full-time job, Ray has put more thought into the subject and had more practical experience than almost any individual in world rugby. His only possible rival would be Dr Danie Craven of South Africa, who introduced rugby into the physical education degree syllabus at Stellenbosch University. So Ray was able to give Wales an enormous push-start over the other four Home Unions and France, and the fact that he had also had a major hand in England's coaching manual, and knew it backwards, made him possibly the most knowledgeable coach in the world.

This English coaching manual, which extended to ten volumes, had been published in 1951–52 – a couple of years before Cliff Jones's working party first assembled. It was so thorough that they decided it would be a waste of time to compile one of their own. Instead they acknowledged it as a masterpiece of radical and progressive thought on the philosophy of the game and a clear guide to its fundamental principles. By simply adopting it they could concentrate their efforts on organization and practical coaching. Ironically this gave Wales a tremendous start on England, and Cliff Jones has always been the first to admit the debt to their old rivals. The England coaching manual became a vital blueprint for Wales's second Golden Era.

Fortunately, too, Cliff Jones was more enlightened about press relations than previous members of the Union, and, as chairman of the coaching and selection committees, he recognized the value of the media in expanding and promoting the game. He was always eager to take the press with him and with Welsh rugby. For the first time in my experience they were treated with respect and not like something which had crawled out from under a stone. This always seemed to be the view of the rugby establishment, not only in Wales, during my early days in the press box. Another of Cliff Jones's beliefs was that knowledge should be derived not only from the written word, but also from the hard school of competitive football at all levels. I particularly liked an utterance of his which indicated that coaching would retain some humanity: 'The soft cursing of sweating forwards will always be a permanent and welcome feature of the game, even under coaching.'

So, within a few years there was the framework of a coaching structure which was to revitalize Welsh rugby. A wind of change had swept in new attitudes; laws had been effectively altered to rid the game of many of its frustrations; teams were being well prepared at every level; above all, the hitherto reactionary establishment of rugby had been broached by vital people who recognized that standards could only be improved by more efficient organization, application and thought. The next stage was to introduce the squad system for the national side, and this was done in 1967.

In essence the squad system is simply a method of intensive coaching in which the senior team and the shadow team of reserves and substitutes train side by side. They also train more often and for longer periods than used to be thought appropriate to the spirit of the game. The first advantage of this approach is that the national team achieves a higher standard of fitness and technique and a clearer sense of common purpose. The second is that any reserve promoted from within the squad finds himself among friends; he is familiar with, say, their lineout calls, their tactical signals and their individual traits.

Up to 1976, teams had always got by with a run-out on Friday. This was under the sole command of their captain, who could not possibly in that time cover all the necessary detail. I well remember my first game for Wales in 1949 against France in Paris when my captain, Haydn Tanner, did not speak more than a couple of words to me throughout the weekend. His team talk was of such brevity that I was totally unaware of any tactics to be employed. The result was we played like a scratch team and lost. The squad nowadays ensures that every player knows his function, the potential of his side and its capacity to react in any given situation. The squad usually numbers twenty-five to thirty players, and selection for the national team usually comes from within. Only occasionally, for reasons known only to themselves, the selectors go outside the family.

At first the squad system was criticized for introducing a too-professional attitude and was thought to transgress the spirit of International Board resolutions on the assembly of national sides. This was another manifestation of the reactionary and out-dated attitudes at that time. The whole logic of the squad system was to raise standards at the level where rugby, shown to millions on television, should be at its very best.

The Welsh squad session is directed by the national team coach, and it usually takes the form of discussions and analyses of one's own and opponents' strengths and weaknesses. There is a review of the tactical options which are available for the next game, and this is backed up with two practical sessions taken up with the detailed organization of the team, lineouts, scrums, rolling mauls etcetera, and the deployment of resources from any situation. International referees are also invited to give their observations and so reduce the number of penalties given away.

Considering Ray Williams's qualifications as a coach, and his role in setting up the squad system, it is ironical that some members of the WRU sought to prevent him lending a hand in preparing the national side. In their eyes, he was a professional who could not be allowed to taint the amateur status of the Welsh XV. There were also those diehards in the four Home Unions who conducted their own watching brief and at rugby dinners throughout the land made pointed references to the dangers of professional coaching. There was an objection only this year against the paid South African coaching organizer preparing their test team. The dread of professionalism still seems alive, particularly among the older members of the rugby establishment. While I would defend to the death the ideal of the amateur status of players, the idea of professional administration and coaching holds no terror; it only assists the lot and performance of the players. Fortunately, the resistance to such professionalism and commercial sponsorship – which has not harmed the game in any way but only enhanced and improved facilities, is rapidly disappearing.

Therefore, Ray Williams had no say in the national team in 1967 or 1968. Gradually, however, in 1969, after long custom and familiarity through his attendance at all squad sessions and practices, he began to have some influence in an advisory capacity. He also played an important part, together with Cliff Jones and Clive Rowlands, in deliberately fostering a family atmosphere within the squad. This had the enormous value of creating intense loyalty among the players, that essential ingredient of close and cohesive teamwork on the field. The Welsh, whose enthusiasm and love for the game is their major asset, now found it properly harnessed, and it was no coincidence that within two years of Ray Williams's arrival Wales were to set out on an era more glorious than that of 1900–11.

The Welsh Union next set a precedent with the revolutionary appointment of David Nash of Ebbw Vale, who had won six caps in 1960–62, as a selector and coach to the national team. He was the first man ever to be recruited from outside the Union. He had been on the short list for the coaching organizer's post, and being a nice guy was promoted by WRU members as the only possible candidate. The job came to him largely on a sympathy vote by a committee who were voting on an issue about which they knew precious little. The more logical choice would have been Carwyn James, who, apart from Ray Williams, was the only other intellectual rugby mind in Wales – a point which he went on to prove both with his club Llanelli, whom he carried through their most prosperous post-war period, and with the astonishingly successful 1971 Lions in New Zealand.

After a disappointing season in 1968, when Wales won only the match against Scotland in Cardiff, there was a considerable and unfortunate reaction against David Nash as coach, and the apathy of the WRU towards coaching became apparent yet again. No coach was appointed for the tour to Argentina in the summer. Instead the WRU general committee chose their president, Glyn Morgan, as the tour manager, and Harry Bowcott, a shrewd and forceful selector but with no coaching qualifications, as assistant manager. This so incensed Alun Thomas, who was chairman of the Welsh selectors at the time and a pugnacious fighter for the cause of coaching, that he promptly decided to make a stand and resigned from the Big Five. It must be said that none of his fellow selectors showed equal determination or commitment.

This immediately produced another trauma for the general committee who received a further lesson in democracy and another rebuke from the clubs at the annual general meeting. The Union was told to rethink the situation. Having already appointed Harry Bowcott as the assistant manager, they found themselves in a cleft stick, but they wriggled out of the difficulty with a compromise, adding Clive Rowlands to the party as the team coach.

This was the watershed as far as the issue of coaching was concerned, and from here on the members and officials of the WRU were left in no doubt about the wishes of the Welsh clubs on coaching. Recognizing the political danger of swimming against the rising tide of opinion, they became confirmed supporters of the principle – simply replacing David Nash with Clive Rowlands – and there was no further obstruction put in the path of coaching. The triple crown success of 1969 and the grand slam of 1971 finally ensured total acceptance, not only of the advantages of coaching, but its absolute necessity.

Clive Rowlands, who won fourteen Welsh caps from 1963 to 1965, and captained Wales on his first appearance, was a substantial influence on the period. He continued to play for Pontypool and Swansea until April 1968 when, at the first attempt, he was elected vice-president of the WRU with a popular vote which reflected the high regard for his talent and personality. Immediately on his return from the tour of Argentina – and despite its lack of success – he was nominated as national coach for a three-year period. When that was completed he went on for another three years and was therefore in charge of the Welsh team from 1968 to 1974. 'Top Cat', as he was known to his fellow players in the Welsh side, was an extraordinary motivator who, in his pre-match diatribes invoked every known influence from past tradition and the family down to distant relatives, girlfriends and his trump card, the Welsh people. The power and humour of his pre-match talk is described beautifully and wittily by Gerald Davies in his penetrating autobiography.

Apart from being a master of emotive appeal, Clive was also the shrewdest judge of a player. It was he who realized that the light frame of Gerald Davies was wasted in the hurly burly of modern centre-threequarter play, and that his scintillating skills could be better employed on the wing. He converted a reluctant Gerald to that position in the second Test in New Zealand in 1969, a move which was to give the Welsh three-quarters a new diamond-hard cutting edge. Clive was a thoughtful tactician and nobody recognized the value of tactical kicking more than he. It was an art of which he was personally the master and with which he incurred the wrath of the Scottish crowd on one occasion when he destroyed the game as a spectacle in Murrayfield. Wales won 6–0 from a drop goal and a penalty goal, with some of the most ruthless kicking to touch and into the box that the Edinburgh crowd has ever seen – and which, one imagines, they never wish to see again. His greatest achievements were to captain Wales to her first triple crown for thirteen years, and to coach the never-to-be-forgotten grand slam side of 1971.

Clive always professed that his principal job as coach was to give the players so much confidence that they could not lose. At the end of his term he left important legacies, not least his belief that the team talk should be given some four hours before the game and never in the dressing-room. He also advised other coaches that since players from different parts and different clubs had different ideas – for instance about blocking and scrummaging – considerable attention had to be paid to these details. He thought the coach should be young enough to be closely involved with the players, and this he believed gave him more authority; and strangely, although he was a product of a time when Wales played nine-man rugby, he nevertheless came to believe in the fifteen-man game. But that was only because he had the shrewdness to appreciate that the players under his command had such extraordinary ability behind the scrum.

I have found it necessary to examine both structure and the personalities involved in the coaching revolution because I believe entirely that this amazing period of Welsh rugby evolved from this new phenomenon, and that the new disciplines imposed created a climate for success. Welshmen at large have never been noted in the past for their self-control; by nature they are often as volatile as the French, which is part of the attraction in their play.

Every generation in Wales has had its share of extraordinarily talented players, but they always seemed to lack the tight control on performance and emotion which wins matches. When I was captain for Wales, I can remember losing the triple crown by drawing the game at Twickenham in 1958, and again by losing by one point against Scotland in 1959. In those days, as captain you were in entire charge of the team, you decided all the tactics and it was usually too big a task to mould a side into single-minded thought and cohesion. At Murrayfield in 1959, I remember that our tactics were to play the game tight in the first half, until we had established control and dominance over the Scottish forwards, who were always a handful on their own patch. However, the Welsh halves, sensing a change, slipped the ball quickly early on and Malcolm Price scored a beautiful try. After congratulating Malcolm and the halves on their work, I remember warning them not to try it again but to kick for a while until we had cracked the Scottish pack. But the damage had been done, and the halves thought they could repeat the move. Of course, Scotland, now waiting for them, began knocking them down and we became too loose. At half-time and in the strongest possible terms, I spoke to the half-backs to put our tactics back on course, but it was too late and we lost by six points to five against a side which we should have beaten easily. Had we had a squad system in those days, I have little doubt that we would have won the triple crown. The value of the squad system and coaching, in my view, is that it has curbed our waywardness and allowed this superb generation of players to express themselves and to create a period of immense prosperity for Welsh rugby.

B

The Crown Princes

Hemingway once defined courage as 'grace under pressure', which definition suggests that any other behaviour in difficult circumstances is cowardice. This view caters only for the immensely talented, the immortals of sport who possess those inherent gifts of skill and perception. Nevertheless many of the players in the period from 1969 did possess these attributes and qualified for their heroic status. The achievements of these young men were so breath-taking and at times such sheer delight, that it was the greatest pleasure to report their deeds in the press boxes of the British Isles. That so many of them were also good friends magnified the privilege. However, you did not have to know them or be a member of their race to appreciate the exquisite pleasure they gave. Excellence is instinctively and instantly recognized, whether it takes the form of a Russian gymnast, a Swedish tennis player, an American golfer or a West Indian cricketer. It is sufficient to be privileged to watch the very best.

James Baxter, chairman of the English selection committee in 1922–23, wrote in his preface to a book by the great England outside-half W. J. A. Davies, 'The rugby player of today must have plenty of sense and complete co-ordination of mind and body. Brain, eye, hand or foot must be completely in harmony with each other.' This remains as true in the higher gear of the modern game, and it epitomizes the qualities of our era of great players.

The Welshmen of the last decade possessed style in every sense, for not only did they impress with their presence on the field of play but off it too. They began to set new standards in the way they presented themselves with their sense of fashion in clothes and smartly styled hair, complemented by beautiful wives and girlfriends, and an intelligent appreciation of life-style. From their generation emerged the first great rugby superstars. They achieved not only recognition but moderate riches as well. It was a period which produced an abundance of backs, who were indisputably the greatest of the whole hundred years of rich Welsh rugby history. To select the finest is perhaps ungenerous to those who help make the whole. However, four names predominate over all others: Barry John, Gareth Edwards, Gerald Davies and J. P. R. Williams. Close behind come others such as Phil Bennett, John Dawes, S. P. Fenwick, J. J. Williams, Maurice Richards, Ray Gravell, Arthur Lewis and John Bevan, all in their way contributing to this period of amazing success. Of those first four each was the best ever seen in his respective position, but in view of the different characteristics of their roles it would be invidious to single out any as the greatest.

Before I saw Barry John I believed that Bleddyn Williams was the most accomplished mid-field back I had ever seen. Then in the mid-sixties I watched a deceptively frail young outside-half playing for Llanelli, and immediately recognized an instinctive genius for the game. That genius gradually developed until in 1971 Barry became the principal authority of the fabulously successful Lions side which destroyed the previous New Zealand dominance over the British Isles. With good reason the Lions gave him the nickname of 'The King', a title he deserved and, with his great sense of fun, still enjoys. I remember that after he came back from New Zealand I asked him for his address, and before I knew what I was doing I had written down at his dictation, 'Barry John, West Wing, Cardiff Castle.' Only then the penny dropped and I looked up to observe his delighted and ingenuous grin. His lively sense of fun was also manifested in his play on the field, though it was often misconstrued as arrogance. Once, whilst playing for the Lions against Hawkes Bay in 1971, he showed his complete disgust for the nature of the rugby – he had spent much of the afternoon as the target for late tackles – by slowing the game down and, much to the amusement of his fellow Lions, holding the ball out to his opponents.

Barry John learned his rugby at Gwendraeth Grammar School but, strangely, failed to play for the Welsh Secondary Schools. He was born and raised in the West Wales village of Cefneithin, which was also the home of Carwyn James, his mentor and coach in the 1971 Lions. Barry began playing for Llanelli when he was a student at Trinity College, Carmarthen, before he moved to work and play in Cardiff. He played in the Welsh Trials in 1965–66, and was reserve to David Watkins for the Welsh team. He got his first cap in 1966 against Australia, and went on to win twenty-five caps for Wales before he retired at his peak, a retirement due to what he believed was the excessive pressure imposed upon him by the Welsh rugby public. In his early days for Wales his play was occasionally variable, and he was the subject of continual controversy. However, his cool computer-like rugby brain blossomed to produce the greatest tactical control I have ever observed in any outside-half. On one occasion, while appearing in a charity game at Cardiff, he was wired for sound by Harlech Television, and from a particular situation he had the blithe effrontery to announce that he was about to score – and promptly did so with a scything run which left the opposition clutching at thin air.

His true talent began to blossom with the Lions in South Africa in 1968, but then tragically he was tipped up in the first Test by that great Springbok flanker, Jan Ellis, and broke his collar bone. This gave him time to observe and think; and when in 1968–69 the Welsh XV adopted squad training, he began to play rugby of ethereal quality. It was a major catalyst in opening an amazing decade for Welsh rugby, beginning with the triple crown in 1969 and followed by the triple crown and the grand slam in 1971.

At that time, due to his cool confidence, he became the senior partner in one of the greatest half-back firms of all time: Edwards and John. I love the story of their first practice together, when Gareth asked him how he wanted the pass, to be told, 'You just throw it, and I'll catch it!' It was Barry who dictated the tactics of the Welsh side during their partnership; it was not until Barry retired that Gareth Edwards himself took over this role. Both went to New Zealand on the ill-fated Welsh tour of 1969, which failed largely due to the lack of commitment by the Welsh forwards. When the two were chosen for the Lions tour in 1971 they had a burning desire for revenge, and Barry in particular was determined to get his own back. Subsequently, on that tour he became the first of the rugby superstars when, at twenty-six years of age, he plotted the defeat of the legendary All Blacks and scored thirty points out of forty-eight in the four Tests. On tour he scored seven tries, eight dropped goals, thirty-one conversions and twenty-eight penalties, a tally which brought a new dimension to his now rapidly increasing stature.

Barry is the first to point out that his skills and assurance flowered because of the astute captaincy of John Dawes, and the incredible performances of Mike Gibson at his elbow in the best mid-field ever produced by the Lions. No less an authority than Gibson declares that John was the greatest outside-half of our time, and we will be fortunate if we ever see his like again. At the end of 1972 he retired, prematurely in the view of most of his contemporaries, after one of the most exciting rugby careers that I have been privileged to see; and now, as well as enjoying a successful business career, he is one of our most perceptive critics and commentators on the game.

When Barry John was King, Gareth Edwards was the Prince, and when Barry John retired many said that Gareth would never be the same again. How wrong they were! For he promptly built a new partnership with Phil Bennett which many believe was even greater. He went on to become a legend throughout his playing days, which included an astonishing fifty-three consecutive appearances for Wales. During that eleven-year period he scored a record-breaking twenty tries, and contributed hugely to three grand slams and five triple crowns.

Nobody has appealed more to the Welsh rugby public than Gareth Edwards; not even Barry John. Not only did they enjoy his bright-eyed charm and modesty, but they had watched him develop his skills from an early age, when there were distinct gaps in his play; his distribution for instance was often erratic and there were even doubts about his temperament. However, his determination was such that he filled in the gaps to become the most complete scrum-half we have ever seen. During his career there were many others as gifted as Gareth in some aspects of scrum-half play. Ken Catchpole of Australia got the ball away quicker than any scrum-half in our time. Sid Going of New Zealand was the more aggressive and durable and, playing behind All Blacks forwards, he had the better of Gareth except in 1971. Chris Laidlaw, also of New Zealand, had as good a pass, and indeed Edwards paid Laidlaw the highest compliment of all when he decided to copy his spin pass, thus enormously increasing the length of his service. The Springbok Dawie de Villiers, nowadays the South African Ambassador in London, was as instinctive a footballer with a beautifully balanced game. But in the end I thought that Gareth had the edge on them all, for after 1974 there was never a weakness in his game; his armoury was complete and he could produce more fire-power than any scrum-half of his time.

Gareth came to maturity after the abdication of Barry John. He was still only twenty-five, and I felt at that time in his career that he was determined to prove he was at least the equal of if not a greater player than his close friend. After all they had come from a similar background, the anthracite-mining areas of West Wales, and Gareth particularly had acquired the immensely competitive feeling that exists in those valleys. With the 1974 Lions in South Africa he perfected the stabbing kick to the diagonals which proved mortal to the Springboks. Then he came back to support many a suspect Welsh pack by creating a platform for them to run on to and build up impetus, a vital factor in the three successive triple crowns of 1976–77–78. He had become a scrum-half without a peer in Welsh rugby, a man of great charm and charisma. He will have many epitaphs, but none more fitting than two of his greatest tries, jewels in his crown. Those who were there will never forget them: that long lung-tearing burst to complete an unforgettable try for the Barbarians against New Zealand in 1973, and before that truly marvellous try against Scotland in 1972 which epitomized the deadly thrust and competitive drive of his play.

I had the privilege of playing under the captaincy of the great Haydn Tanner in 1949, and I am often asked to compare the two. While one hates to draw comparisons between different eras I would, in the final analysis take Edwards as the better man because of his sustained power and pace, and because his dedication to winning every major game he played in never faltered, not even at the very end of his career. He was the archetypal Welshman, both in appearance and temperament – dark, quick and intensely competitive. He always struck me as having similar attributes to Cliff Morgan, who himself recognizes a kindred spirit in Gareth and is therefore one of his greatest fans. Above all, Gareth has remained unchanged, modest and knowledgeable. He is now garnering the fruits of twelve years of tremendous endeavour and astonishing performance by becoming the greatest rugby superstar among so many superb contemporaries. Indeed, his involvement with the commercial superstar organization brought about a change of laws regarding the game's amateur status. His continuing success as a businessman and a commentator of the game which he so dearly loved is assured, and is no less than he deserves, now that he has entered the mythology of Welsh rugby.

I was present in New Zealand in 1969 when T. G. R. Davies, Gerald to his Welsh fans and Reames to his Lion colleagues, was pressed reluctantly into service as a wing threequarter in the last test. His reluctance could also be described as intense annoyance; but that day a great new star was born and for the next nine years travelled through the Welsh rugby firmament with such dazzling brilliance that he will remain as one of the unforgettable memories of those brilliant years. His devastating running in the first half of that test, which had New Zealand at panic stations, was something I shall always remember, even though Wales lost badly. He became the 'Winged Mercury' of Welsh rugby, delighting the senses with his audacity and quick-silver vivaciousness. He had a breath-taking capacity to sear the ground with his electrifying outside bursts or to jink inside with such blistering pace. He seemingly had the capacity too for going through the eye of a needle, even in the stormiest conditions, to score tries that only one player, Peter Jackson of England, might have scored.

He holds the record of forty-six caps for a Welsh threequarter, and jointly holds the record of twenty tries for Wales with his great friend Gareth Edwards. He captained Cambridge, the Barbarians and Cardiff with distinction and commanded enormous respect from all his contemporaries, both for his genius at wing threequarter and for his balanced intelligent lifestyle and personal integrity. Apart from the great tries he scored for Wales, he will be remembered for the hat-trick of tries he scored for the British Lions in that bad-tempered game against Hawkes Bay in 1971; and for the four fabulous tries he scored for Cardiff in the quarter-final of the Welsh Cup in 1977. That last feat produced an anomalous win for Cardiff whose forwards were getting the mother and father of a hiding at the hands of a Pontypool pack so impressively coached and fired by the remarkable Ray Prosser.

Gerald is no less unforgettable than Gareth or Barry for the great excitements he brought to Welsh rugby.

During this or any other era, there was no greater example of total commitment and audacious courage than the 'Flying Doctor', J. P. R. Williams. He was the ultimate bulwark, the fiercest competitor of his time. The confidence he instilled into the Welsh team during his fifty-two games for them, and into the Lions of 1971 and 1974 was again one of the most telling factors in their success. Fearless almost to the extent of fanaticism, he was an inspiration to all who played with him or saw him play.

One can never forget the way in which he seemingly terrorized the All Black pack during the Lions tour in 1971. I did not think I would see the day when All Black forwards would hesitate in the face of a single individual. The well-developed New Zealand ploy of putting the ball high to the opposing full-back for their forwards to thunder on to, became useless as JPR caught everything unerringly and then, choosing his target (usually the nearest All Black forward) thundered at him with an almost crazed joyful abandon. This struck such fear into the minds of some of his victims that they became hesitant, and gave a new meaning to the joke expression, 'a Maori side-step'.

I am sure he will forgive me if I say that he possessed less charisma in the public eye than Barry, Gareth or Gerald, stemming from a tendency to be dour which he himself ascribes to his own strangely shy nature. Nevertheless, he commanded no less respect or hero worship than the others, for his bravery was without equal and will remain a byword in the folklore of Welsh rugby.

He was immensely strong, a magnificent catcher and handler of the ball. For a man so unusually burly for his position (he was over fourteen stone), he was a tremendous ball player, as befitted a top-class tennis player who had won the British junior title at Wimbledon. He was often the subject of controversies, which were self-inflicted, due to strange moments of aberration on the field, and to his occasional unthinking outspokenness. The first real example I saw was at Durban in 1974 when the Lions were playing what is considered to be the most pro-British South African province, Natal. For some unaccountable reason he took umbrage against Tommy Bedford and had to be forcibly restrained by a touch judge and by spectators from a fierce physical assault. I was present in the marquee after the game when his lovely wife gave him one of the biggest dressing-downs he has probably ever received, and I can still remember his sheepishness.

His most controversial moment came in the Irish match at Lansdowne Road in 1978, when he took out the greatest Irish threequarter of all time, Mike Gibson, with such a palpably late tackle that it brought a roar of censure and disapproval from the Irish crowd. Instead of showing any remorse for his action, he went on television and stated that it was a professional foul and that he was not ashamed of it. This, of course, brought down the wrath of the rugby establishment, for the very idea of the professional foul, something which is overt and seemingly acceptable in soccer, was totally unacceptable to them and to most lovers of the game. Few knew that in fact JPR had apologized to his old comrade-in-arms, and that Gibson, with a typically generous gesture, had dismissed the tackle as being unintentional. When I once asked JPR about these uncharacteristic moments (for nobody can ever suggest that over the span of his fabulous career JPR was in any way a dirty player) he found them hard to explain, claiming that everybody at some time does something stupid.

He was always a difficult man to know because he was preoccupied with a full life to which he felt he could only contribute by maintaining the highest standards. Apart from his sporting achievements he is a fine musician, and now a Fellow of the Royal College of Surgeons. For those who bothered to know him he was a sensitive, articulate man, aware of what he had accomplished and the effort it had cost him. For all that I found him modest, but always with a strongly outspoken point of view.

In my opinion, there is only one other full-back of my time who came anywhere near his class as a full-back – Bob Scott of New Zealand in the late forties and early fifties. In his eleven years in the Welsh team and the Lions JPR never asked or gave any quarter, and I can recall him only twice making any complaint. One occasion was when Ashworth, the New Zealand prop, stamped on him during the All Blacks game against Bridgend in 1978, an incident which unfortunately soured an otherwise well-behaved tour, JPR was lying out of a ruck when a boot drove down on him and the stud went right through his cheek, causing a terrible wound. Being a doctor, he realized what the consequences might have been, say, to the eye, if the injury had been three inches higher. It even prompted his father, Dr Peter Williams, to remark that if he had thought that this would happen, he would not have encouraged his sons to play rugby.

The only other time that I heard JPR complain about physical danger was at Dublin in 1978 when, sitting in the dressing-room after the match, he said that, 'If rugby is going to be as hard as this, then somebody is going to get killed.' I too had felt that this was one of the most vigorous international matches I have ever seen, and when a player as fearless as JPR remarked upon it then I knew my opinion was confirmed. Such was his physical commitment that I often felt he was a frustrated forward, an idea illustrated by the fact that he was always the first to volunteer to play in the forwards in practice games on tour, and by his elation at being pressed into service as a flanker for the final Test of the Welsh tour to Australia in 1978.

I have never seen him more delighted than in 1979 when he was chosen to captain Wales in what we all assumed was his last season. He went on to lead Wales to their fourth successive triple crown, and his club Bridgend to win the Welsh Cup in their centenary year. He is currently contemplating a come-back, both for Bridgend and for Wales; and to those who believe that this is retrogressive I would say that I would rather have JPR on one leg than most other full-backs with two. His game has few limitations or weaknesses: he is not for instance the greatest punter of a ball, for he tends to shunt it rather than to stroke it off his boot; but in every other respect he is the most dominant full-back I have ever seen. All his attributes of fearlessness, competitiveness, timing and determination are without parallel. An unforgettable moment was his forty-five yard drop goal in the final test against New Zealand in 1971, which ensured victory in the series; or his extraordinary though unavailing attempts to win the last test in South Africa in 1974, when a draw became the only blot in an otherwise one hundred per cent winning record.

J. P. R. Williams, a product of Millfield School, of the courageous London Welsh team of the late sixties and early seventies, of Bridgend and Wales, of the Barbarians and the Lions, was a full-back certainly without peer in his time, the bravest player I ever saw, and a man prepared to die for any team that was fortunate enough to include him.

I have selected this 'gang of four' as the senior members of the Welsh squad of their period – perhaps invidiously since the team had all the elements of a happy family – because in my opinion they were the best ever in their positions. I now move on to players who in the opinion of others have equally valid credentials to be so regarded.

Gareth Edwards said that when Barry John went, he thought his right arm had gone. But he also added that when one King is dead there are always one or even two others around the corner. How right he was, for immediately he found an equally royal partner in Phil Bennett, whom many West Walians consider the best outside-half of our time. Phil shrugged off all the criticisms of his early career, when he played for Wales as a wing threequarter and centre before his huge heart confirmed him as the true heir to Barry John. He then went on to win twenty-nine caps and lead Wales to two triple crowns and a grand slam.

His achievements are a legend. He holds the world record of 212 points in all internationals and the Welsh record of 166 points in internationals. For a time he shared – with Roger Hosen, Tony Ward and Steve Fenwick – the record of 38 international points in a season; but in 1980 that was beaten by the Irish stand-off, Ollie Campbell, with 46 points.

My own reason for preferring Barry John was that I sensed flaws in Phil's temperament which occasionally brought breakdowns in his confidence that were reflected in his play. For instance, when he captained the 1977 Lions tour to New Zealand he found the pressures imposed upon him by the management (unfairly, I thought) too great, and this had a disastrous impact on his play. His confidence eroded to such an extent that he fell back into the fault, apparent in his early career, of failing to commit the mid-field; and consequently we saw him crabbing across-field, bunching the threequarters and destroying their opportunity for fluency or effectiveness.

However, these occasional deficiencies in a long and illustrious career are far outweighed by the enormous pleasure he gave to the millions who were enchanted by his brilliantly instinctive running and jinking. There was never a better example of this than when, during the 1973 match between the Barbarians and the All Blacks, he initiated one of the greatest tries in the history of rugby. From deep in his own twenty-five he jinked successively past four floundering All Blacks to inspire a movement which covered the length of the field and led to Gareth Edwards scoring. Then, too, after he had been told that a spinal problem would prevent him ever playing rugby again (which happily proved to be a wrong diagnosis), he went to South Africa with the 1974 Lions: he scored 103 points in eleven matches, including another unforgettable try in the second test, and developed as the cutting edge of the Lions' running and handling attack.

It was in running and try-scoring that many considered him better than Barry John, for apart from those magnificent efforts for the Barbarians and the Lions, he scored many tries for Wales which were collectors' pieces. He was, as Barry John once said, a jack-in-the-box runner, capable of conjuring tries from nowhere with that famous jink, which seems to be a Welsh copyright, and his vivid acceleration. Barry John in my view was the cooler, the more composed and therefore the more complete tactician, but Phil's supporters can point to games where he too was the master of the field. His huge armoury of skills was completed by his prodigious talent for kicking out of the hand, as well as for the place kicking which brought him so many magnificent goals. Had he decided to play soccer at a young age, then in the opinion of many experts, including John Toshack, he could have become a First Division star.

The greatest controversy regarding Phil came in the 1975–76 season when, after the final Welsh trial, he was omitted from the Welsh squad. The man in possession was that magnificently direct outside-half, John Bevan of Aberavon, who had been selected against France, England and Scotland in the preceding season and in December had played superbly when Wales, with a powerful performance, had overwhelmed Australia. The selectors' preference for John Bevan was the result of Phil's worst game for Wales against France in 1973, when he misguidedly stood so far off Gareth Edwards' pass, and so crowded the Welsh threequarters that they found themselves operating laterally with about only twenty yards of room and no capacity for attack. All the same, most people believed that the outside-half position was a straight fight between Bevan and Bennett, and were astonished that Bennett was not included as a reserve when David Richards, the young outside-half from Cardiff College of Education, was brought into the squad.

The decision of the selectors was probably coloured by the fact that when he substituted for Bevan at Murrayfield the season before, Phil performed abysmally. In the event fate and fortune were on his side as both Bevan and Richards withdrew with injury and Phil, to the delight of his supporters, came back to control affairs against England. That encounter will be remembered as J. P. R. Williams's match, but from here on Phil, perhaps smarting from earlier indignities, came into his own. He had found a new strength of character, and a more personally committed dimension to his game. He flowered into a fine leader of both Llanelli and Wales and became devoted to his players, 'the lads' as he always called them. He was the most likeable and friendly of men, and never at any time resented the criticisms directed at him in his early career; this was the true measure of the man and his character, and is a fine example of the way to behave in misfortune. He retired from the international scene when still in his prime because of the strain and pressure imposed upon him and his family by the time-consuming demands of the modern game on the star player. Due to his abiding love for the game, however, he continued to play for Llanelli.

Perhaps the most enigmatic personality during the years under review was S. J. Dawes. Not only was he a player of immense significance, stamping an amazing authority on the attitudes and play of his generation by his extremely thoughtful and intellectual approach to the game, but he was also later to join the Welsh rugby establishment as coach to the national side in succession to that great motivator, Clive Rowlands. Although he finally became so good that he ended his playing career in a blaze of acclaim, at the start he was a much overlooked and criticized player. The early criticisms obviously left their mark, for he became a most difficult person in his dealings with the media, and became over-protective towards his players, something which many saw as a creditable attribute rather than a fault. However, the fact that he became an establishment figure put him in a different category from the players, and made him more open to criticism.

To the press, he seemed to possess a Jekyll and Hyde personality. At times he could be a moderate and reasonable man; and then he would change as rapidly as a chameleon, to become less than charitable, to lash out at those who held a different point of view from his own without understanding that no individual can possibly be a total authority on a game which is forever changing and evolving, or that everybody is entitled to a point of view. All comment on rugby is a matter of personal opinion, and any view must be taken seriously. Consequently, his ill-advised outbursts against individuals or teams occasionally made him unpopular. There were moments when he failed to be magnanimous in defeat or victory; once, after Wales had won at Twickenham, he succeeded in incensing the English establishment with a withering attack on its policies.

I found his behaviour as coach of the ill-fated 1977 Lions in New Zealand totally incomprehensible; he built an impenetrable barrier not only between the Lions and their opponents, but also between the side and the New Zealand public, thus destroying the enormous goodwill created by his predecessor, Carwyn James. The now legendary 1971 Lions, with James as their coach, had proved to the cognoscenti to be the greatest team to leave the British Isles – although there are those who would make a similar case for the unbeaten Lions of 1974 in South Africa. I was always a fan of John Dawes and when, prior to the tour, an article appeared in the *Daily Mail* fiercely attacking the choice of Dawes as coach, I defended him vigorously in *The Observer*. I was amazed, therefore, when early on in the tour he attacked me for comment which he alleged was disloyal to the team. From then on I found I was unable to break his antipathy towards me, and perhaps towards the press in general. I found myself continually under attack, although I believe my writing was always well-balanced.

On one occasion he went so ridiculously far as to black me with the team, by telling them not to talk to me. This arose from an incident when the Lions were on a three-day holiday at Waitangi in the Bay of Islands. EMI, the record company, gave a party at which they were to record the songs of the Lions. During the evening I fell foul of an EMI official, who told John Dawes that not only did I say that the Lions could not sing, but that neither could they play rugby, all of which was entirely untrue. The upshot was that the press were ejected. John Dawes gave me a tongue-lashing and sent me to Coventry. On other occasions he discouraged individual players from speaking to the press, and would sometimes shake his head from side to side when, from the other end of a room, he spotted a player talking to anybody of whom he disapproved. This served only to embarrass the players whose destiny on the tour was almost entirely in his hands.

Subsequently the tour, from a public relations point of view, deteriorated into a disaster. The players found themselves in an increasingly hostile environment and, depressed by this, by the ghastly weather and by their lack of success they began to find solace only in their own company. Except for a few independent souls, they failed to embrace the rugby public of New Zealand who were dying to give them a good time. They

Gareth Edwards in action: *(above)* bringing down the Argentinian Carracedo at Cardiff in 1976; *(below)* moving the ball with intent concentration from the ruck.

(Right) Gareth Edwards shaping up for one of his raking diagonal kicks.

Barry John: *(opposite)* for once not getting away with the ball in a 1971 match for an International XV against the Saracens; *(right)* slipping his tackle and getting the kick in.

John Dawes, the influence at the centre of Welsh rugby in the seventies.

became tribal, turning in on themselves; and regrettably in such a situation the main culprits were the Welsh who by the end of the tour were predominantly the major group with eighteen out of thirty-three players, since Charlie Faulkner and Alun Lewis had been flown out as replacements. This added further support to the argument that Welshmen on the whole do not make the best tourists.

The worst moment provided by John Dawes's unpredictable nature came on the last night of the tour when, at the farewell party held by the New Zealand Union, he suddenly spotted some pressmen (who had been invited by that most popular New Zealand liaison officer, Peter Wilde) talking to his long-time colleague Mervyn Davies, who had soldiered brilliantly through so many major campaigns shoulder to shoulder with him, for London Welsh, Wales and the Lions. Dawes came over and asked the pressmen to leave; two of them complied, although a furious Peter Wilde begged them to stay, and Chris Lander went straight to the phone to file a vitriolic account of the incident to the *Sunday Mirror*. The following summer, when Dawes was the coach of yet another disastrous overseas tour by Wales to Australia, matters again disintegrated into chaos on the field and bitter acrimony off it.

Nevertheless, the best of John Dawes is more than sufficient to outweigh the criticism, for as a player and coach his record with the Welsh team was second to none. After a chequered early career, he was reinstated as captain against France in 1970 to mastermind a famous win with a single-minded tactical purpose, and the vindication must have made it a very satisfying day for him. Subsequently Wales won the championship, and only the now-typical disaster in Dublin, generated by an Arkle-type performance from Ken Goodall, kept Wales from the triple crown and the grand slam. However, the following season Dawes captained Wales to their first grand slam since 1952, before his final retirement.

He was a very special player and captain, who commanded enormous respect from his fellow players. More than anyone he was the inspiration of that magnificent London Welsh side of the sixties and early seventies, impressing on them the necessity of courage, thoughtfulness and the will to play fifteen-man attacking rugby. He established the Old Deer Park as a Mecca for those who wished to see club rugby at its best.

One could never hope to see a better handler or distributor of the ball in the mid-field; his timing of a pass was impeccable and the model for any aspiring young player. These skills more than compensated for the lack of real pace which held him back in his early career, although his will ensured that he found that sharp burst when it was most needed. As he grew in experience and strength he became one of the best catalysts of exciting threequarter play, and his partnership with Mike Gibson in New Zealand was as great as any the game has seen.

His greatest achievement was the coaching of Wales to their finest hours in history, when between 1976 and 1979 they won their unparalleled four triple crowns in succession, and two grand slams in 1976 and 1978. Now that he has succeeded Ray Williams as the Welsh coaching organizer, and gets further away from the players, perhaps he will be more ready to see other points of view; and certainly Welsh rugby, at the start of its centenary year, can be helped by the thoughtfulness of one of its most gifted men.

The contribution of another centre, Steve Fenwick, must not be under-estimated. He gained his first cap against England in 1975 and played in every one of those sixteen winning triple crown matches.

In aesthetic terms, his style as a centre could never be regarded as having much beauty. He had critics and detractors who felt that Wales could not develop fluency in the threequarters due to his presence; and there was always a reaction against the Welsh crash ball tactics when he played alongside Ray Gravell in 1976 and 1978. Yet, in truth, this was a superb physical partnership. It finally lost its credibility when David Richards of Swansea was introduced into the centre in 1979, bringing a new dimension and a new injection of pace into the Welsh mid-field, but it had been highly effective in its day. In particular it had responded to the demands of the prevailing system which required that pressure be imposed at every point.

Although there was nothing classical about Fenwick, time and again he proved a match winner with his innate sense of what needed to be done, and if at times he appeared brusque he possessed an inner man who had the tenacity of a bull terrier. His competitive nature rivalled that of J. P. R. Williams, and you cannot go higher than that. He would always rise to the occasion, and even on losing sides his determination often stemmed the rout, as his defensive qualities for the 1977 Lions in the first test in New Zealand showed. Many of his critics said that he was an appalling passer of the ball, with no pleasing swing of the arms and the hip in opposite directions; but we remember those incredible and instinctive flick passes, like the one in Dublin in 1978 for that critical try by J. J. Williams, which put the Welsh back in control; or the swift hand between David Burcher and Phil Bennett at Murrayfield in 1977 for what Bill MacLaren at the time called the try of the season.

Steve Fenwick was one of the most effective players of his generation, and in 1978 he equalled Bennett's record of 38 points in a season in the international championship. In Australia in 1978 he scored 55 points, the highest ever on a Welsh overseas tour. If he lacked grace, and a yard or two, there were no other gaps in his weaponry. Once the ball was in his hands he had a great capacity for always doing the right thing. I well remember seeing him collect a kick on the halfway line in a Welsh Cup semi-final for Bridgend against Llanelli in 1980. Promptly he raced down the touch line with the power of an express engine, and he timed and calculated his cross-kick to the posts so perfectly that when the ball dropped among the Llanelli defenders, he was up there to break their resolution; from this pressure Chris Williams scored a crucial try. He was a courageous and fearsome tackler, the mid-field banger *par excellence*, often making opponents spill the ball and enabling his team to counter-attack. Steve Fenwick was a player whom Wales could never leave out, for he was one of the greatest competitors of his time and a highly effective match winner.

Another player who not only made a large contribution to the Welsh success, but who also left his mark on the memory of this period due to an unusual style of play, was J. J. Williams; he became Wales's third most-capped wing threequarter, with thirty caps. He began his Welsh rugby career as an outside-half for the Welsh Secondary Schools, which perhaps explains the dexterity of his mind in a difficult situation, and the extraordinary ease with which he occasionally conjured up tries from nowhere.

He will always be remembered for that favourite party trick of his – racing up to his opponent and chipping ahead, before roaring past the bemused defence to re-gather and score many an astonishing and often crucial try, for both Wales and the British Lions. It was as a substitute against France in 1973 that he won his first cap, and it was against France the following year that he scored his first typically magical try for Wales, when he got the ball from the game's only movement along the Welsh line and conjured a try from air thick with French defence. He grub-kicked past Bertranne and, racing on, fly-kicked over the full-back to grasp the bouncing ball head-high over the French line and touch down. This led to his well-deserved selection for the Lions tour to South Africa, where his game made enormous progress and he became the second highest try-scorer of a tour. This tour, although hugely successful, was not renowned for fluent threequarter play or for bringing wings into the game; but he scored twelve tries including two in the second test at Pretoria, and two in the third test at Port Elizabeth where he played one of the best games of his career. Only Tom Grace of Ireland, with thirteen tries, got over the line more often than J. J. during the tour. Against South West Districts at Mossel Bay he scored six tries to beat the previous record of five by a British Lion, set by W. Wallace in 1924. He began the following season with five tries against Australia, and established himself in Wales as another personality and hero of his time, becoming another well-oiled cog in the Welsh machine and a fixture in the team until he retired after the England match in 1979. His value can be assessed by the difficulty the Welsh selectors have since found in replacing him and Gerald Davies.

If these were the most famous of a fabulous generation of Welsh backs there were nevertheless other immensely talented players, such as Maurice Richards and John C. Bevan on the wings, who merit consideration. Both became highly respected professionals in the northern code. Richards was an extremely talented and graceful runner, while Bevan was an enormously strong and fearless crash runner, and probably one of the hardest wings to stop ten yards from the line. In the centre, one must never forget the superb technique of Arthur Lewis of Ebbw Vale, who could draw a man with the style of a matador before releasing an exquisite pass to his wing three-quarter. Then there was the great-hearted play of Ray Gravell, who on the day could be the most ferocious of centres; if occasionally his exuberant play lacked a little in control, he will always be recalled as an enthusiastic and effective centre who gave nothing less than his all for his beloved Wales. His club colleague, Roy Bergiers, was another fine forthright runner, whose career never really flowered because he was susceptible to injury and lacked some skill in distributing the ball. There was also Ian Hall, now coach to the Welsh Youth team, who could play centre or wing and who perhaps in another period would also have been a fixture in the Welsh side.

Last but not least, one should not forget the superbly direct play at outside-half of John Bevan of Aberavon, who played four times for Wales in 1975 during that hiccup in Phil Bennett's career. But for Phil's outstanding brilliance, Bevan would also have gained many more caps. It is significant that due to Bevan's personal commitment in the mid-field and the intelligent marshalling of his threequarters, Wales scored over twenty points against France, England and Australia. A hundred per cent record of wins was broken unhappily at that most difficult of Welsh hunting grounds, Murrayfield, where Wales lost by two points. John Bevan's club partner at Aberavon was that superb scrum-half, Clive Shell, who also had to live in the shadow of true greatness as reserve to Gareth Edwards; Clive, too, was unfortunate in getting only a solitary cap for Wales, when he came on as a substitute for Gareth against Australia in 1973.

The retirement of this amazing crop of players was happily made comparatively painless by the emergence of Terry Holmes who, in his first full season of international rugby in 1979, was elected player of the year by the Welsh rugby writers, and was considered by many critics to be better than Gareth Edwards at the same age; and by the simultaneous arrival of Gareth Davies, whose cool calculated play was so reminiscent of Barry John; and of David Richards, whose conversion from outside-half to the centre brought a new and exciting dimension to the Welsh mid-field.

Even so, it will be remarkable if in the next hundred years the Welsh rugby public witnesses another decade of such superlative backs as those we were so privileged to watch during the seventies.

4
The Donkey Workers

Barry John, with a joking irreverence, always used to call his forwards 'the donkeys'. It was, of course, an affectionate affectation for he, more than anybody, realized that without their donkey-work and their physical endeavours at laying the foundations by imposing the initial pressures, his talents and those of the other Welsh backs could never have reached fruition. However, there was more than just the suspicion of a put-down in this mildly derogatory description; intuitively he probably sensed that the true greatness of the Welsh teams of his period lay behind the scrum. His view was tainted possibly by the total failure of the Welsh forwards in New Zealand in 1969 to contain the superlative All Black pack, which destroyed the high Welsh expectations of that tour; and Barry never forgot or forgave their deficiencies on that occasion. It left a scar on his mind, but one which he was able to heal on the 1971 tour.

I tend to agree that the forwards of the period were never as decisively superior as the backs, but at the same time they usually managed well enough; even on occasions they rose to such heights that they deserved to share in the success. Among them there were those who were accorded the idolatry the Welsh rugby public usually reserved for its heroes behind the scrum.

Without question, the immortal Welsh forward from this period was Mervyn Davies. He possessed talents far beyond the reach of ordinary men and was another who helped take London Welsh to their halcyon days. Deceptively lazy, this massive man, six foot six inches tall, was like a steel spring, all tensile strength and unbreakable resolve, an absolute hammer of a player who could devastate his opponents. There is no finer accolade than the view of Colin Meads that 'Merve the Swerve' as he was so affectionately known on the Welsh terraces, was without question as great a No 8 as Wales, or any other country, has seen, due to his majestic authority and a superb rugby brain; and although he was an absolute killer of a man and ball he always achieved his aim without committing any outrage.

He was seemingly indestructible but then, after he had led Wales to the triple crown and grand slam in 1976 a sub-arachnoid haemorrhage during the semi-final Cup match between Pontypool and Swansea on Sunday 28 March blew out the light on a dazzling season and on a career which had already brought him every honour in the game except the captaincy of the Lions. He would undoubtedly have achieved that in 1977. He had played thirty-eight times for Wales, sustaining only eight defeats; and in his twenty-six games for the Lions, he was the automatic choice in the eight tests of his two tours in 1971 and 1974.

The only deficiency that one could see in his play was in his loose distribution when it came to the more traditional pass. However, this was more than compensated for by his ability to flick out passes from the ruck and maul, and by his incredible basket-ball technique from the top of the jump at the tail of the lineout. This was an area which he unfailingly dominated and which was crucial to the success of Wales and the Lions. His impact, too, on the scrummaging was also remarkable, for although he ranged the field to appear unerringly where he was needed most in attack and defence, he never failed to push his weight.

After only a few months with London Welsh, who had plucked him from a junior London side, Mervyn won his first cap against Australia in 1969. By 1976 his enormous experience had given him a tremendous belief in his own infallibility, and I well remember how, just before his tragic illness during which he was in great danger of losing his life, he had reached the stage where he had complete confidence in himself, in his Swansea club and in his beloved Welsh team.

After winning the grand slam in 1976 he stated that his aim was now to win three grand slams in a row, and he had also told the Swansea committee, with a jocular laugh, 'This is my lucky season. Just give me fourteen men for the Cup Final, and we will win it.' His illness, which at first was interpreted as an injury, at least served to accentuate the fact that Welsh rugby players were grossly under-insured, and caused the Welsh Rugby Union to review the whole question of insurance.

At the end of his curtailed career he played his rugby with the same majestic authority as Colin Meads of New Zealand, who was the only forward of our time able to lay claim to being greater even than Mervyn. He employed a strange economy of effort, which belied his athleticism. He possessed a wondrous and indomitable courage, which saw him unflinchingly kill any threateningly dangerous loose ball. His tackling was definitive, and he always defended the ethics of the game; I recall him sticking out an inordinately long arm to waggle a terrifyingly stern finger at any transgressor who went over the narrow line of vigour in the direction of undue violence or brutality; and, to crown it all, he had an uncanny football sense. Colin Meads was one of his greatest admirers, and named him and Mike Gibson as the players who contributed most to the defeat of the All Blacks in 1971.

I remember Mervyn not only for his domination at the end of the lineout, but also for his killer tackles – like the one in the first Test on the Newlands ground in Cape Town in 1974, when he hammered that great South African flanker, Jan Ellis, into the ground. It set a standard for the tour and precipitated the impending doom and eclipse of South Africa in the test series. There were also his great forward surges, such as his imperious arrival to score an unstoppable try in the closing moments of the Barbarian game against the All Blacks at Twickenham in 1974, and so draw the game.

In the late sixties and throughout the seventies Wales never lacked for truly superb and effective back-row forwards; and with Mervyn in the back row of the scrum for much of that period were two of the liveliest and most splendid marauding wing forwards of our time. They were W. D. Morris of Neath, who became the most capped Welsh wing forward with thirty-four caps from 1967 to 1974, and John Taylor of London Welsh, who played as a back row unit with Mervyn Davies for the first time in the triple crown side of 1969.

Dai Morris was a man as hard as the anthracite coal of the West Wales coalfield in which he worked as a colliery blacksmith. He was the nearest thing to perpetual motion on the field that I ever saw; he revelled in the loose game, snapping up more than his share of tries. But he was also never found lacking in the tighter forward game, where he was courageous in the tackle and immensely quick to the breakdown. He was a model flanker, possessing astonishing stamina, a lovely pair of hands and an acute sense of position. Like many strong men he hardly ever spoke unless he was asked a direct question and for such a great player, he was an incredibly retiring and modest man.

Only once can I remember severe criticism of Dai Morris and John Taylor – when they were out-played in a hard forward game against the All Blacks in Cardiff in 1972. On this occasion they were beaten for size and physique by Ian Kirkpatrick and that old grizzly, Alex Wylie. The only tragedy in Dai Morris's magnificent career was that he never went on a Lions tour, for which he was eminently qualified – indefatigable, tireless in attack and defence, and ever eager to drive forward. He was yet another player who graced his era, and whose approach to the game and behaviour at all times was irreproachable.

John Taylor, who won his twenty-six caps from 1967 to 1973, was known to his contemporaries as Basil Brush because of the fuzzy hairstyle which made him look for all the world like a white Fijian. He epitomized the term 'break away forward' for he was supreme in the loose – quick to the breakdown, and with a gift for re-starting movements and playing in support. Often we saw him running like a centre threequarter, a position in which he played his junior rugby. Obviously, he had never forgotten the art of selling a dummy or the side step. Small for a flanker by modern standards, he had an iron will which London Welsh had helped to forge and which carried him on to the Lions tour to South Africa in 1968, then to New Zealand in 1971, where he played with distinction in all four Tests.

He was a controversial selection in his early days for his small stature was thought to make him ineffective, and he was often dropped from the Welsh side. But as he grew in experience he developed into a fine player. He will be remembered above all for his incredible performance at Murrayfield in 1971, when the lead changed hands an astonishing seven times. Apart from playing splendidly throughout the game, Taylor went over for a crucial try under the posts just before half-time. Then, after Gerald Davies had scored wide out in the dying moments, Taylor at the very last tonk of the bell and with the coolness of the veteran he now was, handsomely converted the try with his left foot. This gave Wales the narrowest of victories and contributed to a triple crown and grand slam. Here was a player who, so to speak, punched every ounce of his weight, thus establishing himself as a flanker with the highest credentials.

The only two flankers to challenge Morris and Taylor in this period were Dennis Hughes of Newbridge, who played against New Zealand in 1967 and 1969 and had four caps in 1970, and Tommy David, that mighty man from Pontypridd who, although playing only four times for Wales, toured South Africa with the 1974 Lions. Both were terrific club men who kept the Welsh flankers of their time constantly on their toes. They were lovely men and both went on to give tremendous service to their clubs for many years.

The next in succession in the back row was Derek Quinnell, who got his first cap as a replacement against France in 1972 and in his earlier internationals played at lock forward. Not until 1977, after the sad retirement of Mervyn Davies, did he establish himself as the natural and only successor. Here was one of the most versatile Welsh forwards of our time, but strangely he was never accorded recognition as being one of the really great forwards of the period.

When he was selected as the only uncapped player for the 1971 Lions tour, he became known as 'Sloppy' to his colleagues, after Carwyn James had jokingly chastised him for turning up to a training session in dirty gear. On that tour Carwyn, with typical insight and imagination, blooded him in top international rugby by selecting him as a flanker for the third test, specifically to blot out Sid Going, the most durable scrum-half who ever played for New Zealand. Derek did the job to perfection, enabling the Lions to go 2–1 up in the series.

His career has been punctuated by injury, for he has broken both collar bones, an ankle, a wrist, five ribs and his cheek bone – some measure of his tremendous physical commitment. This chapter of accidents, and a general lack of recognition meant that up to 1979–80 he had won only twenty-two caps; it might have been fifty had he not cried off on three occasions, and been twenty-five times a substitute for Wales. Known as Quinners to his contemporaries he reflects the philosophy of the true amateur, always recognizing that there are more important aspects of life than rugby – which is why he is always fighting for recognition in certain quarters. In 1980 he was the natural captain for Wales, but he was thwarted by an operation which made him unavailable for the first two internationals; and then, controversially, the selectors failed to select him for the last two games. It remains open to question whether under his leadership the disastrous events at Twickenham, when Paul Ringer was sent off, would have occurred, and whether the debacle in Dublin might have been avoided.

Being a heavyweight he has always looked slow in the back row, but so did Bastiat of France; and no-one in his right mind could prefer lightweights before the great skills, presence and commitment of such memorable players. Derek was another link, perhaps the most critical, between Phil Bennett and the try by Gareth Edwards for the Barbarians against the 1973 All Blacks, when he picked the ball up literally from his boot laces for the final pass that sent Edwards on his memorable way. I remember, too, his blind side plunge for a try against Scotland at Cardiff, and the mighty part he played in Llanelli's defeat of the All Blacks. The greatest strength in his game is his instinctive recognition of whether or not to feed the ball, but whenever he chooses to set up a ruck or a maul then nine times out of ten one can guarantee that the ball will come back on his side. Although you could not compare him with Mervyn Davies as a pure No 8, he is nevertheless a player that you have to find room for in your pack.

The next fine flanker to appear was T. J. Cobner, who won nineteen caps from 1974 to 1978 and was to become as highly regarded as Morris and Taylor. He was another player who, astonishingly, was not recognized until late in his career; he did not play for Wales until he was twenty-eight years old. He became captain of Pontypool in 1969 and, remarkably, continued to captain them for nine consecutive seasons. Together with Ray Prosser he built their pack into the most potent club force in Welsh rugby. He belonged to the tighter school of Welsh flankers; incredibly fit and strong, he was a marvellous mauler and turner of a man to make the ball available for his side. He was also a tremendous link player between his forwards and backs, adept at standing out and distributing the ball to the best effect. The only flaw in his game was as a running ball carrier, but here again was a flanker with a fine rugby brain and a born leader by example. It was he and Quinnell who, a third of the way through the 1977 Lions tour, rescued it from total disaster by taking matters into their own hands and determining the forward policy. He was also a fearless stopper, as he illustrated in Dublin in 1978 when, together with Price and Quinnell, he stemmed the avalanching play of an Irish pack which was threatening to over-run the Welsh team. For so hard a player, he was a remarkably sensitive man. Always a players' player, he too belonged in the top drawer of Welsh flankers.

Another hard man on the flank of the scrum was T. P. Evans of Swansea, who won eleven caps from 1975 to 1977. For sheer physical hardness he was probably the toughest of them all; resolute and fearless he possessed an incredible drive which on occasions required a deep wall of defenders to stop. However, he was not a reliable handler of the ball, which possibly was due to defective eyesight.

Although R. C. Burgess of Ebbw Vale got only four caps in 1977, he made a considerable contribution to winning the triple crown that year and scored a very good try under the Irish posts.

At the moment of writing, the Welsh back row seems at the crossroads, with Quinnell coming to the end of his career, Paul Ringer paying a heavy price for his recklessness against France and England and only Jeff Squire, a most reliable and honest craftsman, left to inspire a new generation. It remains to be seen now whether Wales possesses players of the flair and effectiveness of Morris, Taylor and Cobner to fill what is a decisive role for any top-class side.

Although the situation had been alleviated by the introduction of what was once known as the Australian dispensation (which means no direct kicking into touch outside your own twenty-five) the lineout still remains the most decisive area of ball winning in modern rugby. Rarely does a side lose the lineout and win the match. The lock forwards, traditionally the power house of the scrum, and the main jumpers at Nos 2, 4 or 5 in the lineout, are therefore crucial factors to the success of any side. Over the years from 1969, Wales has not been badly served in these vital positions, particularly in comparison with the other nations in the international championship.

At the beginning of our period Wales still had the services of Brian Price who, between 1961 and 1969 won thirty-two caps. However, his last season was marked by controversy; he flattened Noel Murphy with an ugly left hook in front of the referee, and was exceedingly fortunate on that occasion not to go for an early shower; again in contrast, he lacked commitment and aggression during the Welsh tour that summer in New Zealand. These were the only blots on the otherwise unblemished career of one of the outstanding lineout jumpers of the post-war years. Nobody since has equalled his two-handed catching in the lineout, or the height to which he jumped with magnificent timing to win so much consistent ball.

His partner in his last year was Brian Thomas, who also blighted another highly respected career as a hard forward by failing to measure up to the challenge of a great New Zealand pack led by Colin Meads. The presence of Price and Thomas, however, was fundamental to winning the championship in 1969, and their withdrawal left a huge gap for the Welsh selectors to fill in the following season.

Fortunately, however, Delme Thomas now emerged with the new technique he had learned in the southern hemisphere: that of palming with the outside arm while using the inside elbow as protection, a method which is now firmly established throughout the British Isles. He had had a long apprenticeship which began with his controversial selection for the 1966 Lions tour in place of the current England coach Mike Davis; he won seven of his twenty-five Welsh caps between 1966 and 1974, and on another Lions tour to South Africa in 1968. In 1970 Delme Thomas had Geoff Evans, the popular London Welshman, as his partner in the second row, but at the end of an indifferent season Wales did no more than share the championship with France. Then in 1971 he came through in the grand slam team – another London Welshman, Mike Roberts, at his side – to play the best rugby of his career and inspire the rest with some marvellous lineout jumping. In 1973 he was joined by Alan Martin, who to date has won thirty-one caps.

However, it was not until 1975 that Wales was to put together their best lineout team – Geoff Wheel at No 2 and Alan Martin at No 4. While neither was probably the equal of Brian Price or Delme Thomas, they became a well-tried combination, crucial to the Welsh success in winning four consecutive triple crowns. Alan Martin was a fine technician in the lineout but was sometimes lacking in real aggression, though on occasions he rose to great heights, both literally and metaphorically. This lack of aggression was badly exposed in New Zealand in 1977, and for this reason many thought him fortunate to be selected for what was bound to be an equally hard tour to South Africa in 1980. He had the added facility of being able to kick the occasional important long range goal.

Geoff Wheel of Swansea could be described as only a competent jumper at No 2, but in the matter of rucking and mauling he became the best in the business. By the end of the 1979–80 season he already had twenty-six Welsh caps, largely earned by his performance and reputation as a phenomenal ripper of the ball from the ruck and maul. He had a tendency to wildness in his younger days but, like all veteran players, he began to mellow; though he was always capable of the occasional aberration, such as the wild kick which saw him so severely criticized in the now infamous Twickenham game in 1980.

Front rows of this period will always be identified with the memory of that exceptional Pontypool front row of Graham Price, Bobby Windsor and Charlie Faulkner. The trio became a legend during their playing days and were written into the folklore of Welsh rugby by Max Boyce's ballad, beginning with the aggressive words which they so typified: 'Up and under, here we go.' To the Welsh public they were like the three musketeers, intensely loyal to each other, to Pontypool and to Wales – and probably in that order. When occasionally Charlie for any reason was out of the side they grieved with him and then consoled him and each other, and whenever he re-emerged, as when he flew out as a replacement for the Lions in 1977, the other two were as overjoyed as puppies who had found a lost member of their litter.

They were wily on and off the field, and all strong personalities. R. W. Windsor, alias the Duke or Bobby, was always the senior wrangler, and he tended to be the brains and the mouthpiece of this team within a team. It was Bobby who instilled into them their belief in their own invincibility and who was their publicist; if a pressman were near, he was always sure to hear from Bobby what magnificent props Pricey and Charlie were.

Bobby began before the others, winning his first cap in 1973 against Australia, when he scored a try on his début. Controversially, in 1974 when Wales had a bad season by their standards (they lost to England and drew with France and Ireland –

Phil Bennett: *(above)* making the break with JPR Williams as ever in support; *(below)* offering a touch-me-not gesture as he steps out of Strickland's tackle at Old Deer Park; *(overleaf)* kicking one of his four penalty goals against Argentina in 1976.

ohn Williams

and Bobby was having to hook on the retreat) he was selected for the Lions before John Pullin. The oddity of this was that Pullin had been captain when England beat the All Blacks 16–10 in New Zealand in 1973 and also when they beat the Springboks 18–9 in South Africa in 1972 (two anomalous victories which came during one of England's most sterile periods in the championship). However, Bobby vindicated the selection by becoming the Test hooker in what developed into the greatest Lions pack ever; so within ten months of his first cap he had come to be regarded as a world-class hooker.

He was not only a brilliant hooker technically but he was also one of the most intelligent and accurate throwers of the ball at the lineout, and a powerful and highly combative forward in the loose maul and ruck. The game could never get too hot for Bobby, but unhappily it was a burn from lime, applied to mark the field in a Welsh cup-tie against Cardiff, which was prematurely to end his career; he was a bed-ridden television spectator when Wales won the triple crown against England in 1979.

Bobby was joined in the Welsh side by his good friends, G. Price and A. G. Faulkner at the start of the 1975 campaign. The opening match was against France in Paris and brought a surprising 25–10 win – the greatest number of points scored by Wales against France since 1931. This victory established not only the living legend of the Pontypool front row, but also the basis of the pack which contributed handsomely to Welsh accomplishments over the next five years.

Graham Price, destined to be the greatest of the trio, made a devastating début that day in Paris. It was climaxed by a remarkable lung-bursting try which he scored after a surging seventy-yards pursuit of a fly-kick ahead by Geoff Wheel. This prompted Donald Steel of the *Sunday Telegraph*, after describing the late score in some detail, to finish his copy hilariously with the deliciously succinct words, 'But, as they say in Pontypool, *"C'est la vie."*' Graham, who is still practising his craft as the best tight-head prop in world rugby, is a strong silent man who will stand amongst the finest craftsmen of his trade. Enormously powerful, he so weakens his opponents that, like boxers who have received too many body blows, they tend to fade away. This has unfairly brought criticism of him as a collapser of the scrum. In 1980 there was so much suspicion about him that at Twickenham the Irish referee, Mr Burnett, was often to be seen running around to his side of the scrum when the ball was being put in on the opposite side. Because he is such a hard scrummager he has often been the butt of some outrageous violence; he was kicked in the face by a New Zealand prop in the Christchurch test in 1977, and was floored, through a cowardly punch from behind, which broke his jaw, by an Australian forward who was, of all things, a barrister. But although Price's face is a crochet of scar tissue, I have never heard him complain, and to me he embodies the spirit of that most secret of societies, the front row.

The third man, Charlie, like Harry Lime, is the most mysterious for he arrived in the Welsh side at an age when players had sold their boots for charity and replaced them with fire-side slippers. When Charlie came into the reconstructed Welsh pack in January 1975, after a disconcerting display by the Welsh forwards against Tonga in the previous November, he was of an indeterminate age. It was as closely guarded a secret as the number of tickets issued to members of the Welsh Rugby Union, but he was certainly over thirty years old. The programme for his first match in Paris gave his date of birth as the 27 February 1945, but by 1977 it had been amended to the 27 February 1943. Still, who cares, for a man is as young as he feels and performs. It was assumed at the time that he had been carried into the team by the selectors' need to field a stable, experienced unit in the front row, and many people thought that he was only a stop-gap player. He was soon to prove us all wrong, as the Welsh pack that season, with the Pontypool front row, provided the most concrete foundation to a side which won the championship and laid the base for four years' unparalleled achievements. When Charlie scored one of the four tries against Ireland in the last game of the 1975 season, the smile on his face was a picture, and the great delight with which it was hailed by the crowd showed that the Welsh knew a character when they saw one.

Charlie, which is a nickname, was almost thirty when he joined Pontypool from Cross Keys and he went on to win nineteen Welsh caps. He possessed strangely spindly legs for a prop, but he had enormous upper body strength. Although from time to time many critics advocated that he be dropped for a more mobile prop, he always remained the junior but hard-working efficient member of that famous trio. Collectively they were regarded by all who played against them as slightly wicked, but friendly and amiable. Max Boyce referred to them in song as the Viet Cong. Their aggressive and skilful ball winning in the set scrums and the rucks, together with their beavering at the front of the lineout, were of fundamental value to the Welsh team for four years, and they were destined to become a popular part of the mythology of Welsh rugby as the most famous front row of all time.

Wales was represented by many other fine front-row forwards from 1969. The foremost was another superlative player from Gwent, Denzil Williams of Ebbw Vale, who finished an illustrious career on the highest of notes with the grand slam side of 1971. His thirty-six Welsh caps were easily the record for a Welsh prop forward, but though it still exists, it will probably be broken in the next two seasons by Graham Price.

Denzil was big in every sense of the word, one of the biggest props who has played for Wales. He was almost six foot three inches tall, had the dimensions of a barn door and weighed about sixteen and a half stones. He played in the triple crown side of 1961, but although he was dropped after a typically dramatic defeat in Dublin in 1970, he was reinstated for the 1971 grand slam team as a key member of a truly massive front row. His partners were the hooker, Jeff Young, who weighed fourteen and a half stones, and Barry Llewelyn who was also six foot two and a half inches tall and over sixteen stones.

Denzil also belonged to a long list of Welsh props, like W. O. (Stoker) Williams of Swansea and Don Hayward of Newbridge, who converted from the second row because from 1948 onwards the selectors were preoccupied with finding big men, capable of matching the size and power of the New Zealand, South Africa, and French front rows. He captained Ebbw Vale, for whom he played usually in the second row, and also played for Gwent in their famous victory over the Springboks in 1969. An intelligent forward, he had the application and the will to master his new position in the national side, and became an invaluable and popular member of the Welsh team from 1963 to 1971. At the end of the period he had become Wales's most-capped forward, beating Bryn Meredith's record; he was finally overtaken by Mervyn Davies in 1976. Slow to anger, he had the ideal temperament for a position where the battle is always at its thickest and is secretively intense. He never flinched in fierce strife, one rarely saw him losing his temper and throughout his career he was a huge credit to himself and to the game. To this day he is a hard-working, loyal and valuable committee member of Ebbw Vale.

Jeff Young was the automatic choice of hooker from 1968 to 1973 and played twenty-three times for Wales. He would have had a couple more caps but for being on the receiving end of a mighty blow from Colin Meads in the disastrous first test against New Zealand in Christchurch in 1969. His biggest fault was that he always had a terrifying propensity to give away penalties. On that occasion in Christchurch, he held the magnificent All Black prop Ken Gray, by the jersey, and, unfortunately for him, it was Colin Meads and not the referee who spotted his offence. Colin, who in his time too often took the law into his own hands, again became the Lord High Executioner and felled him with a blow which broke his jaw. Subsequently the veteran Norman Gale came on as replacement, and went on to play in the second test in Auckland and in the test against Australia in Sydney.

As well as being a lightning striker for the ball, Jeff was a tough and abrasive forward, who always expressed and proved himself in the loose as well as the tight. A product of the great tradition of St Luke's, Exeter, an institution now sadly defunct having been absorbed into Exeter University, Jeff

Young of Harrogate gave Wales fine and consistent service.

After going on tour with Wales to New Zealand as an uncapped player in 1969, D. B. Llewelyn, known as Barry, became a fixture in the Welsh front row from 1970 to 1972 and won thirteen caps. He would have won many more but for his decision to concentrate on his successful sports shop business. He was another example of the fashion for big props at the time, and another successful conversion – but this time from the back row of the scrum, for at Llanelli he began his career as a No 8 or flanker. It was not surprising, therefore, that he became more renowned for his loose play than for his scrummaging, and his forte was his power and speed on the peel at the back of the lineout.

Another outstanding prop of the early seventies was D. J. Lloyd of Bridgend, who has now succeeded John Dawes as coach to the national side. Known to his contemporaries as 'Greedy' owing to his phenomenal appetite, John played twenty-four times for Wales between 1966 and 1973. He was a quiet and unassuming player but a magnificent thinker about the game. The unhappiest part of his international career came when he was dropped from the great 1971 side and he was never selected for the Lions. Restitution was made in 1972 when, on the retirement of Denzil Williams, he was brought back to captain the side, but although he captained Wales to three victories in three games to head the uncompleted championship of 1972, the fickleness of selection saw him lose the captaincy in 1973 when Wales floundered under three different captains in the season of the quintuple tie.

John Lloyd was another of those rare birds who are not only first-class props but tireless and thoughtful loose forwards, with the intelligence to make the ball readily and quickly available to their half-backs. Strangely, he was always thought too small, yet he was nearly six feet tall and weighed sixteen stone. On reflection, it is also odd that so many props of this period were extremely quiet and reserved personalities, but perhaps, if you consider the nature of their employment in the team, it becomes easier to understand.

In the gap between the period of total supremacy of 1969–72, and the climactic times of 1975–79, Glyn Shaw of Neath, who won twelve caps and ultimately turned professional, was the most consistent, though thought wanting in scrummaging ability. Phil Llewellyn of Swansea earned five caps and Walter Williams of Neath two, but the arrival of the tremendous trio from Pontypool then made the Welsh front row a closed shop until 1979.

Graham Price soldiers on, and Clive Williams, who had the temerity to replace Charlie Faulkner in two matches during 1977 – earning a place on the Lions tour to New Zealand where he sustained a severe knee injury – has re-emerged as an able partner to Graham and to Alan Phillips. The Cardiff hooker, on the evidence of his play, particularly against France and England in 1980, and with his selection for South Africa, where he should gain enormous experience, now seems set for a useful career.

There have been many other fine forwards of this calibre like Stuart Gallacher, who won only one cap before turning professional. If they have not been discussed this is no discredit to their ability; it is simply that they were not around long enough in the Welsh side to have any sustained influence on affairs. It is sufficient to say that since the introduction of the squad system, no forward or back for that matter, has been selected for Wales unless he was worth his salt. The value of the Welsh cap has appreciated considerably since the days when a fluke performance in a Welsh trial on a filthy wet day, or when strength and luck rather than pace and skill, carried many a one-cap wonder into the Welsh team.

If moreover sufficient credit has not been given to the forwards, who so strenuously built the foundations of the Welsh successes of this period, it is because they were found wanting rather more than were the backs. This was clearly illustrated when they played teams from the Southern Hemisphere and failed, sometimes abysmally.

The forwards are only good enough in the European context of the international championship, whereas backs such as

Gareth Edwards, Barry John, J. P. R. Williams, Gerald Davies, Phil Bennett, John Dawes and J. J. Williams measured up to the best in the world – as do Terry Holmes, Gareth Davies and Dave Richards today. It was the kicking skills of the great Welsh halves of the period which so often papered over the cracks in the Welsh forward play, and which provided them with the impetus to go forward according to the gospel of Ray Williams. However the Welsh forwards were consistently the best in the British Isles, and it was only the French who offered a repeated challenge to their supremacy.

I should hasten to add that Ireland also gave them a hard time on occasions. Since 1969, France have beaten Wales three times in Paris, Scotland did so twice at Murrayfield, Ireland twice in Dublin and England twice at Twickenham. On each of these occasions the Welsh pack were beaten away from home in the championship, sustaining only nine defeats in the forty-eight games of the past twelve seasons.

In the final analysis, the donkeys were never asses. They became fine pedigree stock, carrying their onerous burdens with distinction and flair, particularly those packs from 1975 to 1979. During the period, there were forwards of great distinction who held their own or even bettered the achievements of any in the whole hundred years.

5
Pressure Points

It would be naive to imagine that Wales throughout our period always played imaginative, excitingly fluent, running rugby. Much of it was far from that, for what the new system and coaches introduced into the players' consciousness was the necessity to win by playing positive and effective rugby. The new regime set out to ensure that the fundamental objective of ball-winning was achieved by the co-operative method – ensuring that every member of the pack understood the collective purpose. Very quickly the Welsh forwards began to make the ball more available, certainly from the ruck and maul, than any of the other countries in the championship. Even if occasionally they took the wrong option, the fact that they were all taking it together very often turned it into advantage. Enormous care and thoroughness were also applied to the set piece and again the improvement in the scrummaging became immediately apparent. The lineout, which still remains the most confusing and abstract area of forward play (Danie Craven many years ago described it beautifully as 'the illegal child of rugby'), was also rationalized, as far as it ever can be. Learning the lessons dearly bought from the Southern Hemisphere, the Welsh entered into the spirit of compression, always a grey area of legitimacy, improved their throwing skills and techniques and developed their peel and rolling maul. They learned to impose pressure on the opposition's throw, instead of accepting the inevitability of loss of possession. Pressure was to be applied on the opposition not only when Wales were in possession; it was also to be applied at those points where the opposition were expected, as a formality, to win the ball.

Sometimes the Welsh carried the exertion of pressure to

ridiculous extremes. I remember one game against Australia when Gareth Edwards made thirteen consecutive kicks from the ruck and maul. Very often therefore, it was legitimate to criticize Wales for failing to expand their game when they had the capacity to do so. However, it was this single-minded approach to building up momentum by always going forward which created the platform for so many of their victories. And once they had achieved a two-score lead, it allowed them to switch into a free style and unravel opposing defences, to score twenty points or more in the Five Nations tournament on eighteen occasions – seven times against Ireland, six against England, three against Scotland and twice against France.

The most exhilarating spell behind the scrum came between 1969 and 1972, with the half-back partnership of Gareth Edwards and Barry John. At that time Barry was the dominant personality and on occasions he would kick with terrifying frequency and accuracy; but once he knew that the game was won, he would unleash his threequarters with consummate skill which Phil Bennett, although a marvellous match-winning kicker and a tremendous runner from broken play, could never equal. When Roy Bergiers played with Barry John in 1972, he looked an exciting player; but then, when he began playing with Phil, his game failed to develop. We also saw Steve Fenwick and Ray Gravell become obsessed with the crash ball. Not until the advent of Gareth Davies and that exciting runner David Richards in 1979 did we see a release from the stereotyped and predictable midfield play of the mid- and late-seventies. I am assured by all the Welsh coaches that there was never any fault in concept on their part, and that the use of the crash ball and the neglect of Welsh wingers of the quality of Gerald Davies and J. J. Williams were entirely the decisions of the players on the field. Ray Williams tells me that he has attended all the squad sessions since their inception and never has a coach called for a crash ball.

The last twelve years can be divided into two distinct sections when achievement was at its highest. The time from

1969 to 1972 was the more exuberant and satisfying experience in terms of exciting and brilliant rugby; it reached a climax in the 1971 side and also formed the basis of the achievements of the 1971 Lions in New Zealand. The teams in those years had a particular appeal for the Welsh, for although they survived largely on the minimum amount of ball from their forwards, they produced back play which enchanted the crowd. It was impelling and fascinating stuff as the two young Welsh halves, Edwards and John, began to assemble an amazing armoury of skills, convincing so many Welshmen, who have always idolized half-backs, that this was the best pair who ever played for Wales.

Gareth Edwards overcame his weaknesses by working on them until they became his strengths. If his passing had been wayward in the early days, his application saw to it that accuracy and length were achieved together with the right tactical option. Barry John, feasting and revelling at the end of his pass, had the necessary footballing genius to play all the options. There was a precarious wobble against France in 1969, when Wales only achieved a fortuitous draw by unexpectedly going back into their old-fashioned shell of ten-man rugby. However, they ravished England by scoring thirty points and won the triple crown with such a flourish and with such style that the game was hailed as a final justification of the squad system. This, despite the fact that in 1967 Wales had beaten England with the highest score ever achieved against their dearest enemy – 34 points – but then England on that occasion had also mustered a remarkable 22 points.

The show was now on the road, but the bandwagon almost immediately came to an abrupt halt in May and June, when the All Blacks poured cold water and drenched their aspirations by giving them a terrible hiding in the two Tests in New Zealand. The Welsh side, supreme in Britain the previous season, was smashed to pieces, but in retrospect it was good for the soul, for it forced them to go back to the drawing board. It was significant that players such as J. P. R. Williams,

Gerald Davies, John Dawes, Barry John, Gareth Edwards, John Taylor, Mervyn Davies and Dai Morris – all youngsters apart from Dawes and Morris – were among those humiliated by the All Blacks. Most of them were to form the hard core of the huge successes of the next decade. This traumatic experience, which taught them how far they still had to go to become a great side, tempered their minds. The failures in New Zealand had much to do with motivating the players, and it also had a profound effect on the 1971 Lions tour which was to include thirteen invaluable Welshmen.

The other principal controversy of 1969 was a notorious punch by Brian Price on Noel Murphy, which Price claimed was provoked by an Irish player clawing at his eyes in a maul. It became a *cause célèbre* and Tommy Kiernan told the Scottish referee, Doug McMahon, 'If there is any more of this, I'm going to take my team off the field.' Considerable harm was inflicted on Welsh–Irish relations, which have not entirely mended to this day.

There were problems, too, at the end of the season, when those two extremely talented backs, Maurice Richards and Keith Jarrett, turned professional, Gerald Davies took a sabbatical year to concentrate on his studies, and Wales lost two of their hard-core forwards, Brian Price and Brian Thomas, who retired. In addition, the aftermath of the Antipodean tour produced a crisis of confidence and there was a feeling that the players were suffering from a surfeit of rugby. However, the value of the squad system now proved itself and Wales emerged to share the championship with France in 1970.

* *

At this stage, it is important to reflect whether the players who were lured into the professional game were wise in the long term. Surely the rewards gained by the star players who remained were, in the end, far greater. Their prestige in Wales brought them better jobs and opportunities; they travelled extensively at the expense of Rugby Union football, thus widening their horizons; and the superstars among them, like Barry John and Gareth Edwards made small fortunes through their autobiographies and their incursions into the public relations field.

It is a tremendous temptation for a young player without capital, who perhaps is contemplating marriage, to accept the large lump-sum payment for signing as a professional. Unfortunately the lure of Rugby League caused Wales to lose quality players who could have contributed immensely to this period and enhanced the Welsh reputation. Players of the quality of Stuart Gallacher, John Bevan, Maurice Richards, Keith Jarrett and, later, Clive Griffiths were losses of considerable dimension. But the ease with which Wales were able to fill the gaps from the reservoir of talent, now carefully filtered and processed by the squad system, underlined the value of the hard work which had gone into restructuring the whole selectoral system since 1964.

There is also little doubt that rugby at the top level nowadays provides a considerable ego trip for the players concerned. They are feted as heroes and this, together with the commercial advantages gained from their starring roles, is strong motivation. This applies to only a lesser extent in the other four Home Unions and France where the situation in the south-west is a close parallel. However, the concentration of strength in a small area, where the major Welsh clubs are no more than sixty miles apart, gives Wales a distinct selectoral advantage. In addition, the fact that Welsh players are in closer and more regular contact with their public, provides a huge stimulus to their performance. The only disadvantage is that these factors also build up greater pressures on the players.

Such pressures, added to the players' realization of their own worth to the Welsh Rugby Union and to the British Lions (huge sums of money have poured into the coffers in the last decade) have set off a movement by some to gain greater personal reward. In the opinion of most Rugby Union administrators and other responsible observers of the scene, this movement is not only mistaken but could, in the end, be catastrophic for the game. It is essential that in the British

Isles we have one great game in which amateur players can express themselves within the context of normal family life and regular employment. The opportunity for fulfilment in such a game holds great charm. Amateurism is also part of the game's ethic creating a social ambience and a standard of crowd behaviour and attitude which are the envy of many other major sports.

The Welsh Rugby Union has made enormous strides forward. As recently as 1949 I remember the Welsh team travelled third class to Paris while members of the Union were in first class carriages. When they got to the Hotel Terminus, the players were kept milling around the foyer for some time while the more important members of the party, the WRU committee, were allocated their rooms. Nowadays, the WRU care far more for the comforts of their team and the atmosphere is more enlightened. But further progress is necessary, particularly on overseas tours. In New Zealand in 1977, the Lions were not accorded the best accommodation and were even denied the opportunity of an *à la carte* menu. It is complaints such as these which give the players a sense of grievance and which have promoted among them the search for bigger rewards. In our increasingly competitive society we must acknowledge that many players suffer considerable financial hardship in undertaking long tours without payment from their employers. The increase in tour pocket money to almost five pounds a day is still not good enough, particularly in view of the enormous profits which such tours earn. The modern player, therefore, must carefully examine his attitudes, for he must know that he can receive high rewards in other directions. Not least is the vast satisfaction of being involved in the last great amateur sport, and fulfilling his ambitions not only locally but throughout the world.

The international growth of amateur rugby football is largely due to the fact that many people, particularly in North America, wish to express themselves outside the narrow field of professionalism. Professional baseball and football in the United States, for instance, require total dedication and their huge rewards are limited to the very special few.

After making solid progress in the undetermined championship of 1972, Wales faltered during the quintuple tie of 1973, when all the teams won their Five Nations tournament games at home. That year, however, brought the attractive diversion of a visit from the Japanese who, although they were courageous and great fun, lacked the physique and stature to match the Caucasian size and power of the Welsh. Their rugby was as delightfully miniature as their Bonsai trees, conceding nothing in skill or in attitude but clearly a long way from posing a serious threat to Welsh, European or Southern Hemisphere rugby. In 1974 the only comfort was the decisive defeat of Australia. A season which brought a disappointing defeat against England and deficiencies in the front row and centre-threequarter play, saw Ireland winning the triple crown; but in 1975 there was a resurgence of Welsh forward play under the authoritative leadership of Mervyn Davies and the arrival of the Pontypool front row.

Thus began the second and more pronounced period of Welsh supremacy, this time differing from 1971 it was based on the most effective forward play of the decade. This ensured four years of Welsh dominance, blighted only by French victory in the championship in 1977. The results were achieved by superb ball-winning by the reconstructed Welsh pack, which announced its revival in 1975 by providing the biggest Welsh win over France in Paris since 1911. It was all the more gratifying as none of the critics had given Wales the remotest chance of winning, after their substantial defeat in Paris in 1973 and their drawn game in Cardiff the previous year. It was in this match that the Pontypool front row established the foundation which was of inestimable value to the Welsh team for the next four years. The last manager of the All Blacks, the efficient and canny Russ Thomas, said recently, 'British rugby puts too much emphasis on scrummaging' – a view that must never be accepted, as both the Lions of 1971 and 1974, and even the Lions of 1977, proved the value of good scrummaging beyond doubt. It was this very factor which, after the emergence of the Pontypool front row, allowed the remainder of the forwards to play with greater confidence and impact. Subsequently Alan Martin became an invaluable member of the Welsh team at No 4 and, together with Geoff Wheel, a great mauling forward at No 2 and Mervyn Davies to the rear brought Wales more lineout balls than at any other time in the decade. Welsh lineout play became extremely efficient and established its first real authority since 1969. People seem to underestimate the value of the lineout, but due to its greater frequency, it is still the most important set piece for ball-winning.

So the back rows of the next four years had a field day and men like Trevor Evans, Tommy David, Terry Cobner, Mervyn Davies, Derek Quinnell, Clive Burgess, Jeff Squire and Paul Ringer were able to build high reputations for themselves, both in the open field and in complementing the half-back play.

The Welsh forward play, nevertheless, owed much to the imperious kicking of Gareth Edwards, who, by now, had become as authoritative as Barry John in exerting pressure by kicking. With the Lions in South Africa in 1974, Gareth had totally mastered the art of controlling territory and creating momentum for his forwards through his persistent and extraordinary kicks to the diagonal and into the blind-side box.

At this time, John Bevan of Aberavon replaced Phil Bennett for the games against France, England and Scotland in 1975. This followed the defeat of a Welsh XV by the All Blacks in November. No caps were awarded in this match because the All Blacks were on a short tour of Ireland, and the Irish had requested that theirs should be the only full-scale international. The Cardiff fixture was simply inserted to help balance the books, but Wales nevertheless fielded a full-strength side, and its defeat cost Bennett his international place. John Bevan brought a commitment to the Welsh midfield, which had been lacking for two seasons. However, Bennett came on as a substitute against Scotland and was picked against Ireland after Bevan badly injured his shoulder. After the controversy in the following season, when Bennett was astonishingly relegated to fourth Welsh outside-half, it is true to say that Phil, having had food for thought, revitalized his game; from here on he became a vastly different player and a brilliant match winner for Wales. In 1975, the Scots inflicted a typical defeat at Murrayfield – where they always seem to play with far greater élan and pride against Wales – and this combined with the only indifferent performance of the season by the much improved Welsh pack saw the grand slam slither out of Welsh hands.

After their oriental Odyssey to Japan in the autumn of 1975, which was inevitably a simple team-building exercise, Wales returned to take the bounce out of the Wallabies in December, imposing the heaviest defeat that Australia had ever suffered at Welsh hands. From that promising start the 1976 season was one of total fulfilment. The renaissance of Phil Bennett was a major factor in realizing the Welsh threat which, since 1971, had hung as heavily as the sword of Damocles over the other four nations. The grand slam returned to Wales under the compelling captaincy of Mervyn Davies who by now believed implicitly in both his own and the Welsh team's invincibility. If the manner of winning was aesthetically less pleasing to the eye than the brilliance produced by the back play of the 1971 side, it was nevertheless statistically the more emphatic victory; Wales scored more points in the championship than at any other time in its history. This was largely due to the kicking of Phil Bennett, with a record thirty-eight points in a season, thirty-five of them from the boot.

Although the team had scored 102 points in the championship, they scored only eleven tries against the 1971 team's thirteen. To build up so many points meant that they had achieved a massive territorial advantage – largely negotiated by the rising strength and technique of the Welsh pack, and again by the kicking of Gareth Edwards and Phil Bennett. By nature and long practice, Bennett was another fine kicker in both offence and defence and became a great match winner.

Sated by success, it was about this time that Welshmen ceased to be satisfied with anything less than comprehensive victory. They began to expect superhuman, even supernatural, actions from their team, and this put them on the slippery slope to unpopularity in other countries. I remember Mervyn Davies saying that one day Wales were going to annihilate some team by over 50 points, and such was his driving force and his growing confidence in the team that many were inclined to believe him. He also said at the end of the international season in that year, that his ambition was now to win three grand slams in a row. Tragically his playing career was then cut short by a brain haemorrhage, but even without him Wales almost achieved his ambition. To this day, Mervyn is not happy as a spectator he watches the game with all the restlessness of a caged lion, as though he wants to get back on the field to complete some unfinished business.

At the end of the grand slam year in 1976, France had given notice of their great potential when Wales were lucky to scramble a win. It was achieved only by the tactical purpose of Gareth Edwards, who turned France back into the corners, and by the familiar steadfastness of J. P. R. Williams at full-back. Wales won the triple crown again in 1977 after surviving a perilous match against the Pumas of Argentina in October; but for a head hunting tackle by Travaglini which brought them a penalty in injury time, Wales would have lost sensationally. This incident probably did more to eliminate that unattractive feature of Argentinian play, the short-arm tackle, than ten years of criticism. But, Wales relinquished the championship and the grand slam to the French, who remarkably dominated a Welsh pack which badly missed the physical presence of Mervyn Davies.

In 1978 Wales unexpectedly went on to win their third triple crown in succession and their third grand slam in eight years. However, the opposition from the other countries in the championship was now beginning to stiffen, and there was evidence that Wales were beginning to lose much of their emphatic control. The match against England was fraught with pitfalls, and Wales won narrowly by three penalty goals to two. It was only the enormous talent of Gareth Edwards, who by now was the elegant prince of scrum-halves, together with the play of those Welsh barons behind the scrum, Phil Bennett, Gerald Davies and J. P. R. Williams, which saved the day for Wales. Similarly, the match against Ireland in Dublin was played with such Homeric intensity and extreme vigour, that the Welsh team in the dressing-room afterwards were in a state of shock. It was this game which was to precipitate the retirement of Edwards, Bennett and Davies, whose incredible gifts for rugby football seemed irreplaceable. Wales had reached the final apex of their second Golden Era.

The 1978–79 season held little promise. In the summer a disastrous tour of Australia had ended in bitter acrimony which soured relations between the two countries. The Welsh match winners had retired, and there was growing dissatisfaction with recent mid-field play and its devotion to the crash-ball. Yet for all that, Wales marched on to an unparalleled fourth triple crown in succession. Against the rising strength of the other nations, they had to delve deep into their reservoir of experience but in the end only France succeeded in exploiting their weaknesses.

The international season began with the ignominy of a bitter defeat when the black aces of New Zealand once again trumped the red aces of Wales. There was new optimism, however, with the introduction of yet another exciting half-back pair, Terry Holmes and Gareth Davies, who seemed to be as good as Gareth Edwards and Barry John at the same period of development. Later in the season, too, the introduction of an exciting new midfield runner, David Richards, brought an injection of pace into the centre-threequarter play and a new zest for attack after the pallid and sterile crash-ball tactics of the previous two years.

The era finally ended in 1980 on an unhappy note when Wales managed to beat the Romanians in Cardiff by a margin of only 13–12, so thwarting their visitors' brave bid to prove their legitimate claim to a place in the exclusive club of the European championship. Then, after a convincing victory over a French side, cock-a-hoop following their win over New Zealand in Auckland in the summer, the Welsh denouement came. The selectors, ignoring both deficiencies and unacceptable standards of behaviour in their team, made grave errors which led to the sickening events at Twickenham – events which not only enraged the British rugby public but succeeded in drawing the teeth of the Welsh side for the remainder of the season. It was all the more tragic because Wales, in a proper frame of mind, easily had the capacity to beat England. With their spirit damaged beyond repair, Wales struggled on to beat Scotland unimpressively before succumbing to the lively Irish, offering such a muted performance that in some quarters it was interpreted as a surrender without a fight.

Nevertheless, any aberrations in selection, playing standards and ethical conduct during the whole period were remarkably few. They were heavily outweighed by superb achievement and the enormous pleasure that the Welsh players gave to those who love their rugby football, and who were not unduly concerned with ethnic or partisan considerations. The selectors, whose task was very much simplified by the squad system, on the whole made the right choices and were only very occasionally guilty of error. They were involved in only two major controversies – over Phil Bennett and over their failure to spot the problems after the French match in 1980. The players, for their part, subscribed fully to the new concepts, and the isolated incidents violating the unwritten codes of conduct of the game were both exceedingly infrequent and, to a large extent, blown up out of all proportion.

The Welsh teams from 1969 to 1980 reached heights of success and produced rugby of a quality that has probably never before been bettered in the British Isles. One can only say that it has been a marvellous privilege to watch them play. In the final analysis, it was all achieved by collective purpose and organization, induced by the advent of enlightened administration; by men dedicated to the cause of coaching and organization; by the revolutionary concept of the squad system; by the coincidental arrival of players with singleminded loyalty to the cause and huge talents for rugby football; and, finally, by the eagerness and zeal that Welshmen at large possess for a game which they admire before any other.

6
How Others Saw Us

The principal frustrations and failures were those sustained against the mighty men of the Southern Hemisphere, those arch rivals in black jerseys with the silver fern leaf from New Zealand, and the huge men of the green and gold jerseys with the Springbok emblem from South Africa. In seven matches Wales have never beaten South Africa, although they managed to draw in Cardiff in 1970. On three occasions the difference was only three points and, on another, five points. The most decisive defeat came in 1964, when Wales lost by a margin of twenty-one points – a humiliation which provoked the resurgence of Welsh rugby. Against the All Blacks, Wales have won only three out of ten matches, though up until 1963 they had won three out of four. Since then they have suffered a string of six defeats, four of them during their second Golden Era. What was described as a Welsh XV also lost to the All Blacks in an unofficial test in November, 1974.

Of greater concern than the defeats themselves against New Zealand is the appalling deterioration in the relations between the two countries, which basically began during the All Blacks' ill-natured tour of the British Isles in 1972–73. This culminated in the unfortunate affair when Keith Murdoch, the wild man, was sent home after a punch-up with the Gwent security services in the Angel Hotel in Cardiff. In the words of the doyen of New Zealand rugby journalists, Terry Maclean, 'The team took on the character of a body of graceless and ill-humoured men.' Coming from Terry, who to friend and foe alike in the press box is known as 'Poison Pen' and who, for all his urbanity, is a dedicated if not a one-eyed supporter of New Zealand attitudes, this was a surprising admission. It indicated that there were huge problems in the

New Zealand camp. Feeding on the trench warfare, feuding and ill temper of the game itself, the Welsh media also went to town. In *The Observer* I wrote, 'If the total object of a game of rugby is to win, then the least that can be said of New Zealand is that they succeeded. They will be happy but the manner of victory is also part of the folklore and in this they would be regarded without affection.' Subsequently, although the New Zealand rugby public recognized failure in the tour management, they tended to make Murdoch a martyr which, in truth, he never was. The Welsh were presented as the villains of the piece, and this gave rise to the current New Zealand saying that you never beat Wales, you only score more points than them. In 1974, in the game that was an international in all but name, a credible attempt was made to lay the dust of resentment which had lain thick over both sides since the 1972–73 tour. New Zealand had no complaints about the attitudes of their hosts either before or after the 12–6 Welsh defeat. The Welsh had gone out of their way to hold out the olive branch by giving the All Blacks the friendliest of receptions. They sang 'Land of My Fathers' as well as it ever has been sung in Cardiff – though whether this was for the benefit of the All Blacks or an invocation to the Welsh team to bring a yearned-for victory, is a matter of conjecture. Recognizing that they had been well beaten, the Welsh were also generous in defeat, which nails the prevalent lie that Welshmen are bad losers.

Mindful of the fiasco of their last full-blown tour, the New Zealand administration diplomatically appointed one of their shrewdest statesmen, Russ Thomas, for the difficult task of re-establishing the good name of their rugby teams when the All Blacks returned to the British Isles in 1978. (Prior to 1972 they had always been admired for their discipline and conduct on and off the field.) Unhappily, in spite of the strenuous efforts of Russ Thomas as manager and the late Jack Leason, coach (a man responsible for broadening the All Blacks' play in the face of considerable opposition from many New Zealand administrators who firmly believed in their traditionally annihilating forward play), the atmosphere of the tour was tragically destroyed in the test against Wales. It all occurred during that lineout which is now regarded as the most notorious in rugby history. With three minutes to go, including two of injury time, Wales were leading 12–10, a margin which in no way flattered them for at this point they should have been well ahead. Then the referee awarded a penalty against Geoff Wheel, which Brian McKechnie, who had come on as a substitute early in the game, kicked faultlessly to win the game.

The anatomy of this fateful lineout was to be microscopically analysed on television and clearly showed that the All Blacks had cheated – a fact later confirmed by a New Zealand rugby journalist who had been privy to the plot. Although the All Blacks covered up their indiscretion by refusing to comment, the evidence against them was overwhelming. Wales threw a short line and Geoff Wheel jumped for the ball with the intention of deflecting it with his outside arm; in keeping with the modern practice he raised his left elbow to afford protection. Midway through his jump, Frank Oliver backed into him and Wheel, as he felt the barge, fended him off. At this point Oliver threw himself out of the lineout and so did Andy Haden at No 4. The New Zealand expression for acting on the field is known as 'a Hollywood', but for this performance Haden at least earned no Oscar. It was the absurdity of his performance, when he was nowhere near the ball, that ruined the show. I was informed by the touch judge, Welsh referee John Evans, that Oliver, during his dive, shouted at the top of his voice. Understandably enough, the referee, Mr Roger Quittenton was conned by the whole performance and awarded the fateful penalty. In his defence, few people on the ground realized the implications of the whole affair, and it was not until they saw the television replays the next day that Welsh indignation became aroused. However, both Barry John and I in the press box realized at the time that there was something fishy about the whole affair. Five minutes after the match, in my post-match comments on Radio Wales, I stated that

I would await the television replay with interest.

What otherwise had been an impeccably behaved tour was further soured when J. P. R. Williams was savagely stamped on, on the borders of a ruck, by John Ashworth in the match against Bridgend to celebrate the club's centenary year. The result was a grievous wound which required eight stitches after a stud had penetrated the cheek. Again New Zealand management closed ranks by denying that they had seen the incident, and by implying that such injuries were as good as self-inflicted if British players persisted in lying on the ball. In this case, JPR was nowhere near the ball, and the management soon had the opportunity to observe the incident on television; but they still failed to admit that it was an unacceptable action. This, again, received the maximum publicity in the press, and when the New Zealand management compounded the offence by introducing Ashworth as a substitute in the final match against the Barbarians at Cardiff, the predominantly Welsh crowd became incensed by the action. Denying the moral of the banner carried by two New Zealand supporters at the match – 'Rugby, a Way of Making Friends' – they showed their displeasure by booing Ashworth's arrival on the field. So a great tour, otherwise well led by the management and a fine captain, Graham Mourie, and bringing New Zealand seventeen wins in eighteen matches (the only defeat was against Munster), came to grief once again in Wales.

One tends to believe that such events are matters of the greatest misfortune, and it is therefore no wonder that New Zealanders now think so badly of Wales. It must be emphasized, too, that it was the representatives of the media, myself included, who always highlighted these great controversies which caused the Welsh rugby public to react with indignation. The cause of the rivalry lies in the fact that both Wales and New Zealand regard success as the principal virtue; that they both have an enormous passion for the game; and that, by the nature of their social background, both countries provide and accept a greater degree of violence, which perhaps they mistakenly identify as a measure of their virility. There are faults on both sides and it is now time for guidance and statesmanship from the administration of both countries. The first step required is a ban on brutality and untoward violence, together with a statement of intent that the future between the two countries lies in the joy of playing good rugby within the spirit of the game.

The frequency of New Zealand's visits to the British Isles – which have filled the gap so sadly left by South Africa's exclusion since 1970 – have, of course, aggravated the situation. No such antipathy is evident between Wales and South Africa. It is South Africa who have dominated world rugby more than any other country, for they have beaten New Zealand nineteen times, while New Zealand have won thirteen games. These two countries have also enjoyed their considerable differences, particularly in 1976 when New Zealand last toured South Africa and lost the series 3–1. There was a squeal from New Zealand about the violence and the refereeing, which was ironical since New Zealand had spurned South Africa's offer of neutral referees.

Without denigrating the performances of the Southern Hemisphere countries and their successes against Wales, it is possible to put forward a strong mitigation in defence of the Welsh performance. If we begin with the failure in Argentina in 1968 – when Wales lost one test and drew the other – it must be remembered that most of the star Welsh players were in South Africa with the Lions. It was largely an experimental side, thrown into the deep end against the unknown quantity of Argentine rugby, now regarded as a serious rival to the longer-established rugby countries. Wales were surprised by the organization and the hardness of Argentina, and it must also be remembered that during their first game against Belgrano, an Argentine player was concussed and died in hospital, which spoilt the tour and took the edge off the Welsh appetite.

The Welsh tour to New Zealand in 1969 was a suicide mission, for to play Taranaki and New Zealand within eight days of arrival (a period which also included an earthquake in New Plymouth) was complete madness to those who appreciate the debilitating effect of jet lag. Wales struck New Zealand at their very best, for at that time New Zealand possessed their strongest post-war pack, full of all-time greats of the calibre of Colin Meads, Ken Gray, and Kel Tremaine, all hugely experienced and at the height of their powers. If one of them moved in the lineout they all did, which disguised any individual illegality. They were too much of a handful for what, by comparison, was a naive Welsh pack.

Another point of view tendered by Clive Rowlands, who was coach to both the Argentine and New Zealand tours and also manager of the 1978 team to Australia, is that Wales do not take enough players on tour with them. After injuries are taken into account it becomes a struggle to find a full-strength side; therefore there is insufficient competition amongst the players and they tend to enjoy themselves. Rowlands also argues that Wales are regarded with such respect in other countries that the sides they meet are extremely well prepared. Having seen Ivan Vodanovich putting the All Blacks through their paces before the Welsh test in Christchurch, I have no doubt that this is entirely true. In addition, every player in 1969 wanted to play against Wales, and many of them had deferred their retirement until after they had done so. It is interesting to note that the successful 1971 Lions were experienced in the ways and methods of New Zealand rugby, as two-thirds of the side had been to New Zealand before, some of them twice.

The failure of the Welsh team in Australia in 1978 is more difficult to excuse, particularly in relation to the Welsh boast that they were now the best prepared side in European rugby. On this tour the Welsh discipline seemed to disintegrate and there were areas of bitter controversy. On one occasion Clive Rowlands threatened to take the side home, declaring that Australia had broken the tour agreement on the question of the appointment of a referee. Fortunately, having thought about it and discussed it with others, he retracted the ultimatum, but he still lost the argument with the Australian Rugby Union. He was also outspoken when Steve Finnane broke

Graham Price's jaw, which he called 'an act of thuggery'. However, it was evident that Welsh players also lost their heads in that infamous second test in Sydney, and that in so doing they fell on their own sword. This tour served only to increase the feeling that due to ill discipline the Welsh are bad tourists.

It is also interesting to reflect on the view of Ray Williams, that the failures against New Zealand in the last decade have been due to playing too early in the Welsh season; all these matches have been played in October and November. My own view is that the Welsh side now have a complex when they play against the All Blacks. The pressures imposed upon them by the public view that New Zealand are the arch enemy make them inhibited and sap their confidence. This is particularly galling when one considers that most of the All Black teams of the last decade have been far inferior to many of their predecessors.

Another area of grave concern for the Welsh is an apparent failure in public relations. There is an astonishing antipathy towards Welsh rugby by the other nations, much of which can be dismissed as suffering from the green eye. It is the sort of resentment applied to the Arabs and their oil.

The aversion to the Welsh in so many quarters of the British Isles may also find a logical explanation in class distinction. There is a contrast between the more stylish attitudes and atmosphere in areas where the game is still regarded as upper class, and the blunter approach in Wales where rugby is more definitely the working-man's sport. Welsh rugby is far more democratic, but the sociological implications of accent and approach still, it seems, create a barrier in Britain which probably retains more class differences than any country in the Western world. There is resistance to the more aggressive Welsh attitude towards winning their matches.

It is important, therefore, to consider how other people saw the Welsh during the period of their exceptional accomplishments over the last twelve years. John Reason, the highly-respected, long-established and usually controversial journalist who was Rugby Correspondent of the *Daily Telegraph* for over 10 years and is now with the *Sunday Telegraph*, saw the era, in a playing sense, as divided into three distinct sections. 'Wales came to terms with the technical revolutions of their play, outlined by the Rugby Union coaching manual, years before anybody else. As a result they produced a fine selection of team coaches of stature, who genuinely understood the techniques; and they produced a system of clear evaluation second to none as they were able to go to these coaches for advice. Secondly, Wales introduced the squad system to Europe, thus giving themselves an understanding of each other's play which no-one else matched for years and years. They were prepared to slog away on Sunday afternoons after their own fierce club encounters, and this paid enormous dividends. Thirdly and coincidentally, they also had a generation of fine backs, able to take advantage of and to understand the new technical advances – though there is evidence that, in certain areas, coaching has obliterated some of the individual flair.'

In the broader context, Reason believes that Welsh rugby behaviour has declined in all spheres. He illustrates this with the example of Pontypool who have been banned by the WRU from touring abroad for three years, and who disgraced themselves in America when under the captaincy of Jeff Squire. They walked off the field, abandoning the game, which is inexcusable under any circumstances. Reason holds the view that the name of Wales stinks in Australia after their 1978 tour, and that the Australians regard them as squealers, bad losers and bad sports.

He considers that the Welsh in Australia left a trail of wreckage which will take years to rebuild. He also says that the Welsh club tours by Llanelli, Newport and Cardiff to South Africa in 1979 left a unanimous view in that country that Welsh attitudes left much to be desired. In contrast, the North of England, who toured there at the same time, were far more acceptable and welcome. Reason believes that until the mid-seventies there was a universal admiration for Welsh rugby, but since then an anti-Welsh feeling has arisen, because of the spirit in which they have played the game at international level. This has been less than satisfactory and it is to be deplored because of its influence on the young. The Welsh have failed to accept defeat, because of its infrequency. Their behaviour has deteriorated rapidly in the last four years, and this culminated in 1980 in the disgraceful episode at Twickenham from which people turned in horror and disgust.

Reason goes on to say that Welsh players are rapidly becoming isolated by their unfortunate attitudes – from New Zealand and Australia in particular – and this is creating the same laager situation which used to make South Africa feel isolated. His main objections to the Welsh derive from what he believes to be their arrogance, for he believes there is a fine dividing line between justifiable self-confidence, élan and spirit, and arrogance. Physical intimidation, he believes, has become far too big a factor in their game; there was a world of difference between Barry John's supreme vision of his own ability and JPR's late tackle on Mike Gibson, with his acknowledgement of a professional foul, creating one law for himself and another for everyone else.

A kinder reaction to the Welsh comes from Richard Sharp, who so magnificently graced the England team in the early 1960s and is now also reporting rugby for the *Sunday Telegraph*. 'I admired the success of Wales tremendously in the last years, for they have been absolutely wonderful both in club and international football. I am impressed by their tremendous feeling for the game and their knowledgeable crowds, who give them such colossal support. Their standards are so much higher, and certainly in the last decade Wales have been way ahead of the other Home Unions because of their tremendous depth of talent at every level. The atmosphere in England is far less conducive to rugby, for it simply does not have the same enthusiasm or intensity.

'There is definitely an antipathy towards the Welsh when one is among Englishmen, and it is shared by the Irish and the Scots. I find this strange because, frankly, I find Welsh rugby players delightful. When I went on tour with the Lions, some of my very best friends were Welsh. It is not Welsh players but their supporters after the match who disturb me, for when you win they make you feel that you are lucky, and if you lose they are patronizing. The best result to get in Wales is to lose by a score like 24 points to 22, for then the reception afterwards is simply tremendous. I respect the Welsh attitude to winning, but I have been sickened by the hangers-on and the rowdyism after the international matches; so, I believe, has Barry John, and it was this factor which precipitated his retirement. Yet the Welsh are more friendly than any other part of the United Kingdom. In analysing my feelings towards the Welsh, I have nothing but admiration, and to me, of all people, the most enormous pleasure is to watch the extraordinary talent of their outside-half play. Even when I am in a fairly obscure match in a Welsh valley, I constantly see unknown players in this position who are quite amazing. I am impressed by their application and organizational structure, and the future must be fantastically rosy, for they have a marvellous reservoir of young players coming on.'

The rugby correspondent of *The Guardian*, the urbane David Frost, sees the major Welsh strength as their resilience, because they so frequently come from behind with inspiring character as they did at Murrayfield in 1971. He enjoys marvellous memories of the players of the period, and said of Gareth Edwards, 'He was the linchpin. I never knew anybody who controlled or turned a match as well as he did. If things were going well, he would score tries, and, if things were not, then his exuberance and effervescence enabled Wales to change the situation. The Welsh forwards gained a great deal by having Edwards behind them. It was like having a good full-back behind them but they had that as well in the fabulous J. P. R. Williams. Both Gareth and JPR could be relied upon to salvage difficult situations. We seldom saw very spectacular rugby from Wales, but when we did it was breathtaking. One particular period against Ireland in the second half in 1976, when Wales scored three tries in six minutes, was some of the most exhilarating rugby I ever saw, comparable to the best of the Lions in 1971. Barry John was the most accurate kicker of the ball out of the hand that I have observed, with the possible exception of Gareth Edwards. The contribution of Mervyn Davies was immense in so many different areas of the game, and his work in the lineouts, and control and intelligence at the back of the scrum, were remarkable, added to his understanding with Gareth Edwards, which created so many opportunities for attack.

'I feel the antipathy towards the Welsh, certainly by the other Home Unions, is based on envy, and the Welsh were no dirtier than anybody else, although they had moments of aberration. They were generally better organized and better prepared than any other country. Coaching throughout England is in good hands and Don Rutherford has worked tremendously hard at every level to improve it, but it has not produced the same results as have been achieved in Wales.'

The French regard for Welsh rugby is of the highest and born of mutual respect. They recognize a similar earthy attitude to the physical nature of the game, derived from a kindred temperament, which tends to enjoy a robust approach and its attendant risk of the flare-up into warfare. They also realize that only the Welsh match them in the unexpected when individual flair takes over.

Robert Soro, known as 'The Lion of Swansea' after that epic battle which France won there in 1948, is a huge man in every sense, a Basque from the Pyrenees, who in his time possessed breathtaking skills. He is a man of great perception, who can tell a story with his eyes, without uttering a word; and when you mention Welsh rugby, those eyes go through a vast gamut of emotions indicating immense respect, a realization of certain wickedness, seriousness and joy.

The doyens of the French rugby press, Denis Lalanne, Paul Haedens, Henri Garcia and Jean Denis, are all admirers of the Welsh. I remember Paul Haedens telling me, 'If we believe we can beat Wales, then we usually have a very good team, and if we do beat them, then we feel that we have a team which can beat anybody.' When I once asked Denis Lalanne to define Welsh rugby, his succinct comment, delivered with a Gallic shrug and amused eyes, was, 'Serious'.

Peter Robbins, the magnificent English flanker of the early sixties, and now the rugby correspondent of the *Financial Times,* reinforces the credits and discredits by saying, 'I viewed Welsh rugby in the European scale as quite extraordinary. Some of the rugby was astounding, but it was significant that it coincided with a diminution in the standards of the other countries, apart from France. It was also true that Wales had an emotional block whenever they met the All Blacks. Rugby is an expression of nationalism for the Welsh and, like education, it is a way of expressing their basic natural introversions and defensive attitudes. This is a vital part of their nature after years of depression which scarred their consciousness, and they therefore always take up defensive postures against the other countries.

'They have a natural instinct and aptitude for rugby football, and one of their major strengths is their regenerative invention. You have to be good to compete at their level, and to be accepted by them you need both physical courage and technical skills.

'The Welsh *en masse* can be horrid, for they present an image of having lost the art of losing gracefully, and there is no doubt in my mind that the Welsh have become arrogant because of their success. A nation which has always expressed itself admirably in cultural terms has now added another dimension to its self-expression – that of rugby as a physical art – and they have become a target for hostility. Yet individually they are fine players and the nicest of people. Perhaps the real root of the hostility towards them, certainly by the English, is that they envy them their talent and ability and, of course, their success.'

Cliff Morgan, that famous stand-off and demi-god of the fifties, who is an outsider only by virtue of being the most famous expatriate in Welsh rugby, is Head of Outside Broadcasts for BBC Television in London. His views, therefore, are of interest. 'To me, a Welshman in dispersion, who has

JPR Williams: *(below)* making a clearance kick under pressure; *(left)* startled by the shirt-pulling of Selwyn Williams (Llanelli) in a game for London Welsh.

JPR Williams: *(above)* closing in to tackle the England full-back, Alastair Hignell, at Twickenham, 1976; *(below)* passing to his wing for the Barbarians against the British Isles in September 1977.

suffered a certain emptiness by not being able to watch Welsh rugby in his own country, the Welsh performances of the last twelve years produced the most attractive rugby I ever saw. It was because the players played for each other with a discipline and an awareness which no other country rivalled. In the broader context of behaviour and attitudes, I believe that pride is one thing and arrogance another. If the Welsh were guilty of the latter, it was not endemic to them alone; it is symptomatic of our time and abundantly manifest in sport generally. However in Wales we do suffer from provincialism, and there is a tendency to try and win at all costs.

'The greatest sadness for me during the last twelve years has been the commercial exploitation of the game. The Wales versus New Zealand match in November, 1980 is to be known as the Crown Paint Centenary Game. Rugby should not sell its soul in this fashion. Sponsorship is one thing, but when firms give sets of jerseys to famous teams and then put it on the price of jerseys for children, then I want to object. I see a danger of all that was worthwhile in rugby disappearing because of the commercial pressures on the players. In the end it will mean that the game might just as well go totally professional. I have also been saddened by the use of the phrase "professional foul", when it was applied to rugby football. Whenever you see big money coming into sport, it tends to corrupt, and I only hope that amateur rugby players will understand the more basic value – that there is nothing like a bit of a struggle.'

The most flattering opinion comes from Norman Mair, who played for Scotland in the early fifties and now writes brilliant international match previews for *The Scotsman*: 'Much as I believe in coaching, I think some of the current warnings are timely, because there are undoubtedly coaches who have their priorities wrong, and who also do not know what to leave alone. But unquestionably Welsh rugby in general, and Ray Williams in particular, did a great deal to show the way. During the last twelve years at their best, the Welsh provided an excellent example of how to allow individual genius to express itself within the framework provided by modern coaching and

D

squad systems. A perfect illustration of the point would surely be Carwyn James' treatment of Barry John on the 1971 Lions tour, an obvious example of knowing what and whom to leave alone, and to what degree.

'With the set-up existing in Wales, built around that comparatively small number of great clubs, and the fact that it is the national game, players of talent will always be rolling off the assembly line. Even so, one is presumably not too often going to find such a cluster of all time greats as J. P. R. Williams, Gerald Davies, Barry John, Gareth Edwards and Mervyn Davies coming together in the side at the same time. No system can guarantee that. In soccer even the greatest footballing nations have only intermittently succeeded, for no-one can produce a Pele, a Cruyff or a Beckenbauer to order.

'In almost any game, an expectation of success can be the vital ingredient, and that is something Wales have had in recent years against the other home countries – though not against the All Blacks – and it has shown in all the little things that are apt to go to make a result. I suppose it is just another exemplification of the old adage that nothing succeeds like success, and, as Scotland have found, once you get out of the habit of winning, even the close matches are liable to keep going just the wrong way. However, for all Wales's triple crowns, championships and grand slams, it is the players whom one will remember. In the mind's eye, even twenty years from now, I expect still to see Gerald Davies as clearly as in any television recording. Players of genius invariably have their own distinctive style, and, for all the irresistible comparisons that are made when a new player emerges, there can only be one Gareth Edwards, one Barry John or one JPR.

'You ask if there is the same antipathy in Scotland towards the Welsh as there seems to be in other rugby countries. I should have to say that if there is, I have not been conscious of it. Indeed, despite the recent Welsh successes and the understandable reaction of many in wanting to see the top dogs toppled, I have a notion that there is less now than there was in bygone generations, at any rate among the rank and file of the rugby fraternity. Obviously the Scottish Rugby Union down the years have not always felt that their interpretation of the concept of an essentially amateur game was quite the same as the Welsh. Other factors come into it too, such as the mass pilgrimage by the Welsh every second year to Murrayfield, where they are very popular with the people because they mostly behave so well. And of course they have a natural kinship with the folk of the Scottish border where the game has always been as classless as it is in Wales. Finally, there is the fact that though Wales have had their bad results in Murrayfield, even in their vintage era, none of these games has ever really turned ugly. There has been the odd thing, inevitably, but none of those incidents which can sour relations between two rugby countries for years to come.'

If there is any substance in the allegations made against the Welsh during this period – although I regard most of it as being ill-informed – then in future Wales must examine their situation very carefully in order to guard their good name. It is important to observe the highest standards of conduct at all times and meticulously scrutinize the appointment of managers and coaches. In a time when brutality is said to be on the increase, any departure from the most punctilious behaviour, both on and off the field, must be promptly dealt with at all levels of the game. In my experience, Welsh teams are no better or worse in the matter of behaviour than those from any other country, but because in recent years they have presented such high standards of play and success, they are increasingly coming under scrutiny.

It is now evident that their opponents, both in Europe and in the rest of the world, are making strenuous efforts to catch up in organization and preparation, so life is going to be much harder for Welsh teams at the start of their next hundred years. Countries like Scotland and England, by introducing league systems with promotion and relegation, are seeking to raise the competitive element in their game. In the next decade, Wales will have to rely even more on their natural ability to produce players with talents far above the ordinary.

In looking for the final judgement on Welsh rugby, I found it at the twenty-fifth anniversary and reunion dinner of the never-to-be-forgotten Lions team of 1955 – the first to break the grip that the Southern Hemisphere had had on British teams for over fifty years. The words came from the inimitable Tony O'Reilly, and were delivered with his typically whimsical wit: 'Whether we like it or not, and most of us don't, rugby football is simply not a game without the Welsh.'

Part Two

7
The Squad Falls In: 1968–69

In the New Year of 1969 a yard was still a yard, not ·914 metres; a try was worth three points; the matches in the international championship, instead of being staged in pairs at fortnightly intervals, straggled on in ones and twos from early January to mid-April – and for Wales things could only improve.

The previous winter they had been beaten 13–6 by the visiting All Blacks, and in the championship only just managed to hand on to Scotland the wooden spoon pressed upon them in 1967. They had come out of the series with a single victory, 5–0 over Scotland. At Twickenham they had drawn 11–11, at Lansdowne Road lost 9–6, and back in Cardiff for the final game they had gone down to France, the grand slam champions.

Not a season to remember with much pleasure, but altogether it had been a patchy twelve years for the Welsh. Between 1957 and 1963 the title had been lobbed back and fore between England and France. And although there were three consecutive seasons in the mid-sixties when Wales first shared the championship with Scotland, then twice won it outright, France had bounded back with their usual resilience.

Still, a few straws drifted in the wind. The programme for transforming Cardiff Arms Park into the national stadium had already been launched in 1968. So had the new national training scheme. Instead of relying on a last-minute get-together on the Friday afternoon before the match, Wales were now beginning to hold regular weekend squad sessions at the Afon Lido sports centre in Port Talbot.

Collectively the International Board approved this development; individually some of the more conservative countries deplored it. But when Wales finished the 1969 season with the championship and the triple crown, most people managed to put cause and effect together. The *Playfair Rugby Football Annual,* in a style already as dated as a Movietone News commentary, talked of Wales's 'special training', and went on: 'Some of their plays were intricately rehearsed and could never have come off without concerted attention beforehand – the dividends are, of course, in the results. Richards' four tries against England was a magnificent performance, but it was still essentially a team effort, with every man clearly briefed in exactly what was expected of him. No-one failed in his duty.'

The creation of the national stadium was a mixed delight. For a while the removal of the old north stand made the ground disconcertingly lop-sided. Teams played to applause on one flank and to a wall of silence on the other. But at least the expensive alterations were an act of faith in the expanding future of Welsh rugby.

As it happened, the team was also in the process of rebuilding. Over the next decade we were to get used to seeing only familiar figures trotting out to represent Wales. But in 1969 half of the players who opened the season against the Scots at Murrayfield were just beginning to make their names.

The pack was reasonably experienced, at least at prop and lock, and Brian Price, who captained Wales from the second row, was a veteran of nine seasons and twenty-six caps. But the hooker, Jeff Young, was in only his second season; Morris and Taylor were starting their third; and Mervyn Davies, who was to become the most distinguished No 8 of his time, was making his first appearance.

Among the backs the only old-timer was the 6ft 2in Newport right wing, Stuart Watkins, with nineteen caps. At half-back Edwards and John, with seven caps apiece, were, for all their evident and abundant talent, still maturing as internationals; so was Gerald Davies, then playing at centre. The other centre, Keith Jarrett, had three caps, and Maurice Richards on the left wing, two – although both had been precociously selected for the Lions' South African tour the previous summer.

Since he had played most of his adult rugby in London, the new full-back was little known in Wales – except perhaps on the tennis circuit; he had been junior Wimbledon champion. At first the press referred to him as John Williams. It was only later, when a Llanelli wing of the same name began to share the stage with him, that they converted John Peter Rhys into the most familiar initials in the game.

Finally, a development which helped to change the game for Wales, for everyone else, but particularly for JPR: the general adoption of what was then called the 'Australian dispensation'. This rule laid down that, except when he was taking a penalty, a player outside his own twenty-five might not gain ground by kicking directly into touch. The ball had to strike the ground or an opposing player before it went over the touchline, otherwise the lineout would be taken back up the field opposite the spot from which the ball had been kicked.

It meant an end to those dreary foul-weather games in which teams did little more than pound the touchline to death. Players as skilful as Edwards and John, of course, soon developed a tantalizing knack of bouncing and rolling the ball out of play. But a thump to touch was no longer the half-back's automatic response under pressure. And for the full-back the new rule created a new role, provided he had JPR's inclination to attack. He was no longer the howitzer behind the lines but the armoured car poised to break through them.

Wales In Argentina

Wales paid their first visit to Argentina – indeed their first to South America – in September 1968. It was not a tour exactly, for though the side did some incidental travelling, all their six matches were played in the same stadium at Buenos Aires. There they beat Belgrano 24–11, a Provincial XV 14–3, a Combined XV 9–6, and drew 8–8 with Argentine Juniors.

But they were unable to impose themselves on the national side, losing the first unofficial test (14 September) 9–5 and drawing the second (28 September) 9–9.

The results expressed the growing strength of Argentinian rugby as well as the comparative weakness of the Welsh party which had left out all the players recently returned with the Lions from South Africa. That still left nine internationals among the thirteen forwards, but only one international in the backs. This was the centre and captain, John Dawes, who with ten caps already was just approaching the significant years of his career. Of the other backs only JPR and Phil Bennett went on to achieve any real distinction, and Bennett had still to wait his turn before coming in to John's kingdom.

The International Championship

In the first two matches of the series France, the 1968 champions, forfeited any claim to this season's title. At Stade Colombes on 11 January they lost 6–3 to Scotland, and at Lansdowne Road on 24 January went down 17–9 to Ireland.

Scotland 3 pts Wales 17 *Murrayfield, 1 February 1969*

Wales had won only four of their eleven matches at Murrayfield since the war, and Scotland, having beaten France in Paris, were all the greater favourites to win their first home match. Instead Wales put together their highest score against them since 1947, winning by a goal, two tries and two penalties to a single penalty. It was not that Scotland had slackened the stubborn defence which saw them through against the French; but that Wales, without developing any fluent or sustained attacks, steadily nagged away until the Scots made mistakes, and then exploited them ruthlessly. The game was not enjoyable to watch; the Scots were effectively killing the loose ball. But on the Welsh side it was a model of efficient control by the pack and spontaneity by the halves.

Penalty kicks by Jarrett in the eighth and fourteenth minutes gave Wales a 6–0 lead which carried them through to the interval. And since they had been playing into the wind in the first half, it was a sufficient return on their forty minutes' effort. There was also some relief at having stopped two bull charges from Carmichael and Arneil, two more strong runs through the centre by Rea and a perfectly executed scissors between Frame and Colin Telfer.

All the same the danger of similar attacks remained and it took Wales another thirteen minutes to compromise Scotland further. Then they half-wheeled the scrum as the Scots heeled near their line. McCrae was harassed into a hasty pass which failed to reach Colin Telfer. Edwards, snatching up the ball, dived over for a try.

Scotland retrieved those points when Blaikie kicked a forty-five yard penalty (this time they had wheeled to lure Taylor offside); but then followed a Welsh try which caused a few hard feelings. At a lineout within the Scottish twenty-five Brian Price noticed McHarg moving to No 3, and stepped into No 2 to intercept the throw. He tapped the ball down to Maurice Richards, and the wing ran past the front of the lineout to score before the Scots rumbled him. Cleverly done, unless the ball went forward, and afterwards Price agreed with those who thought it had done.

The score stood, however, and fortunately it had little bearing on the result. Wales were now pounding ahead, and typically John conjured up the try which put them beyond reach. He charged down an attempted clearance by Colin Telfer forty yards out from the Scottish line, gathered the ball and, as the defence converged on him, curved his way through with untouchable elegance to score near the posts. Jarrett converted and Wales, who would be playing the other two home countries at Cardiff, could already think optimistically of the triple crown.

Scorers SCOTLAND – penalty goal: Blaikie. WALES – tries: Edwards, Richards, John; conversion: Jarrett; penalty goals: Jarrett 2.

Scotland C. F. Blaikie (Heriot's FP); A. J. W. Hinshelwood

(London Scottish), J. N. M. Frame (Gala), C. W. W. Rea (West of Scotland), W. D. Jackson (Hawick); C. M. Telfer (Hawick), I. G. McCrae (Gordonians); N. Suddon (Hawick), F. A. L. Laidlaw (Melrose), A. B. Carmichael (West of Scotland), P. K. Stagg (Sale), A. F. McHarg (London Scottish), T. G. Elliot (Langholm), J. W. Telfer (Melrose, capt.), R. J. Arneil (Edinburgh Academicals).

Wales J. P. R. Williams (London Welsh); S. J. Watkins (Newport), K. S. Jarrett (Newport), T. G. R. Davies (Cardiff), M. C. R. Richards (Cardiff); B. John (Cardiff), G. O. Edwards (Cardiff); D. Williams (Ebbw Vale), J. Young (Harrogate), D. J. Lloyd (Bridgend), B. Price (Newport, capt.), B. E. Thomas (Neath), W. D. Morris (Neath), J. Taylor (London Welsh), T. M. Davies (London Welsh).

Referee K. D. Kelleher (Ireland).

It was five weeks before Wales played again. On 1 February Ireland beat England 17–15 at Lansdowne Road, and on 22 February there were two games. At Twickenham England beat France 22–8, and at Murrayfield Ireland beat Scotland 16–0.

Wales 24 pts Ireland 11 *Cardiff, 8 March 1969*

This match could have won Ireland the triple crown. Instead it ended in their comprehensive defeat by three goals, a try, a dropped goal and a penalty to a goal and two penalties – the greatest number of points that Wales had ever scored against them. A triumph for Welsh method and skill? Perhaps; but also an afternoon of some embarrassment.

The Irish had previously won six consecutive matches for the first time in their history, and with a highly experienced side, which had collected a record two-hundred-and-ninety-four caps between them, they were strongly fancied to take their first crown in twenty years. There was fierce commitment on either side, and the opening exchanges between the packs were savage and at times lawless.

After ten minutes came the most blatant act of violence when Brian Price, the Welsh captain, was clearly seen to strike Noel Murphy to the ground. It may have been a wild retaliation for some hidden incident. Price later explained that he had felt someone whom he couldn't identify clawing at his face in a maul. But to the limited crowd of twenty-nine-thousand, which included the Prince of Wales, and to the millions more who were watching on television, it was a matter of amazement that the blow resulted in nothing more than a caution and a penalty. Price might well have been the first Welshman ever ordered off in an international.

The ructions didn't end there. Later there was a mass brawl in which nearly all the forwards were involved. Again no individual was punished, and it was only gradually that the anger subsided as the Welsh forwards won increasing possession from the lineouts and the loose, and so opened the way to a more open, skilful and agreeable second half.

Ireland made a good start. Although they chose to play the first half into the wind, they took, lost and then regained the lead shortly before the interval – Kiernan kicking two penalties with a dropped goal by John sandwiched in between. But the half was wearily prolonged by injury, and in the forty-seventh minute Jarrett caught the Irish by surprise. Instead of taking an expected penalty kick at goal, he tapped the ball and fed it out to Denzil Williams, the big prop, who celebrated his twenty-third cap with a first international try. Jarrett converted to make it 8–6.

After that Wales began to run the Irish off their feet. John, with his deceptive pace, broke away to the right and, ignoring his centres, sent a long scoring pass out to Watkins. Edwards, having seized a loose ball and twice kicked ahead, performed the same service for Morris. Finally Taylor, from a strong build-up by J. P. R. Williams and Watkins, crossed in the corner. Jarrett added his contribution, two conversions and a penalty.

No side with Gibson playing at centre is ever totally eclipsed, and before the finish he had kicked through from sixty yards for a magnificent try which Kiernan converted. But already the game had been long decided and Wales had become the new candidates for the triple crown.

Scorers WALES – tries: D. Williams, Watkins, Morris, Taylor; conversions: Jarrett 3; dropped goal: John; penalty goal: Jarrett. IRELAND – try: Gibson; conversion: Kiernan; penalty goals: Kiernan 2.

Wales J. P. R. Williams (London Welsh); S. J. Watkins (Newport), K. S. Jarrett (Newport), T. G. R. Davies (Cardiff), M. C. R. Richards (Cardiff); B. John (Cardiff), G. O. Edwards (Cardiff); D. Williams (Ebbw Vale), J. Young (Harrogate), D. J. Lloyd (Bridgend), B. Price (Newport, capt.), B. E. Thomas (Neath), W. D. Morris (Neath), T. M. Davies (London Welsh), J. Taylor (London Welsh).

Ireland T. J. Kiernan (Cork Constitution, capt.); A. T. A. Duggan (Lansdowne), F. P. K. Bresnihan (University College, Dublin), C. M. H. Gibson (North of Ireland F.C.), J. C. M. Moroney (London Irish); B. J. McGann (Lansdowne), R. M. Young (Queen's University, Belfast); P. O'Callaghan (Dolphin), K. W. Kennedy (London Irish), S. Millar (Ballymena), W. J. McBride (Ballymena), M. G. Malloy (London Irish), J. C. Davidson (Dungannon), M. L. Hipwell (Terenure College), N. A. Murphy (Cork Constitution).

Referee D. C. J. McMahon (Scotland).

A week later England beat Scotland 8–3 at Twickenham.

France 8 pts Wales 8 *Stade Colombes, 22 March 1969*

France had lost ten games in a row and chosen forty-one different players in seven matches. Few of their supporters would have put a sou on them making any showing in their last match of the championship. Wales, twice victorious, were fielding an unchanged side for the third time running. Most Welshmen would have put their shirt on them winning the grand slam. Which only proves once again that you should never bet on the French – either way.

With five Narbonne players introduced at hooker, in the back row and at half-back, and with one of them, Walter Spanghero, working hard at the leadership, France found something like their native wit and resilience. Wales, however, lost theirs. They did not play badly, but they turned in upon themselves, producing a rather sterile form of ten-man rugby in which Edwards and John took too much upon themselves. John in particular kicked away a great deal of possession which might have been put to better use; Wales could ill afford to let France get their hands on the ball even deep in their half. Meanwhile the potential of the Welsh wings and centres was largely ignored.

Even so, Wales were 8–0 up at half-time. Their opening score came after twenty-four minutes when John moved to the blind side of a scrum, found his way blocked and neatly doubled back to send Jarrett away on the open. Taylor came up alongside to take the next pass, and then found Edwards on the outside twenty yards from the line. The French cover had now regrouped, yet Edwards forced his way through the thicket, twisting out of one tackle and struggling through another, to score a try by sheer strength and momentum.

It was Edwards, too, who set up the second try just before the interval. He took the ball to the open side, then saw there was more to be gained from kicking it back across the top of the scrum and down into the corner. Richards ran on to it for the touchdown, Jarrett converted, and the worst of the Welsh problems seemed to be over.

Instead their game began to unravel in the second half. France moved the ball with a pace and dexterity which Wales could only counter at the final tackle. Twenty-five minutes on, Villepreux landed a forty-five-yard penalty, and it was he, after a dazzling mid-field run by Maso, who sent up the high diagonal kick which led to the French try. The bounce beat Watkins and J. P. R. Williams, and it was Campaes who gathered to burst through for a try. Villepreux completed his good work with the conversion.

That was the final score, and under the present points

system, of course, it would have meant the narrowest of wins for Wales. But in the circumstances, with John missing an easy drop at goal and Jarrett a perfectly kickable penalty, the Welsh, now under considerable pressure, were happy enough to settle for a draw.

An injury to Gerald Davies just before the end is worth an historical footnote. Phil Bennett came out to replace him, winning the first cap of a career which broke many records, by playing for sixty seconds without touching the ball. And since Davies did not recover in time to play in the final championship match, John Dawes was recalled, an event of some significance to Welsh and British rugby.

Scorers FRANCE – try: Campaes; conversion: Villepreux; penalty goal: Villepreux. WALES – tries: Edwards, Richards; conversion: Jarrett.

France P. Villepreux (Toulouse); B. Moraitis (Toulon), C. Dourthe (Dax), J. Trillo (Bègles), A Campaes (Lourdes); J. Maso (Narbonne), G. Sutra (Narbonne); J. L. Axarete (Dax), R. Bénésis (Narbonne), J. Iraçabal (Bayonne), E. Cester (Toulouse OEC), A. Plantefol (Agen), J–P. Biemouret (Agen), G. Viard (Narbonne), W. Spanghero (Narbonne, capt.).

Wales J. P. R. Williams (London Welsh); S. J. Watkins (Newport), K. S. Jarrett (Newport), T. G. R. Davies (Cardiff), M. C. R. Richards (Cardiff); B. John (Cardiff), G. O. Edwards (Cardiff); D. Williams (Ebbw Vale), J. Young (Harrogate), D. J. Lloyd (Bridgend), B. Price (Newport, capt.), B. E. Thomas (Neath), W. D. Morris (Neath), J. Taylor (London Welsh), T. M. Davies (London Welsh). Replacement: P. Bennett (Llanelli) for T. G. R. Davies, 79 min.

Referee R. P. Burrell (Scotland).

Wales 30 pts England 9 — *Cardiff, 12 April 1969*

Rounding off the season, this match, with its second-half rout of England and its star-burst of scoring by Wales, seemed the final vindication of squad training. Whatever opposition there had been to the system, other countries would now have to take it up or else accept a lower return on their resources. It clearly helped to bring the Welsh their biggest victory over England since 1922, and both the championship and triple crown. Their points' total was seventy-nine, their average almost twenty. If England still held the record with eighty-two points, set in 1914, the sixties had been a decade of generally low-scoring internationals. Even the French, with their phenomenal work-rate, had averaged only thirteen and fourteen points a game in taking the last two titles.

What also justified faith in the new Welsh approach was that in this game they scarcely noticed the absence of two great players, their lock and captain, Brian Price, and their centre, Gerald Davies. Delme Thomas and John Dawes, who replaced them, were admittedly internationals already. But more significant, they had remained in training with the squad and so fitted into the team and its strategy at once. Every man might have his unique value, but nowadays nobody was irreplaceable.

England postponed their fate by winning the toss and taking first advantage of a stiff wind. But already there were warning signs which would develop into distress signals. The front five England forwards were conceding the ball in every phase which was their special responsibility. Their halves were outclassed by Edwards and John, who again showed the completeness of their talents. And the Welsh backs had already cast suspicion on the myth that England had the most dangerous threequarter line in the championship.

At half-time England needed a substantial lead as insurance against the more difficult conditions of the second half. Instead they changed ends at 3–3. The imperturbable Bob Hiller had kicked the first of his three penalty goals, but Maurice Richards had also scored the first of his four tries which were to equal the Welsh records of Willie Llewellyn in 1899 and Reggie Gibbs in 1908.

After the interval it was Jarrett's two penalties which steered Wales ahead, but all the while Edwards's long, precise pass kept the backs in continuous probing movement. Jarrett's next contribution was a kick ahead, a neat gather and a pass outside which sent John through on one of those remarkable feinting stop-go sprints in which he beat four men before touching down. A conversion – Jarrett again – and Wales were 14–3 up and free to run whatever ball and whatever risks they chose.

Still to come – with Hiller's remaining penalties as the only interruption – were a left-footed dropped goal by John and another three tries from Richards. In most cases these tries were the culmination of fast, freewheeling moves among the Welsh halves and threequarters, their attacking full-back, J. P. R. Williams, and their back row, in particular the small terrier figure of Taylor. But the final try Richards created on his own, surging through from thirty-five yards, splitting the defence and shaking off three or four intended tacklers.

Richards was seen at his best in his home city that afternoon. But he was also seen in a Wales jersey for the last time. Before next season's championship, Richards, together with Jarrett, had gone north.

Scorers WALES – tries: Richards 4, John; conversions: Jarrett 3; dropped goal: John; penalty goals: Jarrett 2. ENGLAND – penalty goals: Hiller 3.

Wales J. P. R. Williams (London Welsh); S. J. Watkins (Newport), K. S. Jarrett (Newport), S. J. Dawes (London Welsh), M. C. R. Richards (Cardiff); B. John (Cardiff), G. O. Edwards (Cardiff, capt.); D. Williams (Ebbw Vale), J. Young (Harrogate), D. J. Lloyd (Bridgend), W. D. Thomas (Llanelli), B. E. Thomas (Neath), W. D. Morris (Neath), J. Taylor (London Welsh), T. M. Davies (London Welsh).

England R. B. Hiller (Harlequins); K. C. Plummer (Bristol), J. S. Spencer (Headingley), D. J. Duckham (Coventry), R. E. Webb (Coventry); J. F. Finlan (Moseley), T. C. Wintle (Northampton); K. E. Fairbrother (Coventry), J. V. Pullin (Bristol), D. L. Powell (Northampton), P. J. Larter (Northampton), N. E. Horton (Moseley), R. B. Taylor (Northampton), D. M. Rollitt (Bristol), D. P. Rogers (Bedford, capt.).

Referee D. P. d'Arcy (Ireland).

Championship Table 1969

	P	W	D	L	For	Ag	Pts
Wales	4	3	1	0	79	31	7
Ireland	4	3	0	1	61	48	6
England	4	2	0	2	54	58	4
Scotland	4	1	0	3	12	44	2
France	4	0	1	3	28	53	1

Welsh tour of New Zealand and Australia

It was the prospect of this tour which had prompted Wales to begin squad training. And since the system had already helped convert them into European champions, they set out for New Zealand in May with reasonable confidence. This was soon dissipated. After no more than drawing their opening match 9–9 with Taranaki on 28 May, three days later in the first test they were treated by New Zealand as brusquely as they had recently treated England. They lost 19–0.

The next two provincial matches they won comfortably enough, beating Otago 27–9 (3 tries for Richards, 15 points for Jarrett) on 4 June, and Wellington 14–6 on 7 June. But the second test brought even costlier defeat than the first: 33–12. It was a relief to move on to Sydney where they salvaged something by beating Australia 19–16, and then to wind down with a friendly game in Fiji which they won 31–11.

Short tours are notoriously hard on players, and this one made life more difficult than most with a fifty-two-hour non-stop flight to New Zealand, the first match within four days and the first test within a week of arriving. It was asking for trouble.

Yet even allowing for the punishing schedule, and for a hamstring injury to Edwards which only allowed him to play at reduced tempo, the Welsh had to admit uncompromising defeat in the real terms of world rugby. They might have the faster, cleverer backs, but their forwards were both more static and less committed than New Zealand's, and their place-kicking skills infinitely less reliable.

New Zealand 19 pts Wales 0 *Christchurch, 31 May 1969*

Wales travelled thirteen-thousand miles to discover how far behind New Zealand they still were in terms of all-round rugby efficiency and physical prowess. Lochore's forwards – six of them farmers – were supreme on this day, and would probably have beaten any other pack of any other period. They won the first sixteen rucks in succession, and throughout the game Wales took only three or four.

Although in muddy conditions the New Zealand half-backs, Going and Kirton, handled with remarkable assurance, they invariably played back to their forwards. And as the All Blacks pack drove on to the ball chipped over their heads, the Welsh had nothing but courage to deploy in return. J. P. R. Williams had a particularly heroic game, taking every kick that rained down on him; and John, who received liability ball from start to finish, made the most of each unrewarding chance.

New Zealand went ahead with a try by Dick after the ball had passed via the forwards from the other wing. And before half-time they had scored two further tries to which McCormick added the conversions to make it 13–0. During the second half the Welsh hooker, Jeff Young, went off with a broken jaw after being punched. And to that blow was added New Zealand's fourth try and a penalty.

Scorers NEW ZEALAND – tries: Dick, McLeod, Lochore, Gray; conversions: McCormick 2; penalty goal: McCormick.

New Zealand W. F. McCormick (Canterbury); M. J. Dick (Auckland), W. L. Davis (Hawkes Bay), I. R. Macrae (Hawkes Bay), G. S. Thorne (Auckland); E. W. Kirton (Otago), S. M. Going (N. Auckland); B. L. Muller (Taranaki), B. E. McLeod (Counties), K. F. Gray (Wellington), C. E.

Meads (King Country), A. E. Smith (Taranaki), A. A. Kirkpatrick (Canterbury), B. J. Lochore (Wairarapa, capt.), T. N. Lister (S. Canterbury).

Wales J. P. R. Williams (London Welsh); S. J. Watkins (Newport), K. S. Jarrett (Newport), T. G. R. Davies (Cardiff), M. C. R. Richards (Cardiff); B. John (Cardiff), G. O. Edwards (Cardiff); D. Williams (Ebbw Vale), J. Young (Harrogate), D. J. Lloyd (Bridgend), B. Price (Newport, capt.), B. E. Thomas (Neath), W. D. Morris (Neath), J. Taylor (London Welsh), T. M. Davies (London Welsh). Substitute N. R. Gale (Llanelli) for J. Young, 64 min.

Referee J. P. Murphy (New Zealand).

New Zealand 33 pts Wales 12 *Auckland, 14 June 1969*

It was little consolation to the Welsh that they gave Fergus McCormick, the New Zealand full-back, an opportunity to set a world test record of twenty-four points. But the fact that all but nine of their opponents' points came from kicking puts the disastrous-looking scoreline in a certain perspective. In the matter of tries, New Zealand were only 3–2 up.

All the same, the All Blacks' hundredth win brought another display of driving, crushing forward play which the Welsh could not match. And McCormick's place-kicking – five penalties and two conversions – plus a magnificent dropped goal from the touchline, simply put the seal on their overall efficiency. In contrast Jarrett crucially missed three penalties and two conversions from within twenty-six yards of the New Zealand line.

The first twenty-five minutes were encouraging to Wales when, after an exchange of penalties, Richards put them into a 6–3 lead with a try which followed some brisk passing along the line. But then New Zealand scored eight points in two minutes, and from there it was downhill until just before the end when Jarrett – whose centre play, if not his kicking, had been excellent – went over for the final try.

It was in this game that Gerald Davies made his first international switch from centre to wing, a move with certain implications for the future.

Scorers NEW ZEALAND – tries: Skudder, Macrae, Kirkpatrick; conversions: McCormick 3; dropped goal: McCormick; penalty goals: McCormick 5. WALES – tries: Richards, Jarrett; penalty goals: Jarrett 2.

New Zealand W. F. McCormick (Canterbury); M. J. Dick (Auckland), I. R. Macrae (Hawkes Bay), W. L. Davis (Hawkes Bay), G. Skudder (Waikato); E. W. Kirton (Otago), S. M. Going (N. Auckland); A. E. Hopkinson (Canterbury), B. E. McLeod (Counties), K. F. Gray (Wellington), A. E. Smith (Taranaki), C. E. Meads (King Country), T. N. Lister (S. Canterbury), B. J. Lochore (Wairarapa, capt.), I. A. Kirkpatrick (Canterbury).

Wales J. P. R. Williams (London Welsh); T. G. R. Davies (Cardiff), K. S. Jarrett (Newport), S. J. Dawes (London Welsh), M. C. R. Richards (Cardiff); B. John (Cardiff), G. O. Edwards (Cardiff); D. Williams (Ebbw Vale), N. R. Gale (Llanelli); B. E. Thomas (Neath), B. Price (Newport, capt.), W. D. Thomas (Llanelli), D. Hughes (Newbridge), W. D. Morris (Neath), T. M. Davies (London Welsh).

Referee J. P. Murphy (New Zealand).

Australia 16 pts Wales 19 — *Sydney, 21 June 1969*

Relieved to be playing against ordinary mortals again, Wales, eleven points down midway through the first half, were confident enough to stage a recovery and win a fine, eventful match by two goals, a try and two penalties to two goals and two penalties.

After their early reverse Wales got back to first principles, curbing the speed of the Wallabies in the loose by making them scrummage and taking a tighter grip on the lineout. A penalty from Jarrett and a try by Morris – from Edwards' explosive blind-side run – put Wales back in the game. At half-time they were only five points adrift with the advantage of the wind to come.

The turning point was reached three minutes later. Missing out Dawes but bringing in JPR, the threequarter line rapidly relayed the ball to Gerald Davies, and the newly-converted wing made a marvellous forty-five yard run to beat the full-back with an inside jink and score beneath the posts. Jarrett converted to make it 11–11, and from that moment Wales were never headed. A fifty-yard penalty followed from Jarrett. Gerald Davies went off on another fine run to set up a try for Taylor. Jarrett again converted and Wales had dug themselves into a position that they could defend to the finish.

Scorers AUSTRALIA – tries: Smith, McGill; conversions: McGill 2; penalty goals: McGill 2. WALES – tries: Morris, T. G. R. Davies, Taylor; conversions: Jarrett 2; penalty goals: Jarrett 2.

Australia A. N. McGill (New South Wales); T. R. Forman (NSW), G. Shaw (NSW), P. V. Smith (NSW), J. W. Cole (NSW); J. P. Ballesty (NSW), J. N. B. Hipwell (NSW); J. Roxburgh (NSW), P. Darvenzia (NSW), R. B. Prosser (NSW), P. N. P. Reilly (Queensland), A. Abrahams (NSW), H. A. Rose (NSW), G. V. Davis (NSW, capt.), A. J. Skinner (NSW).

Wales J. P. R. Williams (London Welsh); T. G. R. Davies (Cardiff), K. S. Jarrett (Newport), S. J. Dawes (London Welsh), M. C. R. Richards (Cardiff); B. John (Cardiff), G. O. Edwards (Cardiff); D. J. Lloyd (Bridgend), N. R. Gale (Llanelli), D. Williams (Ebbw Vale), B. Price (Newport, capt.), W. D. Thomas (Llanelli), W. D. Morris (Neath), J. Taylor (London Welsh), T. M. Davies (London Welsh).

Referee C. Ferguson (NSW).

8

Conquer and Divide: 1969-70

This was a difficult year for Wales. The New Zealand tour the previous summer had left some of the players glutted with rugby; Barry John, for one, didn't appear to get back his appetite for the game until well into the winter. Some changes were forced on the selectors by the retirement of their captain, Brian Price, and the veteran hooker, Norman Gale; by the temporary withdrawal of Gerald Davies, who wanted a year away from international rugby to concentrate on academic life at Cambridge; and by the move north to rugby league of Keith Jarrett and Maurice Richards. Other changes the selectors brought upon themselves by indecision. As a result they called upon twenty-six different players compared with only seventeen the season before, and occasionally played some of them out of position. To their credit it was not a mistake they were often to repeat during the seventies.

Wales got away with it all the same. In early January they drew 6–6 with South Africa in Cardiff, the first time in seven meetings that they had managed to avoid defeat. It was a result in which they might have taken more pride, however, if Scotland and England hadn't already beaten the Springboks and Ireland hadn't also drawn with them.

In the international championship Wales finished level with France at the top of the table, but only after painful moments of suspense. They were 9–0 down against Scotland at Cardiff before winning with a flourish of four tries. At Twickenham they came from even further behind, 13–3, to win by four points in what, for all its other dramas, will always be remembered as Chico Hopkins' match. But twice having managed the last word they ran out of repartee completely in Dublin, offering no reply at all to Ireland's fourteen points.

This ineffectual performance meant that France, with two victories behind them, became favourites to win Wales's last game. But even before it started Christian Carrere, the French captain, described Cardiff Arms Park as 'the mausoleum – so many of our hopes have died there.' They perished once again. Although France scored two tries to one, the Welsh kicking brought them an 11–6 win and the certainty of at least a share in the title.

By devouring England in the final match of the championship, France made sure that a share was all that Wales got. But the French had been so plainly the more consistent side that winter that really Wales could only feel flattered to divide the prize with them.

The Sixth Springboks

This turned out to be the last visit to Britain by the Springboks during the seventies, and was a pretty depressing experience for everyone involved. Mainly outside the game, and particularly among students, great hostility was felt towards the South African apartheid system, and this feeling was channelled into a series of demonstrations against the all-white tourists. The most violent, in fact, took place in Wales – at the St Helen's ground, Swansea, on 15 November – when protesters clashed with police and stewards, and there were several injuries on either side. No games were abandoned, but some were switched to more secure grounds, and most were interrupted, however briefly, by demonstrators running on the pitch. Even where there were no stoppages, the sight of police surrounding the touchline had its own distracting effect. Whether or not the demonstrations influenced general opinion, the threat to public order was enough to make successive governments oppose any further Springbok tours.

Although South African officials denied that this battle of nerves had any effect on their play or morale, the results suggest otherwise. From a totally unexpected defeat by Oxford University in their opening match (switched for safety's sake from Iffley Road to Twickenham) they went on to lose another four (England, Scotland, Gwent and Newport) of their twenty-four matches and draw four (Ireland, Wales, Western Counties and South of Scotland). Their failure to win a single test on a long tour was unprecedented.

Wales 6 pts South Africa 6 *Cardiff, 24 January 1970*

This was the Springboks' last chance to win an international, and there were two good reasons for thinking that they might pull it off. The weather was the first. Rain had fallen all the week to depress Welsh hopes; the national plan had been to run the ball and avoid at all costs a pitched battle between the two packs. Encouragingly the skies cleared on the Saturday morning, but at noon they closed in again and rain fell stubbornly through the match. The surface of the Arms Park turned to a sticky plasticine.

The Springboks couldn't have been more pleased. In these conditions they would not have to expose the technical limitations of their threequarters, whose job would be simply to chase and tackle if the ball worked loose. By constantly returning the ball to their pack, the halves would ensure that this didn't happen too often.

What also gave them grounds for optimism was that Wales were rebuilding once more. Raybould had returned to the centre in Jarrett's place, and Phil Bennett was making his first scheduled appearance on the wing vacated by Richards. Perrins, Llewelyn and Geoff Evans were all winning their first caps in the pack, and against a side which had been playing regularly together for over eleven weeks they would have little time to settle.

Taking the ball cleanly in the lineout, kicking it into the box and making ground by foot rushes, South Africa adapted naturally to the conditions. Wales did not. Reluctant to give up their original plan, they tried too often to pass the ball out and, in John's case, kicked downfield at the Springboks' full-back instead of keeping the ball close to touch. The Welsh tapping back at the lineout also gave Edwards some bad times.

In a match which was bound to produce little scoring, South Africa twice took what seemed a crucial lead. After ten minutes Henry de Villiers kicked a penalty when John strayed off-side at a lineout. Edwards equalized with another, kicked from a wide angle, to make it 3–3 at the interval, but then eight minutes into the second half South Africa broke the deadlock with a try. They wheeled a five-yard scrum, so keeping the Welsh back row fully occupied, and Lawless fed the ball to the blind side where Nomis went over by the flag.

That seemed to be that. Over half an hour passed without another score and the match drifted wearily into injury time. But suddenly it returned to life as Bennett sent a long pass in from the touchline, John punted diagonally across to the left wing, Hall caught Nomis as he fielded the ball, and Dawes lent his weight to enable Llewelyn to prise away possession. The Welsh were now in hot pursuit of their last opportunity, and as Llewelyn passed the ball back Edwards, full of wiry energy to the last, spurted through to the corner.

Scorers WALES – try: Edwards; penalty goal: Edwards. SOUTH AFRICA – try: Nomis; penalty goal: H. O. de Villiers.

Wales J. P. R. Williams (London Welsh); P. Bennett (Llanelli), S. J. Dawes (London Welsh), W. H. Raybould (Newport), I. Hall (Aberavon); B. John (Cardiff), G. O. Edwards (Cardiff, capt.); D. Williams (Ebbw Vale), V. C. Perrins (Newport), D. B. Llewelyn (Newport), W. D. Thomas (Llanelli), T. G. Evans (London Welsh), W. D. Morris (Neath), D. Hughes (Newbridge), T. M. Davies (London Welsh).

South Africa H. O. de Villiers (Western Province); S. H. Nomis (Transvaal), O. A. Roux (Northern Transvaal), J. P. van der Merwe (Western Province), G. H. Muller (Western Province); M. J. Lawless (Western Province),

D. J. de Villiers (Boland, capt.); J. L. Myburgh (Northern Transvaal), C. H. Cockrell (Western Province), J. F. K. Marais (North Eastern Cape), F. C. H. du Preez (Northern Transvaal), I. J. de Klerk (Transvaal), P. J. F. Greyling (Transvaal), J. H. Ellis (SW Africa), T. P. Bedford (Natal).

Referee Air Commodore G. C. Lamb (England).

The International Championship

Wales played their first match on the third working Saturday of the tournament, by which time France had already scored four championship points. They had beaten Scotland 11–9 at Murrayfield on 10 January, and Ireland 8–0 at Stade Colombes a fortnight later.

Wales 18 pts Scotland 9 *Cardiff, 7 February 1970*

Cardiff Arms Park was the Scots' least favourite ground. Their last win there, in 1962, had been the only one in forty-two years, and even though they now forged nine points ahead, the habit of defeat proved too strong for them. The wind was the decisive factor, and when Scotland turned to face it after the interval, with their lead already reduced to 9–5, they clearly hadn't used it to sufficient effect.

The Welsh forwards were to get the upper hand in the second half – particularly in the lineouts and the loose – but the Scots stood up to them well in the opening half-hour. The first rewards for their resistance were a goal dropped by Robertson as he calmly manoeuvred among the Welsh back row, and a penalty by Lauder which came whistling through from forty-eight yards. But if the Welsh could shrug these off as the rub of the wind, they were more disconcerted by what followed. Robertson fielded a relieving kick by J. P. R. Williams and, setting off innocently, sidled past two challengers, flicked the ball to Young and received it back, and, with a final dummy to bemuse the defence, glided over for a try. In eleven minutes the Scots had scored nine points.

It was only now that Wales reacted, Edwards and John running strongly to carry play into the Scottish twenty-five. There Daniel calamitously missed a penalty from only fifteen yards, but immediately had the chance to make amends when Edwards decided to run the next penalty. Llewelyn charged through; the Welsh pack won the subsequent ruck; and Daniel not only scored a try from John's pass but converted it from the touchline.

With the wind scattering any long mid-field passes, Edwards took it upon himself to initiate most of the attacks, relying on the support of the loose forwards. After thirteen minutes he ordered another short penalty from which Denzil Williams made the running and Llewelyn scored a try. That reduced the Scottish lead to one point, but as time ran out Welsh anxiety remained. Then in quick succession John charged down a kick by Robertson and Dawes picked up the loose ball to score a try, and from a five-yard scrum Morris, in ebullient form, charged over for another. Edwards converted both, and suddenly Wales had accumulated twice as many points as their opponents.

In a fairly pedestrian Welsh threequarter line, Dawes alone won praise for his skill. Bennett, who had been selected in place of the injured Raybould at centre after his brief appearance in Paris the winter before and his game on the wing against the Springboks, was dropped altogether for the next two games.

Scorers WALES – tries: Daniel, Llewelyn, Dawes, Morris; conversions: Edwards 2, Daniel. SCOTLAND – try: Robertson; dropped goal: Robertson; penalty goal: Lauder.

Wales J. P. R. Williams (London Welsh); L. C. T. Daniel (Newport), S. J. Dawes (London Welsh), P. Bennett (Llanelli), I. Hall (Aberavon); B. John (Cardiff), G. O. Edwards (Cardiff, capt.); D. Williams (Ebbw Vale), V. C. Perrins (Newport), D. B. Llewelyn (Newport), W. D. Thomas (Llanelli), T. G. Evans (London Welsh), W. D. Morris (Neath), D. Hughes (Newbridge), T. M. Davies (London Welsh).

Scotland I. S. G. Smith (London Scottish); M. A. Smith (London Scottish), J. N. M. Frame (Gala), C. W. W. Rea (West of Scotland), A. J. W. Hinshelwood (London Scottish); I. Robertson (Watsonians), R. G. Young (Watsonians); J. McLauchlan (Jordanhill College), F. A. L. Laidlaw (Melrose), A. B. Carmichael (West of Scotland), P. K. Stagg (Sale), P. C. Brown (Gala), W. Lauder (Neath), R. J. Arneil (Leicester), J. W. Telfer (Melrose, capt.).

Referee D. P. d'Arcy (Ireland).

A week later England beat Ireland 9–3 at Twickenham.

England 13 pts Wales 17 *Twickenham, 28 February 1970*

Fixtures between these two countries always have a strong element of theatre, but few have been quite so melodramatic as this. England were 13–3 up when they changed ends on their home ground. Gareth Edwards, the saviour of Wales against the Springboks, limped off when the score was still only 13–6. And just as England felt the greatest danger was past, Chico Hopkins, the Maesteg scrum-half – unknown in Britain at large although he had played on the Welsh tour of New Zealand – came on as a replacement and won the match.

There was even a touch of black irony as an England forward stepped on the fallen referee and broke a bone in his leg. M. Calmet's last act was to blow for half-time, after which the touch-judge, 'Johnny' Johnson, came on to replace him – an Englishman to arbitrate over his country's decline and fall.

Without these bizarre events it would still have been a fascinating match because of the contrast in style between the two teams. The English pack was very ordinary but their threequarter line was devastating. This was the height of the Duckham-Spencer partnership at centre and the two could simply unravel the Welsh defence. The Welsh pack, on the other hand, was formidable in its urgency and directness, while the threequarters, with the exception of Dawes's strong defence and Watkins's running on the right wing lacked either flair or pace.

Again the wind played a part and with its aid England built up a seemingly unassailable lead in the first half. Within ten minutes JPR had been tackled in possession by Novak, and the ball played out to the centre where Duckham, with a two-man overlap, raced across for a simple try. Dependably Hiller converted.

Wales won back three points when John kicked deep to the corner flag and Mervyn Davies pounced over from the back of the lineout. But England had not done yet. A breathless threequarter movement sent Novak over in full flight for a try, and Hiller, having converted from the touchline, went on to kick a longish penalty.

The Welsh halves, virtually ignoring their threequarter line, began to take the game in hand in the second half. Soon Edwards had kicked for the corner to create a defensive tangle from which John swept in to score. But England were back on the attack – foiled only by Dawes's magnificent tackle on Spencer – when Edwards was forced to leave the field with a twisted ankle.

England's optimism rose, but they had counted without the quickness and pugnacity of the chunky Hopkins who came out to win his only Welsh cap. It was like the arrival of the Milky Bar Kid. From a scrum he broke on the blind side to send JPR crashing over for a try – only the third ever scored by a Welsh full-back. And in the fortieth minute of the half, Hopkins fastened onto a long ball to the back of the lineout, and while the England defence stood in horror, he swept through for a try of his own to bring scores level. Although everything appeared to hang on the conversion – and JPR made no mistake with it – there proved to be still sufficient time for Wales to win another commanding position and John to drop a final goal.

Scorers ENGLAND – tries: Duckham, Novak; conversions: Hiller 2; penalty goal: Hiller. WALES – tries: Davies, John, J. P. R. Williams, Hopkins; conversion: J. P. R. Williams; dropped goal: John.

England R. B. Hiller (Harlequins, capt.); M. J. Novak (Harlequins), J. S. Spencer (Headingley), D. J. Duckham (Coventry), P. M. Hale (Moseley); I. R. Shackleton (Harrogate), N. C. Starmer-Smith (Harlequins); C. B. Stevens (Penzance & Newlyn), J. V. Pullin (Bristol), K. E. Fairbrother (Coventry), A. M. Davis (Harlequins), P. J. Larter (Northampton), A. L. Bucknall (Richmond), R. B. Taylor (Northampton), B. R. West (Northampton).

Wales J. P. R. Williams (London Welsh); S. J. Watkins (Cardiff), W. B. Raybould (Newport), S. J. Dawes (London Welsh), I. Hall (Aberavon); B. John (Cardiff), G. O. Edwards (Cardiff, capt.); D. Williams (Ebbw Vale), J. Young (Harrogate), D. B. Llewelyn (Newport), W. D. Thomas (Llanelli), T. G. Evans (London Welsh), W. D. Morris (Neath), D. Hughes (Newbridge), T. M. Davies (London Welsh), Replacement: R. Hopkins (Maesteg) for G. O. Edwards, 67 min.

Referee R. Calmet (France). Replacement: R. F. Johnson (England) at half-time.

On the same afternoon Ireland beat Scotland 16–11 at Lansdowne Road.

Ireland 14 pts Wales 0 *Lansdowne Road, 14 March 1970*

Clem Thomas had ended his report of the England game: 'And so to Ireland in an attempt to win the triple crown. What a game that promises to be.' And what a game it proved, if not in the sense that he or anyone else expected. Four times previously Ireland had snatched the crown from Wales's grip at the final moment, so it wasn't so much the fact as the scale of defeat which threw the Welsh. It was their greatest loss since 1951, when they were belaboured 19–0 by the Scots at Murrayfield. And what made it all the harder to bear was that Edwards and John – playing together for the sixteenth time to beat the Dick Jones-Dicky Owen record set before the Great War – had one of their least successful games for Wales. Perhaps they were no more culpable than anyone else, but they were the pilots and for once they salvaged nothing from the wreck.

There was none of the violence which had disfigured this fixture the year before, but the Irish tore into the Welsh with such ferocious energy that even the possession which Delme Thomas regularly won at the lineout proved a bit of a liability. Instead of sticking to ten-man rugby the Welsh halves fed their threequarter line, only to expose their weakness and subject them to Ireland's deadly tackling. And whenever Ireland won the ball, the daunting accuracy of McGann's kicking kept J. P. R. Williams tied down in defence.

Yet Wales survived a scoreless first-half, and had some reason to believe the worst was over. Although they were still living dangerously in the mid-field, they had more of their share of the ball from scrums as well as lineouts – plus a well-earned reputation for the grandstand finish.

Instead it was Ireland who got their blows in first and last, so that their triumph, as well as the Welsh collapse, was total. Seventeen minutes into the second half McGann floated a high ball up towards the Welsh twenty-five, JPR was rudely bundled off it, and from the scrum which followed it was McGann again who dropped a succinct goal.

Four minutes later, as JPR moved into the threequarter line to try to force the issue, John sent out a long pass which dropped behind everyone. Every Welshman, at least. Duggan was able to run onto the ball, and with the Welsh defence committed to attack, shot through for fifty yards to score a try in the corner.

Next Morris was dummied offside by Young at a scrum to give Kiernan a penalty from thirty yards. And finally, when John kicked upfield, Goodall the industrious Irish No 8, took the ball, burst through the centre, kicked ahead and won the touchdown from John and Dawes. Kiernan celebrated his forty-seventh cap, an Irish record, by converting the try and rounding off the sixteen-minute burst of scoring.

Scorers IRELAND – tries: Duggan, Goodall; conversion: Kiernan; dropped goal: McGann; penalty goal: Kiernan.

Ireland T. J. Kiernan (Cork Constitution, capt.); A. T. A.

Duggan (Lansdowne), F. P. K. Bresnihan (London Irish), C. M. H. Gibson (Northern Ireland F.C.), W. J. Brown (Malone); B. J. McGann (Lansdowne), R. M. Young (Collegians); S. Millar (Ballymena), K. W. Kennedy (London Irish), P. O'Callaghan (Dolphin), W. J. McBride (Ballymena), M. G. Molloy (London Irish), R. A. Lamont (Instonians), J. F. Slattery (University College, Dublin), K. G. Goodall (City of Derry).

Wales J. P. R. Williams (London Welsh); S. J. Watkins (Cardiff), S. J. Dawes (London Welsh), W. H. Raybould (Newport), K. Hughes (Cambridge University); B. John (Cardiff), G. O. Edwards (Cardiff, capt.); D. Williams (Ebbw Vale), J. Young (Harrogate), D. B. Llewelyn (Newport), W. D. Thomas (Llanelli), T. G. Evans (London Welsh), W. D. Morris (Neath), D. Hughes (Newbridge), T. M. Davies (London Welsh).

Referee Air Commodore G. C. Lamb (England).

A week later Scotland beat England 14–5 at Murrayfield.

Wales 11 pts France 6 *Cardiff, 4 April 1970*

After that humbling defeat by Ireland, and in the absence through injury of Barry John, the Welsh selectors made seven changes to their side. Bennett came in for his fourth cap, but his first at stand-off. The persistent problem of the three-quarter line was temporarily solved by awarding three new caps – to Arthur Lewis in the centre and to Shanklin and Mathias on the wings. The last two normally played at centre for their clubs, while Mathias had earlier played at flank forward. In the pack Lloyd returned at prop, Gallaher made a storming first appearance (and, as it turned out, last before going north) at lock, and Taylor came back on the flank.

Edwards was relieved of the captaincy, which switched back to John Dawes at centre (as it had in 1968), and Dawes in turn revised the Welsh tactics to allow for the side's weaknesses and play to its strengths. Since the threequarters lacked decisive pace, Wales would return the ball to their forwards with the halves under orders to kick over the advantage line whenever they won possession. This Edwards and Bennett did with great precision, leaving the threequarters to come in quickly and conclusively for the tackle.

To this challenge the Welsh pack responded with remarkable vigour, holding the French tight forwards in the scrums and winning more than their share of the ball – in particular through Gallaher in the lineouts. JPR, running bravely to the blind side instead of the open, a lesson learned in Dublin, added his weight to the onslaught, and the French who had started overwhelming favourites, were harassed into error.

It took Wales some time, however, to build up the pressure and meanwhile France were first to score. Marot and Lux kicked on and Bonal, beating JPR and Shanklin to the touch-down, got a try. But by half-time JPR had kicked two penalties to put Wales ahead, and at the kick-off for the second half they created the pressure which brought the decisive score. The French forwards took the ball, but when they worked it back Puget gave his stand-off a suicide pass. Paries hesitated for a fraction, and was spun round by Dawes as he tried to reach his full-back. The irrepressible Gallaher intercepted the loose pass then lobbed the ball inside to Morris who scored between the posts. JPR converted.

Although the French threequarters were to put Cantoni through for a try to close the gap a little, the Welsh policy of containment had been enough to win the day. Enough too to win at least a share of the championship with – as they would be forced to acknowledge – a rather more talented French side.

Scorers WALES – try: Morris; conversion: Williams; penalty goals: Williams 2. FRANCE – Bonal, Cantoni.

Wales J. P. R. Williams (London Welsh); R. Mathias (Llanelli), S. J. Dawes (London Welsh, capt.), A. J. Lewis (Ebbw Vale), J. L. Shanklin (London Welsh); P. Bennett (Llanelli), G. O. Edwards (Cardiff); D. J. Lloyd (Bridgend),

J. Young (Harrogate), D. B. Llewelyn (Newport), W. D. Thomas (Llanelli), I. S. Gallaher (Llanelli), W. D. Morris (Neath), J. Taylor (London Welsh), T. M. Davies (London Welsh). Replacement: W. H. Raybould (Newport) for J. L. Shanklin.

France P. Villepreux (Toulouse); J. Cantoni (Béziers), A. Marot (Brive), J–P. Lux (Tyrosse), J–M. Bonal (Toulouse); L. Paries (Biarritz), M. Puget (Brive); J. Iraçabal (Bayonne), R. Bénésis (Narbonne), J–L. Azarete (Dax), J–P. Bastiat (Dax), E. Cester (Toulouse OEC), J–P. Biemouret (Agen), C. Carrere (Toulon, capt.), B. Dauga (Monte. de-Marsan).

Referee K. D. Kelleher (Ireland)

A fortnight later France beat England 35–13 at Stade Colombes to share the championship.

Championship Table 1970

	P	W	D	L	For	Ag	Pts
France	4	3	0	1	60	33	6
Wales	4	3	0	1	46	42	6
Ireland	4	2	0	2	33	28	4
England	4	1	0	3	40	69	2
Scotland	4	1	0	3	43	50	2

9
Lions' Share: 1970–71

Wales have never looked more sleek with success than they did this season. October brought the official opening of the national stadium at Cardiff, and a new term into the Welsh rugby glossary: debenture holder – the man who has everything. By the end of March the second triple crown in three years had been followed by the first grand slam in nineteen, on the strength of which, when the British Lions left in May for Australia and New Zealand, it was with thirteen Welsh players in the party of thirty, a Welsh captain, John Dawes, and Welsh coach, Carwyn James. If the selectors at first appeared to have overreacted, the results on that tour were their vindication.

The season began rather slowly, even ceremonially. It was the centenary of the Rugby Football Union, and to celebrate this Wales held a house-warming at their own new stadium in which they beat the RFU President's XV 26–11. There were no major tourists, but a month later Fiji, visiting England as part of the centenary programme, paid a courtesy call on Cardiff where they lost 8–6 to the Wales Under-25. Not a particularly impressive Welsh performance, but a milestone in the progress of Alan Martin, the Aberavon lock, who was not to get the first of his (so far) thirty-one senior caps for another three years, and John Bevan, the wing threequarter who graduated rather more rapidly from Cardiff College of Education *via* Wales to the Lions within a season.

In the championship only Scotland presented Wales with any real problem, the result depending on John Taylor's final conversion. After the indecisions of 1970, Wales were a settled team once more. Only one temporary change was made, at centre, for the Scottish game. And while it may be true that the French respond to the occasional charge of dynamite beneath them, the Welsh generally thrive best when left alone.

With the return of Gerald Davies to one wing and the promotion of Bevan to the other, the confirmation of Dawes as captain and tactical director in the centre with the solid Arthur Lewis at his side, Welsh threequarter play was once again a dominant influence. A total of seventy-three points and thirteen tries was proof of that. The pack, too, having been given the benefit of several doubts after the Scottish match, ended the season as strongly against France as they had begun it against England.

If the Welsh victories were a triumph for teamwork and squad training, they were not gained at the expense of individual expression. This winter saw Barry John grow into the King John of popular legend, his virtuosity in the French game in particular carrying through to the New Zealand tour. If he owed much to the rifled pass and general protection of Gareth Edwards, he appeared to develop almost an invulnerability of his own as he circled and slid past outstretched arms, and brought to perfection the timing and placing of his diagonal kicks to the wing.

This was also the season when the influence of the free-scoring London Welsh reached its peak. Under Dawes the Old Deer Park had become a semi-official nursery and proving ground for techniques which were carried into the national side: tap passing to relay the ball without it even resting in the player's hands; rounding to take a second pass; reversing direction; maintaining a perpetual motion so that players of no more than moderate speed ran opponents off their feet; the regular but varied incursions of JPR from full-back.

London Welsh were top of the England and Anglo-Welsh tables, came second in the Welsh club championship to Bridgend, won all the matches on their Christmas and Easter tours of South Wales, and had six representatives in each of Wales's championship matches: Dawes, JPR, Gerald Davies, Roberts, Mervyn Davies and Taylor. They crowned the season by winning the Middlesex Sevens, even though these six were sitting in the stand with the British Lions party, together with Geoff Evans, a reserve who would later fly out to join them in New Zealand. Still, a club with fourteen past and present internationals on its strength wasn't exactly at its wits' end to find replacements.

The International Championship

Wales 22 pts England 6 *Cardiff, 16 January 1971*

Wales so swiftly and completely took England apart in the tight and rucks that by half-time it was no contest. And sadly for the English in their centenary year Wales, for the first time in fifty years, went ahead in the series 33–32 with eleven matches drawn.

The highly-tuned Welsh pack drove through their opponents like an armoured division through cavalry, and the gifted England threequarters became spectators of the struggle. Llewelyn and Williams buckled the England props at the scrum; in the more closely-fought lineouts Thomas and Mervyn Davies got the cleaner possession at the back and made more aggressive use of it; the loose was controlled by the greater Welsh speed and skill.

To the rear Edwards and John played with a growing understanding and composure, swung the ball with discretion and kicked with precision and effect. In the centre Dawes was an immaculate distributor, and with Lewis set up a great deal of second-phase play. Both wings got tries and J. P. R. Williams was at his most decisive in the catch, tackle, run and kick. It was all too much for England.

It took Wales eight minutes to settle, after which they won two successive lineouts. From the first John kicked into the England twenty-five and from the second dropped a goal. But that lead was thrown away two minutes later when Taylor rashly tapped back from a lineout close to his line and Hannaford pounced to accept the gift of a try. Though

Rossborough missed the conversion, Wales had to start again.

This time they made no mistake. Two minutes more and Lewis, put through on a scissors move with John, deliberately ploughed into the England forwards to set up a second-phase attack. John, after considering another drop at goal, instead swung the ball to his right. JPR came in to make the overlap for Davies to score in the corner, and Taylor kicked the angled conversion.

Almost on the half-hour, John again showed his consummate skill by chipping the ball around Spencer, regathering and putting Bevan over on the other wing. Clearly shaken, England began to contribute their own errors to the score. When Rossborough knocked on in his own twenty-five, Lewis was up at once to feed Dawes whose perfectly-timed pass gave Davies his second try and Taylor his second conversion. At half-time Wales were 16–3 up – all this on a pitch made heavy by a morning of rain – and the rest of the game was a formality.

After the interval Wales relaxed the pressure, though John still managed another dropped goal, while Rossborough and JPR swopped penalties. Half an hour before the finish the crowd were singing Wales home.

Scorers WALES – tries: T. G. R. Davies 2, Bevan; conversions: Taylor 2; dropped goals: John 2; penalty goal: J. P. R. Williams. ENGLAND – try: Hannaford; penalty goal: Rossborough.

Wales J. P. R. Williams (London Welsh); T. G. R. Davies (London Welsh), S. J. Dawes (London Welsh, capt.), A. J. Lewis (Ebbw Vale), J. C. Bevan (Cardiff); B. John (Cardiff), G. O. Edwards (Cardiff); D. B. Llewelyn (Llanelli), J. Young (Harrogate), D. Williams (Ebbw Vale), W. D. Thomas (Llanelli), M. G. Roberts (London Welsh), W. D. Morris (Neath), J. Taylor (London Welsh), T. M. Davies (London Welsh).

England P. A. Rossborough (Coventry); J. P. Janion (Bedford), C. S. Wardlow (Northampton), J. S. Spencer (Heading ley), D. J. Duckham (Coventry); I. D. Wright (Northampton), J. J. Page (Bedford); D. L. Powell (Northampton), J. V. Pullin (Bristol), K. E. Fairbrother (Coventry), P. J. Larter (Northampton), B. F. Ninnes (Coventry), A. L. Bucknall (Richmond, capt.), A. Neary (Broughton Park), R. C. Hannaford (Bristol).

Referee D. P. d'Arcy (Ireland).

On the same afternoon France beat Scotland 13–8 at Stade Colombes. A fortnight later (30 January) Ireland and France drew 9–9 at Lansdowne Road.

Scotland 18 pts Wales 19 *Murrayfield, 6 February 1971*

In all the seventies there was not to be a more exciting match or, for Wales, a more crucial victory than this (even though, had they lost it, they would still have won the title). Four times the lead changed hands, neither side allowing itself to admit the possibility of defeat. The action was continuous, the effort totally draining – not least the effort of watching it.

Often during the decade Scotland's rugby was a good deal better than their results. And although they were to finish bottom of the table this season, nobody would have guessed it by the way their forwards set about the game. Knowing what the Welsh pack had done to England, they set their tactical ambush. From the start they began slewing any scrum with a Welsh thrust behind it. And although they conceded penalties, they took the steam out of the Welsh forward drive, eventually winning three scrums against the head and conceding none. That accomplished, they went on to win the lineouts as well.

It was a match in which the Welsh halves had to retrieve their pack's misfortunes, and John in particular conjured opportunity from the scantiest means. One Scottish newspaper had described him as such a 'ghostly' runner that 'it comes almost as a relief to see him leave a room by the door, rather than simply vanish through a wall'. It was this ability to glide through walls that John had to demonstrate this day.

In the opening spell of probing, Scotland's eighteenth minute lead, a penalty by Peter Brown, was answered with another by John, to which Brown responded in kind. Scotland 6–3. Indeed it was not until just before half-time that Wales went into the lead for the first time. Thomas won a lineout on the left; Edwards, John, Hall and Dawes all handled before JPR plunged through the centre; and Taylor, from a slipped pass, beat two men to run between the posts for a try. John converted. Half-time 6–8.

Wales then extended their lead to 6–11 as Edwards scored a typical try in a breakaway on the blind side of a ruck. But they maintained it only briefly. Scotland came back with two scores in rapid succession – a try by Carmichael who burst upon a rash tap-back by Thomas near the Welsh line, and Brown's third penalty – to make it 12–11.

Wales then extended their lead to 6–11 as Edwards scored a ahead with a try which probably no other player could have scored. He drove the ball past a Scottish defender, picked it up from his toecap, and glided through one tackle after another before dropping over the line. It was 12–14. But again Scotland came back with a brace of scores: yet another penalty from Brown, and then a try by Rea after Bevan had a kick charged down.

At 18–14, with only five minutes' play remaining, it seemed that Wales must go down. But now they were ready to run anything. They swung the ball right from a lineout; by threatening to come into the line JPR wrong-footed the defence; and this gave Gerald Davies just enough room to squeeze over. But he was forced to touch down only a dozen yards from the corner, and so after all the fluctuations it came down to this: a difficult conversion to win or lose the match. The kick went to John Taylor whose round-the-corner approach was still highly suspect at that time. But his left boot (now to be seen in the London Welsh clubhouse) swung in its arc, the ball curved gracefully between the posts, and the game was put out of its splendid misery.

Scorers SCOTLAND – tries: Carmichael, Rea; penalty goals:

P. C. Brown 4. WALES – tries: Taylor, Edwards, John, T. G. R. Davies; conversions: John, Taylor; penalty goal: John.

Scotland I. S. G. Smith (London Scottish); W. C. C. Steele (Bedford), J. N. M. Frame (Gala), C. W. W. Rea (West of Scotland), A. G. Biggar (London Scottish); J. W. C. Turner (Gala), D. S. Patterson (Gala); J. McLauchlan (Jordanhill College), F. A. L. Laidlaw (Melrose), A. B. Carmichael (West of Scotland), A. F. McHarg (London Scottish), N. A. MacEwan (Gala), R. J. Arneil (Leicester), G. L. Brown (West of Scotland), P. C. Brown (Gala, capt.).

Wales J. P. R. Williams (London Welsh); T. G. R. Davies (London Welsh), S. J. Dawes (London Welsh, capt.), I. Hall (Aberavon), J. C. Bevan (Cardiff); B. John (Cardiff), G. O. Edwards (Cardiff); D. B. Llewelyn (Llanelli), J. Young (Harrogate), D. Williams (Ebbw Vale), W. D. Thomas (Llanelli), M. G. Roberts (London Welsh), W. D. Morris (Neath), J. Taylor (London Welsh), T. M. Davies (London (Welsh).

Referee M. H. Titcomb (England).

A week later (13 February) England beat Ireland 9–6 at Lansdowne Road, and on 27 February drew 14–14 with France at Twickenham. On that day, too, Ireland beat Scotland 17–5 at Murrayfield.

Wales 23 pts Ireland 9 *Cardiff, 13 March 1971*

After the debacle at Lansdowne Road the year before, when Ireland rudely jolted Wales's arm as they reached for the triple crown, this game was approached with a little circumspection. It began with a ferocious attack launched by the Irish lock, Hipwell, from the lineout, settled into a trial of strength at the scrums, and saw Ireland six points in the lead after thirty-three minutes. Mike Gibson had put them there with the second of his three penalty goals.

These, however, were Ireland's only scores. In a flattening reply the Welsh put together a goal, three tries, a dropped goal and two penalties – seventeen of those points coming from Edwards and John in another superlative display at half-back. They benefited from the gradual assertion of the Welsh pack which held, though never quite managed to subdue, the Irish forwards. And in turn they were supported by some excellent running from the backs. Dawes played with cool, unobtrusive authority in mid-field, snapping out his passes with a dramatic sense of timing. Gerald Davies's speed and subtlety on the right was balanced by the brisk determination of Lewis and Bevan on the other flank. JPR was his usual belligerent self at full-back.

By the interval Wales had moved into a 9–6 lead. Winning a ruck set up by Bevan, they relayed the ball rapidly to the wing where Davies, cutting first inside then out, scored a try by the flag. Next O'Driscoll was overrun as he fielded a high kick ahead by John, and when the ball re-emerged John dropped a goal – his eighth for Wales, a national record. To this he added his first penalty.

Still nothing conclusive in the scoring, however, until Edwards made two of his familar, low-slung plunges to the blind side, setting up a bout of scoring which brought fourteen points for Wales (plus Gibson's third penalty) in the space of eighteen minutes. Edwards' first run, from a ruck set up by Llewelyn in a peel from the lineout, ended in a try of his own. His second, from a scrum, created another try for Davies, all done by luring in the Irish wing, Grant, and leaving his own unmarked for the scoring pass.

The rest belonged wholly to the halves: a forty-eight yard penalty by John; a second try by Edwards who took the ball as it bounced behind the lineout; a final conversion from John. Beyond that, a twelfth triple crown for Wales, making England's record of thirteen crowns look highly vulnerable.

Scorers WALES – tries: T. G. R. Davies 2, Edwards 2; conversion: John; dropped goal: John; penalty goals: John 2. IRELAND – penalty goals: Gibson 3.

Wales J. P. R. Williams (London Welsh); T. G. R. Davies

(London Welsh), S. J. Dawes (London Welsh, capt.), A. J. Lewis (Ebbw Vale), J. C. Bevan (Cardiff); B. John (Cardiff), G. O. Edwards (Cardiff); D. B. Llewelyn (Llanelli), J. Young (Harrogate), D. Williams (Ebbw Vale), W. D. Thomas (Llanelli), M. G. Roberts (London Welsh), W. D. Morris (Neath), J. Taylor (London Welsh), T. M. Davies (London Welsh).

Ireland B. J. O'Driscoll (Manchester); A. T. A. Duggan (Lansdowne), F. P. K. Bresnihan (London Irish), C. M. H. Gibson (Northern Ireland F.C., capt.), E. L. Grant (CIYMS); B. J. McGann (Cork Constitution), R. M. Young (Collegians); J. F. Lynch (St Mary's College), K. W. Kennedy (London Irish), R. J. McLoughlin (Blackrock College), W. J. McBride (Ballymena), M. L. Hipwell (Terenure College), J. F. Slattery (University College, Dublin), M. G. Molloy (London Irish), D. J. Hickie (St Mary's College).

Referee R. F. Johnson (England).

A week later (20 March) Scotland beat England 16–15 at Twickenham.

France 5 pts Wales 9 *Stade Colombes, 27 March 1971*

Nobody would have questioned the talent and discipline of the Welsh XV this season. But what was proved above all in the match which gave them their first grand slam since 1952 was their character and courage. On a sunny spring day and a dry pitch, the equally gifted French side were in their element. They were also playing with the incentive of selection for their tour of South Africa that summer. There was urgent ambition on both sides, and the result was a game which, if low in scoring, was of the highest spirit and quality.

The waves of French attack came crashing in like breakers on the Atlantic coast, and it was only by fearless tackling that Wales were able to limit their scoring to a single goal. Then, coming from behind as was their custom, they seized their chance – and in one case created a chance from the makings of disaster – to score two tries and a penalty goal. All the points went to Edwards and John, though if there was one man who turned the tide it was J. P. R. Williams.

Wales chose to open against the breeze and accept the inevitable early onslaught. This came mainly from the lineout where Dauga, Biemouret and the Spanghero brothers were supreme. John stopped three seemingly certain tries with his tackles, one of them, aided by Taylor, on the 6ft 5in Dauga, which cost him a bloody nose and a few minutes off the field. JPR engulfed Bourgarel. Bevan forced Lux back through the Welsh posts. Nobody flinched or remained unscathed, and the dressing-room afterwards was like an out-patients' clinic. If one weakness of the French was their finishing, the punishment they received from the Welsh defence was enough to make them lose a little last-minute concentration.

The French try came after thirty-seven minutes. Barrau switched to the blind side from broken play in front of the Welsh posts, Villepreux and Bertranne worked the ball cleverly, and Dauga lent his weight to score a crashing try which Villepreux converted.

In the final minutes of the half it looked as if the process would be repeated as Villepreux and Bourgarel composed an attack. But only a few yards out from the Welsh line, the latter's pass was amazingly intercepted by JPR. He raced through almost to the French twenty-five before cutting inwards. Inside him he saw Denzil Williams, but judging that the prop might lack the pace to complete the move, he turned outward again. There he found Edwards eager and able to take the ball on to the corner. Instead of changing ends nine points down, Wales turned their backs to the wind with only a 5–3 deficit to make up.

The second half was largely a test of stamina, for the French hostility was undiminished. But managing to break out of their own defensive lines, the Welsh set up two good attacking positions and scored from both. Dawes created a ruck in front of the French posts at which Bertranne went off-side and John at last put Wales ahead with a penalty goal. And then, fifteen minutes from no-side, Wales won a heel against the head and John slid through for a try.

Scorers FRANCE – try Dauga; conversion: Villepreux. WALES – tries: Edwards, John; penalty goal: John.

France P. Villepreux (Toulouse); R. Bourgarel (Toulouse), R. Bertranne (Bagnères), J–P. Lux (Tyrosse), J. Cantoni (Béziers); J–L. Berot (Toulouse), M. Barrau (Beaumont); M. Lasserre (Agen), R. Bénésis (Narbonne), J. Iraçabal (Bayonne), W. Spanghero (Narbonne), C. Spanghero (Narbonne), J–P. Biemouret (Agen), B. Dauga (Mont-de-Marsan), C. Carrere (Toulon, capt.).

Wales J. P. R. Williams (London Welsh); T. G. R. Davies (London Welsh), S. J. Dawes (London Welsh, capt.), A. J. Lewis (Ebbw Vale), J. C. Bevan (Cardiff); B. John (Cardiff), G. O. Edwards (Cardiff); D. B. Llewelyn (Llanelli), J. Young (Harrogate), D. Williams (Ebbw Vale), W. D. Thomas (Llanelli), M. G. Roberts (London Welsh), W. D. Morris (Neath), J. Taylor (London Welsh), T. M. Davies (London Welsh).

Referee J. Young (Scotland).

Championship Table 1971

	P	W	D	L	For	Ag	Pts
Wales	4	4	0	0	73	38	8
France	4	1	2	1	41	40	4
England	4	1	1	2	44	58	3
Ireland	4	1	1	2	41	46	3
Scotland	4	1	0	3	47	64	2

British Lions tour of Australia and New Zealand

Although the Welsh submerged their national identity in the British Lions tour that summer, their individual and collective contribution to its success provided more than just a footnote to the season. There had been some criticism of the appointment of Dawes as captain and Carwyn James as coach, and of the selection of so many Welshmen in the party – (fourteen out of thirty-three by the time three replacements had been flown out). A stubbornly received idea in rugby circles was that the Welsh made bad tourists; they tended to be homesick, clannish, bolshie. And perhaps the circumstances of some earlier tours had made them so. But it was not a view you heard repeated on many lips by the time the trip was over.

After disconcertingly losing their opening game at Brisbane – still suffering from jet-lag or, as their manager, the learned Dr Douglas Smith put it, *circadian dysrhythmia* – they went on to lose only one game more, the second test against New Zealand. The first and third tests they won, the fourth they drew, to become the first British Isles team to take a series there. In all they won twenty-three of their twenty-six matches, scoring 580 points to two hundred and thirty-one.

Of the Welshmen, Dawes, Gerald Davies, J. P. R. Williams, John, Edwards, Taylor and Mervyn Davies played in all four tests. John was the highest points scorer in this or any other Lions tour: 191 in seventeen appearances, made up of seven tries, thirty-one conversions, eight dropped goals and twenty-eight penalties. Behind Bob Hiller, the England full-back with 110, came John Bevan who, although he played in only one test, scored 54 points from eighteen tries. And in contrast to some earlier – and later – tours, there was not a hint of warfare between the various Lions tribes.

Gerald Davies: *(above)* attracting the attention of two England forwards, Roger Uttley and Mike Rafter (on the ground); *(overleaf)* trapped but still determinedly looking for a man to pass to.

Steve Fenwick: a more forceful than graceful presence in the Welsh centre.

10

Broken Engagements: 1971–72

The Lions' success in New Zealand during the summer might have had the same impact on rugby as England's World Cup victory in 1966 had on soccer. Instead the following season was a dreadful anti-climax. For the first time since the war, the international championship was interrupted by politics. With an increase in the violence in Northern Ireland and threats of sabotage in the Republic, both Scotland and Wales declined to play their scheduled matches in Dublin. Ireland adamantly and very understandably refused to give up their home advantage and switch to a neutral ground (Stade Colombes was offered). So only two countries played their full programme: England, who for the first time ever lost all four of their championship games, and France, who were little more successful, losing three out of four. Wales and Scotland played three games and Ireland only two.

This was particularly hard on the Irish. They lost the revenue from two internationals, although they recouped some of it when, at the end of April, France came over to play a friendly match before thirty-thousand grateful spectators at Lansdowne Road. But worse, Ireland lost a credible chance of triple crown and championship. Having won their first two games away from home, they were entitled to expect no less success on their own ground. But on 17 February the Scottish Rugby Union, concerned for the safety of their players, cancelled their visit and, despite Irish claims that the dangers were exaggerated, Wales followed suit in March.

Wales did so reluctantly, for they had already won three convincing victories and were only a single win away from scoring, for the first time in sixty-three years, two successive grand slams. Still, it was their choice and although it caused some bitterness at the time, now it is pointless to argue what might have happened on the field or off it.

As often happens after major events, three important figures retired. The one who left the most immediate void was John Dawes, the unobtrusive technician and tactician of the Welsh and Lions threequarter lines. Although he continued to play for London Welsh – who for the first time won the Welsh club championship and again took the Middlesex Sevens – he announced in November that he would no longer be an international candidate.

The other man to bow out before the championship was that unbendable veteran of thirty-six Welsh matches, Denzil Williams. He was succeeded by John Lloyd of Bridgend. In 1971 Lloyd, although he had nineteen previous caps, was not selected either by Wales or the Lions, but now it was he who took over the captaincy from Dawes.

Despite these losses Wales could still call upon ten British Lions – eight of whom had played in the tests – for the opening match against England. The basic structure of the team was still intact. What looked like jeopardizing it was a third retirement just after the season ended. On 7 May, at the age of twenty-seven, Barry John decided to leave the game altogether.

There was a genuine sense of shock at the announcement, even though it had been half-expected. Players are always being urged to quit when they are at the top. Yet while John had no equal at stand-off, people felt he might still not have reached his individual peak. In his final championship, restricted as it was to three games, he had scored thirty-five points to pass his own and Jarrett's joint record of thirty-one, and bring his total to ninety – two better than Jack Bancroft's fifty-eight-year-old record.

Otherwise the season was remarkable for the introduction of the WRU Challenge Cup (which went to Neath) and of the four-point try. Appropriately enough the first Welshman to score one in the championship was J. P. R. Williams.

The International Championship

England 3 pts Wales 12 *Twickenham, 15 January 1972*

With the Lions' triumph still reverberating throughout rugby, there was enormous interest in this opening match of the championship. The Rugby Union had to refund £75,000 to disappointed applicants after the tickets had run out, and among those who managed to get in the ground there was a high expectation of a Welsh win and a masterly display of rugby.

The first was achieved, but a Welshman who had boasted before the match that they would drop the fixture unless England improved spent an uncomfortable first forty minutes. England had improved almost out of recognition. Pullin won six strikes against the head in the first half, conceding only three in the game, and collectively the England pack took the lineouts 23–20. As a measure of the pressure that England put upon them, Wales gave away twelve penalties to five.

By denying Wales possession and by marking strongly, England greatly reduced the opportunity for fluent, open rugby. Especially since, for all their steady supply of the ball, England had little of their own to contribute. Duckham made one fine run through the centre, only to be beaten by the slippery turf as he tried to circle JPR. Webster, their new scrum-half, was also a constant, darting threat. But essentially England were at their best in winning the ball not using it, in countering moves not constructing them.

Wales therefore had to win by making the most of scant chances, and their try was the only one of the match. Of the many penalties only two on either side were close enough to be kicked at goal. Hiller succeeded with his first to give England the lead, but failed with his second. John put both of his across the bar to make it 6–3 to Wales at half-time.

That still left Wales in an anxious situation until nearly mid-way through the second half. Then from a five-yard scrum Edwards fed JPR who was steaming up on the blind side like a dreadnought, and nothing less than the West stand collapsing on him would have stopped him scoring in the corner. John, whose role this day had been largely confined to kicking, was at least able to show his genius for that by converting from the touchline. Any victory at Twickenham must be gratefully accepted, but its style was not quite what the crowds in the old country had been hoping for.

Scorers ENGLAND – penalty: Hiller. WALES – try: Williams; conversion: John; penalty goals: John 2.

England R. B. Hiller (Harlequins, capt.); J. P. Janion (Bedford), M. C. Beese (Liverpool), D. J. Duckham (Coventry), K. J. Fielding (Moseley); A. G. B. Old (Middlesborough), J. G. Webster (Moseley); C. B. Stevens (Penzance & Newlyn), J. V. Pullin (Bristol), M. A. Burton (Gloucester), A. Brinn (Gloucester), C. W. Ralston (Richmond), P. J. Dixon (Harlequins), A. Neary (Broughton Park), A. G. Ripley (Rosslyn Park).

Wales J. P. R. Williams (London Welsh); T. G. R. Davies (London Welsh), R. T. E. Bergiers (Cardiff College of Education), A. J. Lewis (Ebbw Vale), J. C. Bevan (Cardiff); B. John (Cardiff), G. O. Edwards (Cardiff); D. J. Lloyd (Bridgend, capt.), J. Young (Harrogate), D. B. Llewelyn (Llanelli), W. D. Thomas (Llanelli), T. G. Evans (London Welsh), W. D. Morris (Neath), J. Taylor (London Welsh), T. M. Davies (London Welsh).

Referee J. Young (Scotland).

On the same afternoon Scotland beat France 20–9 at Murrayfield, and a fortnight later (29 January), Ireland beat France 14–9 at Stade Colombes.

Wales 35 pts Scotland 12 *Cardiff, 5 February 1972*

Early in the second half, two tries in two minutes by Gareth Edwards, both cleverly worked for, but the second a remarkable display of ball control, timing and acrobatics, turned a 12–10 lead for Scotland into a 12–20 uphill struggle. For all the promise of their opening forty-five minutes, the Scots weren't equal to it, and by the end they had suffered their worst defeat ever at Welsh hands – three goals, two tries and three penalties to a goal and two penalties.

The game began in a mean and savage mood, and though a lecture from the referee limited the excesses – well, more or less, there were still thirty-one penalties, seventeen to Scotland and fourteen to Wales – the game simmered on into the second half. Only then was the anger finally spent and rugby began to make the running.

From their kick-off Scotland began ominously to win everything, and though Wales survived some of the dangers, Renwick gave the visitors the lead with a fifteen-yard penalty. John evened that up with another, and in the eighteenth minute Wales, regaining their composure, put together a fine try. From Mervyn Davies at the back of the lineout the ball was sent to John who threw a deep pass missing out the centre. JPR came into the line to make the overlap, and Gerald Davies, first beating his wing and chipping ahead, picked up neatly on the line to score.

Again before the interval a Scottish penalty – this time a hefty fifty-yarder from Peter Brown – was cancelled out by one from John. But in between Wales were dealt a greater blow when JPR broke his jaw in a tackle on Steele. Even he couldn't play on with that disability (though he did talk his way out of hospital that night to attend the match dinner). Fortunately Phil Bennett, who had previously played at wing, centre and stand-off for Wales, had been thoroughly trained as a utility man at Llanelli, and came out to do an accomplished job at full-back.

Scotland, too, lost Biggar just after the interval – but also regained the lead. While still reduced to fourteen men they won a ruck near the Welsh line and Arneil sent the hooker, Clark, bursting over on the blind side for a try which Brown converted. But the Scots weren't back in the game for long. Moments later Llewelyn peeled away from the back of the lineout within their twenty-five and was stopped only a yard from the goal-line. Wales won the ruck, and Edwards made a typical broad-shouldered charge for the try. John's conversion put Wales ahead once more at 16–12, and the Scottish collapse had begun.

To the Scots' way of thinking, and to some others', the preliminaries to that try had included a knock-on by Mervyn Davies in the lineout and an accidental off-side by Llewelyn as he peeled away. They were still seething about it when Edwards broke through once more to score one of the most memorable tries of his career.

It began near his own twenty-five when he moved away from a ruck, bursting through the tackle of Arneil. Then he kicked over the full-back's head to begin a race with Jim Renwick for the touchdown. By the time the ball slithered over the line, Edwards had covered eighty yards of heavy ground. But at the end of the run he produced a perfect gymnastic dive, stretching out to ground the ball just before it reached the dead-ball line.

From that point the Welsh were irresistible, the Scots on a hiding. John kicked another penalty, this time from forty-five yards; Bergiers scored near the posts for John to convert; Taylor sold a stylish dummy and cut inside to score; a final conversion by John and he was well on his way to a record with fifteen points from this match alone.

Scorers WALES – tries: Edwards 2, Bergiers, T. G. R. Davies, Taylor; conversions: John 3; penalty goals: John 3. SCOTLAND – try: Clark; conversion: P. C. Brown; penalty goals: Renwick, P. C. Brown.

Wales J. P. R. Williams (London Welsh); T. G. R. Davies (London Welsh), A. J. Lewis (Ebbw Vale), R. T. E. Bergiers (Cardiff College of Education), J. C. Bevan (Cardiff); B. John (Cardiff), G. O. Edwards (Cardiff); D. B. Llewelyn (Llanelli), J. Young (Harrogate), D. J. Lloyd (Bridgend, capt.), W. D. Thomas (Llanelli), T. G. Evans (London Welsh), W. D. Morris (Neath), J. Taylor (London Welsh), T. M. Davies

(London Welsh). Replacement: P. Bennett (Llanelli) for J. P. R. Williams, 25 min.

Scotland A. R. Brown (Gala); W. C. C. Steele (Bedford), J. N. M. Frame (Gala), J. M. Renwick (Hawick), A. G. Biggar (London Scottish); C. M. Telfer (Hawick), D. S. Paterson (Gala); A. B. Carmichael (West of Scotland), R. L. Clark (Edinburgh Wanderers), J. McLauchlan (Jordanhill College), I. A. Barnes (Hawick), G. L. Brown (West of Scotland), N. A. MacEwan (Gala), R. J. Arneil (Northampton), P. C. Brown (Gala, capt.). Replacement: L. G. Dick (Loughborough) for Biggar, 45 min.

Referee G. A. Jamieson (Ireland).

England suffered consecutive defeats in the next three matches, a week later losing 16–12 to Ireland at Twickenham, 37–12 to France at Stade Colombes on 16 February, and 23–9 to Scotland at Murrayfield on 18 March.

Wales 20 pts France 6 *Cardiff, 25 March 1972*

After beating Scotland with so much exuberance, Wales made a thoroughly – though to some people's tastes, a coldly – professional job of their final match. France are nearly always the side to beat in the championship, and Wales did so emphatically by four penalty goals and two tries to two penalties. This meant they had known nothing but victory for two seasons, which was, to say the least, satisfactory. So was Barry John's capture of Jack Bancroft's record with his twelve penalty points. But the Welsh, who had the upper hand, were not prepared to take any risks. And from Europe's two most gifted running sides, playing in the late spring, the crowd had hoped for a little more gaiety.

Considering that, because of the Irish troubles, Wales had not played for seven weeks, they settled into the game remarkably quickly. The pack took almost complete control of possession at scrums, lineouts and rucks, channelling the ball exactly where they wanted it. Edwards's passing was at its most precise, and John kicked austerely for position, forcing the French to attack from deep or not at all.

When the Welsh allowed the ball beyond their halves, the threequarters responded briskly, Lewis taking over Dawes's old role as the mid-field distributor. But their hour was yet to come. For the moment Bergiers was mainly seen as a solid defender, occasionally tackling two and even three Frenchmen at a time, and the first half resolved into a goal-kicking duel between John and Villepreux. This John won by hitting three penalties and a post from close range but difficult angles, although Villepreux, playing in his last championship game, was the more spectacular with two penalties from sixty yards.

In the second half Wales at last broke loose to score two fine tries with John's fourth penalty sandwiched in between. Both tries were scored on the wing. Davies went first, fed on the blind side of a scrum won against the head and forcing through a narrow gap to reach the line. Then came Bevan's turn: a sudden break, a beautifully balanced fifty-yard run, a kick over Villepreux and a final surge for the touchdown.

A minute or two from the end Mervyn Davies went off the field with a rib injury. And it says much for the quality of the competition to get into this Welsh side that the man who came out briefly to replace him was already a Lions test player but only now winning his first Welsh cap. It was that other great back-row tactician, Derek Quinnell.

Scorers WALES – tries: T. G. R. Davies, Bevan; penalty goals: John 4. FRANCE – penalty goals: Villepreux 2.

Wales J. P. R. Williams (London Welsh); T. G. R. Davies (London Welsh), A. J. Lewis (Ebbw Vale), R. T. E. Bergiers (Cardiff College of Education), J. C. Bevan (Cardiff); B. John (Cardiff), G. O. Edwards (Cardiff); D. B. Llewelyn (Llanelli), J. Young (Harrogate), D. J. Lloyd (Bridgend, capt.), W. D. Thomas (Llanelli), T. G. Evans (London Welsh), W. D. Morris (Neath), J. Taylor (London Welsh), T. M. Davies (London Welsh). Replacement: D. L. Quinnell (Llanelli) for T. M. Davies, 79 min.

France P. Villepreux (Toulouse, capt.); B. Duprat (Bayonne), J. Maso (Narbonne), J–P. Lux (Dax), J. Sillières (Tarbes); J–L. Berot (Toulouse), M. Barrau (Beaumont); J. Iraçabal (Bayonne), R. Bénésis (Agen), J–L. Azarete (St-Jean-de-Luz), A. Estève (Béziers), C. Spanghero (Narbonne), J–C. Skréla (Toulouse), B. Dauga (Mont-de-Marsan), J–P. Biemouret (Agen).

Referee M. H. Titcomb (England).

Uncompleted Championship Table 1972

	P	W	D	L	For	Ag	Pts
Wales	3	3	0	0	67	21	6
Ireland	2	2	0	0	30	21	4
Scotland	3	2	0	1	55	53	4
France	4	1	0	3	61	66	2
England	4	0	0	4	36	88	0

11

The Quintuple Tie: 1972–73

During the next two seasons Wales won their share of matches but no special prizes. And to the pessimists (76.8 per cent of the population at a rough estimate), the great days were over. In the event nothing cataclysmic happened. Wales's unbeaten home record in the championship was extended from four years to six. The All Blacks were made to sweat for their narrow victory at Cardiff, and next season Australia, as well as Japan, were beaten. By 1975 Wales were champions once more and the best years of the decade were just beginning. In retrospect this two-year dip in the graph of Wales's onward and upward progress looks no more than a breathing space.

Natural wastage and certain swings in the balance between the clubs brought changes to the national side. Where London Welsh had been the great provider in the early seventies, it was now Llanelli which stepped up its production of internationals. Seven of their men – J. J. Williams, Roy Bergiers, Phil Bennett, Delme Thomas, Derek Quinnell, Barry Llewelyn and Tom David – played for Wales this season. And though a hard core of veterans remained in the side, it took some time to adjust to the departure of John Dawes and Barry John.

After the stable, consistent leadership of Dawes, it was John Lloyd who had first inherited the captaincy. This season the job passed to Delme Thomas, then Arthur Lewis and on, yet again, to Gareth Edwards. In 1973-74, Edwards continued to lead the side (John Taylor deputizing once in his absence), but great individual and team-man that he was, the dual role of tactician and strategist didn't really suit him. It was not until the 1975 championship that Wales discovered another born captain in Mervyn Davies.

The loss of Barry John was even more immediately felt, and it was at least three seasons before Phil Bennett, who had already played in four positions for Wales, was accepted as his true heir at stand-off. In fact his first full season was a good deal more profitable to Wales than John's had been. Bennett kicked thirty-one points in five matches, nineteen of them in the championship. John had averaged little more than a point a match in his first sixteen appearances. It was only afterwards that his really prolific period began, and the talents of his running and tactical kicking brimmed over. But that's what most people remembered and made him such a difficult man to follow. Inescapably, too, Wales lost three of their matches this winter (to New Zealand, Scotland and France), which they had not done since 1967.

Indeed they finished bottom of the championship table – though only in alphabetical order. They won both their home matches and lost twice away. So did everyone else, and for the first time ever the five nations finished all square.

The Seventh All Blacks

This young New Zealand side – average age only twenty-three – was neither as fearsome as most of its predecessors nor as entertaining as it might have been. Relying on subjugation by the pack, with the aid of that stocky 'ninth forward', Sid Going at scrum-half, it largely ignored the potential of its talented stand-off, Bob Burgess, and the ambitions of its threequarter line. It also found opponents better rehearsed than on previous tours and had few easy matches. This made it difficult for players to relax, and the strain was both expressed and aggravated by the sending home of Keith Murdoch for indiscipline.

Yet the tourists achieved most of their objectives. In the UK and Ireland they lost only four of their secondary matches – to Llanelli, North-Western Counties, Midland Counties and 23–11 to the Barbarians led by John Dawes in one of the great rugby classics of the decade. They drew with Munster, and the other eighteen they won. In the tests they were unbeaten, though a 10–10 draw with Ireland denied them the grand slam. Their full record in the home countries was P 26, W 20, L 4, D 2; points for 521, against 227. In France it read P 4, W 3, L 1; for 47, against 27.

Wales 16 pts New Zealand 19 *Cardiff, 2 December 1972*

New Zealand won the first half 13–3; Wales won the second 13–6 but consequently lost the match by five penalties to four with a try to either side. So much for the pattern of the game, but the Welsh failure was their habitual slow start during which they were unable to check the All Blacks' surging forward thrust, and their recklessness in conceding penalties. All told they gave away fewer than the tourists – the balance was 13–9 but crucially half were in kickable positions and the twenty-one-year-old New Zealand full-back, Joe Karam, didn't need asking twice.

Offering nothing in the way of constructive rugby, New Zealand relied on Going's kicks across the gain-line to keep up the forward momentum, and the pack's voracity in the rucks to complete the destruction. It was by these means that they scored their first-half try: an up-and-under by Going from the lineout, hard tackles on Bevan and JPR, and the forwards driving the ball on for Murdoch to get the touchdown. Karam kicked his first three penalties to one by Bennett, and New Zealand's position seemed unassailable.

Wales came back at them, however, in the second half, and with a new-found confidence began winning possession in the loose and launching one threequarter movement after another. One try came from their efforts as Edwards, spoiling Going in the middle, got the ball away to Bevan who beat three men into the corner. Many more of their moves were sabotaged by blatant late tackles and obstruction by the All Blacks who preferred the risk of being penalized to the greater danger from the quickness of the Welsh attacks. As a result Bevan was able to score from three more penalties, but Karam kicked two in reply to keep the tourists invariably ahead. And so they won the match, though few admirers.

Scorers WALES – try: Bevan; penalty goals: Bennett 4. NEW ZEALAND – try: Murdoch; penalty goals: Karam 5.

Wales J. P. R. Williams (London Welsh); T. G. R. Davies (London Welsh), R. T. E. Bergiers (Llanelli), J. L. Shanklin (London Welsh), J. C. Bevan (Cardiff); P. Bennett (Llanelli), G. O. Edwards (Cardiff); D. B. Llewelyn (Llanelli), J. Young (London Welsh), G. Shaw (Neath), W. D. Thomas (Llanelli, capt.), W. D. Morris (Neath), J. Taylor (London Welsh), D. L. Quinnell (Llanelli), T. M. Davies (Swansea).

New Zealand J. F. Karam (Wellington); B. G. Williams (Auckland), D. A. Hales (Canterbury), R. M. Parkinson (Poverty Bay), G. B. Batty (Wellington); R. E. Burgess (Manawatu), S. M. Going (N. Auckland); K. Murdoch (Otago), R. W. Norton (Canterbury), J. D. Matheson (Otago), G. J. Whiting (King Country), H. H. Macdonald (Canterbury), I. A. Kirkpatrick (Poverty Bay, capt.), A. J. Wyllie (Canterbury), A. R. Sutherland (Marlborough).

Referee R. F. Johnson (England).

The International Championship

The series began on 13 January with France's 16–13 win over Scotland in the first international to be staged at Parc des Princes, rebuilt at a cost of £8 million.

Wales 25 pts England 9 — *Cardiff, 20 January 1973*

To some spectators, who perhaps weren't making sufficient allowance for the slippery grass and greasy ball, this game was a disappointment. And it's true that it wasn't until the last four minutes, when Wales scored two tries and ten points in injury time, that the great difference in merit between these two sides was properly expressed. But from the start it was clear that Wales had the beating of England for the fifth year running. The English forward play was extremely loose, and it was only a matter of time before Wales fully exploited it.

As so often Wales conceded the opening lead when Cowman dropped a goal for England. It was short-lived, however, Taylor grabbed a loose ball behind the lineout, and with Lloyd and Quinnell drove for the line. From the ruck – the source of four of Wales's five tries – Edwards sent a long pass to Bergiers, and Bevan, with great determination, burst through a couple of tackles to score.

By half-time Wales had scored two further tries – by Gerald Davies from Bennett's diagonal kick, and by Edwards in support of his loose forwards – and though Doble kicked a penalty in reply, Wales changed ends with a comforting 12–6 lead.

In the final quarter, after Taylor and Doble had exchanged penalties, leaving matters where they stood, the Welsh began to move with increasing freedom and complexity, although scoring was slow. At last, in quick succession, came a try from Lewis in a scissors with Edwards, which Bennett converted, and another from Bevan in a dazing series of passes back and fore across the field.

Scorers WALES – tries: Bevan 2, T. G. R. Davies, Edwards, Lewis; conversion: Bennett; penalty goal: Taylor. ENGLAND – dropped goal: Cowman; penalty goals: Doble 2.

Wales J. P. R. Williams (London Welsh); T. G. R. Davies (London Welsh), R. T. Bergiers (Llanelli), A. J. Lewis (Ebbw Vale, capt.), J. C. Bevan (Cardiff); P. Bennett (Llanelli), G. O. Edwards (Cardiff); G. Shaw (Neath), J. Young (London Welsh), D. J. Lloyd (Bridgend), W. D. Thomas (Llanelli), D. L. Quinnell (Llanelli), J. Taylor (London Welsh), W. D. Morris (Neath), T. M. Davies (Swansea).

England S. A. Doble (Moseley); A. J. Morley (Bristol), P. J. Warfield (Rosslyn Park), P. S. Preece (Coventry), D. J. Duckham (Coventry); A. R. Cowman (Coventry), J. G. Webster (Moseley); F. E. Cotton (Loughborough Colleges), J. V. Pullin (Bristol, capt.), C. B. Stevens (Penzance & Newlyn), C. W. Ralston (Richmond), P. J. Larter (Northampton),

J. A. Watkins (Gloucester), A. Neary (Broughton Park), A. G. Ripley (Rosslyn Park). Replacement: G. W. Evans (Coventry) for P. J. Warfield, 25 min.

Referee G. Domercq (France).

Scotland 10 pts Wales 9 *Murrayfield, 3 February 1973*

After eight successive wins in the championship, and six years' dominance over Scotland, Wales went down with colours drooping in their next match to lose by a goal and a try to three penalties.

The Welsh betrayed their well-known failing, the sluggish start – they seemed to need opponents' points on the board to convince them it was all in earnest – and the Scots played on it ruthlessly. By the end of the first quarter they had scored all their points, and from there on they strangled any reply that Wales considered by the ferocity of their tackling and their commitment in the loose. The rucks, from which Wales had won so much useful possession against England, were dominated by the Scots, under their new captain, Ian McLauchlan. And with the scrums and lineouts breaking roughly even, the Welsh couldn't claw their way back into the game.

Scotland's first try came after eight minutes, with Telfer their scorer in a dummy scissors with Morgan. Their second, in the twentieth minute, followed a ripping blind-side run by Steele. Morgan converted the first of these to give Wales a great deal to do. It was not until the thirty-seventh minute that Bennett narrowed the gap with a penalty for offside – the error that the eager Scots were always liable to commit. But in first-half injury time Taylor kicked another for the same offence, and given Wales's capacity for the second-half revival, the game seemed far from over.

Instead of developing it simply disintegrated into a spoiling match. The more the Welsh tried to pass the ball, the more determinedly the Scots broke up the play. Unable to bring the game under control and let it flow, all that Wales could piece from the fragments was a second penalty by Bennett, again for offside.

Scorers SCOTLAND – tries: Telfer, Steele; conversion: Morgan. WALES – penalty goals: Bennett 2, Taylor.

Scotland A. R. Irvine (Heriot's F.P.); W. C. C. Steele (Bedford), I. R. McGeechan (Headingley), I. W. Forsyth (Stewart's F.P.), D. Shedden (West of Scotland); C. M. Telfer (Hawick), D. W. Morgan (Stewart's-Melville F.P.); A. B. Carmichael (West of Scotland), R. L. Clark (Edinburgh Wanderers), J. McLauchlan (Jordanhill, capt.), A. F. McHarg (London Scottish), P. C. Brown (Gala), J. G. Millican (Edinburgh University), N. A. MacEwan (Gala), G. M. Strachan (Jordanhill).

Wales J. P. R. Williams (London Welsh); T. G. R. Davies (London Welsh), R. T. E. Bergiers (Llanelli), A. J. Lewis (Ebbw Vale, capt.), J. C. Bevan (Cardiff); P. Bennett (Llanelli), G. O. Edwards (Cardiff); D. J. Lloyd (Bridgend), J. Young (London Welsh), G. Shaw (Neath), D. L. Quinnell (Llanelli), W. D. Thomas (Llanelli), W. D. Morris (Neath), J. Taylor (London Welsh), T. M. Davies (Swansea).

Referee F. Palmade (France).

A week later, on 10 February, Ireland beat England 18–9 at Lansdowne Road. On 24 February Scotland beat Ireland 19–14 at Murrayfield, and at Twickenham England won 14–6 against France.

Wales 16 pts Ireland 12 *Cardiff, 10 March 1973*

Again this was not a particularly convincing display by Wales. But the difference between the two scores was a try – otherwise two goals and four penalties were equally shared – and the difference between the two sides was Gareth Edwards. Wales did just enough to win another untidy spoiling match, but without Edwards they would probably not have earned the points to prove it.

The first half was a virtual stalemate, with the Welsh unable and the Irish unwilling to move the ball far from their forwards' sphere of influence, and most attacks reduced to tentative probing kicks. Two Bennett penalties, the first from fifty-two yards, and one penalty from McGann left Wales 6–3 ahead at the break with rather better things to come.

In the second half Wales began to construct their game, moving the ball freely and forcefully. What helped reinforce their confidence was Bennett's decision, a couple of minutes after the restart, to take the risk of running the ball out of defence. He had just fielded a deep kick by Grace, and he had to beat three men in order to reach the safety of his own forwards. But they responded by developing a momentum which carried them through to a ruck they quickly won, and from there the ball went to Edwards. Probably nobody else could have prised open such a narrow gap on the blind side, but Edwards took the ball almost to the line before slipping a scoring pass back to Shanklin.

Another McGann penalty left the score at 10-6, but Edwards, now in overdrive, handled twice in a cunning manoeuvre which outflanked the Irish defence and brought him a try far out. Bennett converted, and Wales were proof against Mike Gibson's belligerent late try and McGann's conversion.

Scorers WALES – tries: Shanklin, Edwards; conversion: Bennett; penalty goals: Bennett 2. IRELAND – try: Gibson; conversion: McGann; penalty goals: McGann 2.

Wales J. P. R. Williams (London Welsh); T. G. R. Davies (London Welsh), R. T. E. Bergiers (Llanelli), A. J. Lewis (Ebbw Vale, capt.), J. L. Shanklin (London Welsh); P. Bennett (Llanelli), G. O. Edwards (Cardiff); P. D. Llewellyn (Swansea), J. Young (London Welsh), G. Shaw (Neath), W. D. Thomas (Llanelli), M. G. Roberts (London Welsh), J. Taylor (London Welsh), W. D. Morris (Neath), T. M. Davies (Swansea).

Ireland A. H. Ensor (Dublin Wanderers); T. O. Grace (St Mary's College), R. A. Milliken (Bangor), C. M. H. Gibson (North of Ireland F.C.), A. W. McMaster (Ballymena); B. J. McGann (Cork Constitution), J. J. Moloney

F

(St Mary's College); J. F. Lynch (St Mary's College), K. W. Kennedy (London Irish), R. J. McLoughlin (Blackrock College), W. J. McBride (Ballymena, capt.), K. M. A. Mays (University College, Dublin), S. A. McKinney (Dungannon), J. F. Slattery (Blackrock College), T. A. P. Moore (Highfield).

Referee T. F. E. Grierson (Scotland).

A week later, on 17 March, England beat Scotland 20–13 at Twickenham.

France 12 pts Wales 3 *Parc des Princes, 24 March 1973*

The main complaint against Bennett this season was that he kicked too often and ran too little, and that when he ran he tended to move crabwise, crowding the man he intended to pass to rather than advancing on his opponent and drawing him in. On the first Welsh appearance at Parc des Princes Bennett had one of his less effective afternoons. By not confronting the French with the ball in his hands, he allowed their defence to fan out and obliterate the Welsh threequarters. It was a fault he would overcome, but for the moment it helped to lose Wales this game, and left doubts, which lingered on for another two seasons, about his suitability as leader of the Welsh attack.

As it happened, too, neither Bennett from the left nor John Taylor from the right, was able to score from their four crucial penalty kicks. Bennett did drop a goal, but so did Romeu, and the French stand-off also landed three penalties to put together all his side's points in an unmemorable game.

Not unmemorable, of course, for the other John Williams – J. J. Williams – who came on at half-time, after Lewis had injured his shoulder, to win the first of his thirty Welsh caps.

Scorers FRANCE – dropped goal: Romeu; penalty goals: Romeu 3. WALES – dropped goal: Bennett.

France J–M. Aguirre (Bagnères); J–F. Philiponneau (Montferrand), C–F. Badin (Chalon), J. Maso (Narbonne), J.

Cantoni (Béziers); J–P. Romeu (Montferrand), M. Pebeyre (Montferrand); J. Iraçabal (Bayonne), R. Bénésis (Agen), J–L. Azarète (St-Jean-de-Luz), E. Cester (Valence), W. Spanghero (Narbonne, capt.), J–C. Skréla (Toulouse), J–P. Biemouret (Agen), O. Saisset (Béziers).

Wales J. P. R. Williams (London Welsh); T. G. R. Davies (London Welsh), A. J. Lewis (Ebbw Vale), R. T. E. Bergiers (Llanelli), J. L. Shanklin (London Welsh); P Bennett (Llanelli), G. O. Edwards (Cardiff, capt.); P. D. Llewellyn (Swansea), J. Young (London Welsh), G. Shaw (Neath), W. D. Thomas (Llanelli), M. G. Roberts (London Welsh), T. P. David (Llanelli), J. Taylor (London Welsh), T. M. Davies (Swansea). Replacement: J. J. Williams (Llanelli) for A. J. Lewis, 40 min.

Referee D. P. d'Arcy (Ireland).

In the final championship match on 14 April, Ireland beat France 6–4 at Lansdowne Road.

Championship Table 1973 (alphabetical order)

	P	W	D	L	For	Ag	Pts
England	4	2	0	2	52	62	4
France	4	2	0	2	38	36	4
Ireland	4	2	0	2	50	48	4
Scotland	4	2	0	2	55	59	4
Wales	4	2	0	2	53	43	4

Welsh tour of Canada

In May a strong Welsh party of twenty-three, including almost all that winter's regular caps, made a five-match tour of Canada, winning all their games by almost embarrassing margins and beating Canada itself 58–20 at Toronto on 9 June. In all Wales scored 288 points and conceded 41, though what they or the Canadians gained from the experience is less easy to add up.

12

Marginal Losses: 1973–74

If two draws are inferior to a win and a loss – and surely they are in terms of excitement and satisfaction, if not in championship points – then this was a more disappointing season for Wales than the last. For the first time in six years they won only a solitary match, against Scotland, in the tournament. They then drew consecutively with Ireland away and France at home before losing at Twickenham, an unexpected and galling defeat this, for England scored only one other championship point and took the wooden spoon.

There was one other draw, between England and France, and generally results were close. The fine balance of rugby power, or impotence, between the five nations, which had produced the tie in 1973, was prolonged for another winter. After all those years of profligate scoring, two match points in the right places would have given Wales the title, seven would have meant a grand slam. But equally the other countries could have indulged in much the same kind of special pleading as they saw a whole season's opportunity fade away in a single knock-on or a mis-kicked penalty. Ireland finished on top. Even though only two points separated them from England at the bottom of the table, they were outright champions for the first time since 1951. And they deserved to be if only for their four tries in a match of untypical high spirits at Twickenham.

As so often the top country in the championship provided the captain for the British Lions, and it was Willie John McBride who led them on an unbeaten tour of South Africa in the summer. There Phil Bennett was the highest scorer in the tests with twenty-six points, and Wales provided most of the backs in these and other major games. Together with rather devalued victories over Japan and Australia, it was Wales's small consolation for an undistinguished season.

Japan's tour of Wales and England

Fast, athletic, ingenious, brave and impeccably behaved, the Japanese were always enjoyable to watch, even in defeat. Unfortunately defeat came only too often; skill and commitment could not wholly compensate for lack of physical bulk, and winning possession was their problem. Of five matches in Wales and two in England, Japan won only against the Welsh Western Counties, 12–9, at Llanelli. In France they won one game in four.

Unlike the English, who fielded an Under-23 team against them, the Welsh paid the Asiatic champions the compliment of a senior game. But although it was an international in title, and a full-strength Welsh team was picked, no caps were awarded. Predictably it was Japan's heaviest defeat. But if you deduct that score from the overall points total for the British leg of the tour, you get a balance of 61 for and 106 against, which was certainly no disgrace.

Wales 62 pts Japan 14 *Cardiff, 6 October 1973*

Japan had made such a sympathetic impression that thirty-five thousand people turned up for their final game. And it wasn't simply to see Wales score nine goals and two tries against two tries and two penalties. The Japanese, apart from their tireless teamwork, had two or three players of genuine class, and a wing, Itoh, who would have held his own in most company. Although he was forced to move to full-back in the second half when Yamamoto was injured, Itoh remained their most dynamic player and scored both their tries. The first completed a forty-three-yard run, the second involved a masterly evasion of J. P. R. Williams, not a man normally passed with impunity.

As a contest, however, it was disastrously one-sided. The Japanese were not only outweighed but outplayed since, for all their tenacity, they continued to buy dummies whenever they were offered. This made it hard to know by what standards to judge the Welsh performance. After their stereotyped play the previous season they had been encouraged to improvise more, which posed no problems in this context. But even so there was criticism of the alignment of their backs, Hughes in particular; against harder opposition they would have been taking the ball at a standstill with the defence staring into the whites of their eyes. But Bergiers looked leaner and hungrier than he had the previous winter, while Bennett's twenty-six points from two tries and nine conversions was remarkable enough on any day. It might well have given him the confidence to expand his play as he'd done more often for Llanelli than so far he had for Wales.

Scorers WALES – tries: Bennett 2, Hughes 2, J. J. Williams, Bergiers, Shell, Taylor, J. P. R. Williams, T. G. R. Davies, Windsor; conversions: Bennett 9. JAPAN – tries: Itoh 2; penalty goals: Yamamoto 2.

Wales J. P. R. Williams (London Welsh); T. G. R. Davies (London Welsh), K. Hughes (London Welsh), R. T. E. Bergiers (Llanelli), J. J. Williams (Llanelli); P. Bennett (Llanelli), R. C. Shell (Aberavon); P. D. Llewellyn (Swansea), R. W. Windsor (Pontypool), G. Shaw (Neath), A. J. Martin (Aberavon), D. L. Quinnell (Llanelli), J. Taylor (London Welsh, capt.), T. P. David (Llanelli), T. M. Davis (Swansea). Replacement: I. Robinson (Cardiff) for T. P. David, 35 min.

Japan I. Yamamoto; T. Itoh, M. Fujiwara, A. Yokoi, (capt.), Y. Sakata; T. Kamohara, H. Shukuzawa; S. Hara, K. Ohigashi, K. Yoshino, K. Shibatâ, T. Terai, H. Akama, Y. Izawa, Y. Murata. Replacement: B. Shimazaki for I. Yamamoto, 57 min.

Referee G. Guilhem (France).

The Wallabies in England and Wales

By their own rather higher standards and expectations, the Australians – who arrived just after the Japanese left and covered much the same ground – were equally unsuccessful. On their last major tour, in 1966–67, they had won half their British Isles matches and beaten both England and Wales. But that was in the days when they had world-class halves in Catchpole and Hawthorne, and reliably kicked their goals. In this autumn's short tour the Wallabies won only two of their eight matches, against the English Metropolitan Counties and West Wales, and lost both internationals: 24–0 to Wales and 20–3 to England.

John Hipwell, who had been Catchpole's deputy at scrum-half seven years earlier, was their outstanding player. But except for Fairfax as an attacking full-back, they had no other player of comparable authority among the backs. Their pack was too easily shoved around. And Jeff McLean, who played at wing threequarter, was out of touch in his place-kicking.

Wales 24 pts Australia 0 *Cardiff, 10 November 1973*

Wales won this game comfortably but not as expansively as some had hoped. They played the first half cautiously – mindful perhaps of their 1966 defeat and of the fact that Wales hadn't beaten a major touring side at Cardiff since 1958. But when Bennett had kicked them into a twelve-point half-time lead with four penalties (McLean failing with his four attempts), and they began to open up their game, they had to work surprisingly hard to score three tries.

It wasn't lack of possession. They won the rucks cleanly 20–4, the lineouts 19–11, and at the scrums made three strikes to one against the head. The fault lay with their backs. Only the wings and J. P. R. Williams had the confidence to make the running in attack. Bergiers and Hughes were most unsharp at centre. And Bennett, a gifted and relaxed player with his club, was still not wholly at ease with the Welsh side. This may explain why the Welsh continued to play an over-physical game with Edwards and the forwards repeatedly taking the ball to the blind side instead of paying it out to the open.

It was on the short side of a ruck that Morris scored the first Welsh try. The second came from JPR's intervention, which gave Davies the overlap and scoring pass. The third went to Bobby Windsor, who was winning his first cap and blazing the trail for the Pontypool front row. Clive Shell, a fine player unlucky enough to be understudy to such a durable man as Gareth Edwards, came on to win his one cap in injury time when the maestro limped off with a leg injury.

Scorers WALES – tries: Morris, T. G. R. Davies, Windsor; penalty goals: Bennett 4.

Wales J. P. R. Williams (London Welsh); T. G. R. Davies (London Welsh), K. Hughes (London Welsh), R. T. E. Bergiers (Llanelli), J. J. Williams (Llanelli); P. Bennett (Llanelli), G. O. Edwards (Cardiff, capt.); P. D. Llewellyn (Swansea), R. W. Windsor (Pontypool), G. Shaw (Neath), D. L. Quinnell (Llanelli), A. J. Martin (Aberavon), T. P. David (Llanelli), W. D. Morris (Neath), T. M. Davies (Swansea). Replacement: R. C. Shell (Aberavon) for G. O. Edwards, 83 min.

Australia R. L. Fairfax (New South Wales); O. Stephens (N.S.W.), R. D. L'Estrange (Queensland), G. A. Shaw (N.S.W.), J. J. McLean (Queensland); G. C. Richardson (Queensland), J. N. B. Hipwell (N.S.W.); J. L. Howard (N.S.W.), M. E. Freney (Queensland), R. Graham (N.S.W.), G. Fay (N.S.W.), S. C. Gregory (N.S.W.), P. D. Sullivan (N.S.W., capt.), M. R. Cocks (Queensland), A. A. Shaw (Queensland).

Referee K. A. Pattinson (England).

The International Championship

Wales 6 pts Scotland 0 — *Cardiff, 19 January 1974*

The Welsh side's neglect of its wings at this period, its preference for running the ball back to cover, seemed more than usually perverse after this match. It was only the peculiar genius of Gerald Davies which won it for them (though admittedly the defensive courage of J. P. R. Williams did a lot to stop them losing it). Midway through the first half Gareth Edwards ran to the open side and slipped back a pass to Bennett who was going to the blind. Bennett at once unleashed Davies who veered inside and side-stepped both Telfer and Irvine, leaving them grasping. McEwan, the Scottish flanker who was covering across, Davies couldn't evade. But even as he accepted the tackle he turned and tipped back the ball to Terry Cobner who found himself joining that small band of players who have scored a try in their first international. Bennett converted, and that was the end of the scoring, though certainly not of the match.

This was the hundredth international played at Cardiff, and despite that try it looked for a long time as though the Scots, not the Welsh, would celebrate it. They elected to open against the wind, and by out-scrummaging the Welsh pack they were able to limit Bennett's chances of worrying Irvine and the Scottish wings with deep kicks. When they changed ends only six points down they might well have been halfway to winning. But the Welsh held their attack early in the second half, JPR bringing off two deadly tackles on Gill just short of the line, and by the end Wales were taking the game back to the Scots to keep them at their distance.

Scorers WALES – try: Cobner; conversion: Bennett.

Wales J. P. R. Williams (London Welsh); T. G. R. Davies (London Welsh), K. Hughes (London Welsh), I. Hall (Aberavon), J. J. Williams (Llanelli); P. Bennett (Llanelli), G. O. Edwards (Cardiff, capt.); P. D. Llewellyn (Swansea), R. W. Windsor (Pontypool), G. Shaw (Neath), A. J. Martin (Aberavon), D. L. Quinnell (Llanelli), T. J. Cobner (Pontypool), W. D. Morris (Neath), T. M. Davies (Swansea).

Scotland A. R. Irvine (Heriot's F.P.); A. D. Gill (Gala), J. M. Renwick (Hawick), I. R. McGeechan (Headingley), L. G. Dick (Jordanhill); C. M. Telfer (Hawick), A. J. M. Lawson (Edinburgh Wanderers); A. B. Carmichael (West of Scotland), D. F. Madsen (Gosforth), J. McLauchlan (Jordanhill, capt.), A. F. McHarg (London Scottish), G. L. Brown (West of Scotland), W. Lauder (Neath), N. A. MacEwan (Highland), W. S. Watson (Boroughmuir F.P.).

Referee R. F. Johnson (England).

This season, for the first time, championship matches were played in pairs at fortnightly intervals. On the same afternoon France beat Ireland 9–6 at Parc des Princes.

Ireland 9 pts Wales 9 *Lansdowne Road, 2 February 1974*

The wind from the city was strong enough to keep the goalposts swaying like masts on their moorings. And for the Irish the vagaries of this blast of air created an exercise in pure frustration which they pursued with a dogged persistence that amounted almost to genius. Despite the fact that their full-back, Ensor, scored three penalty goals – to a goal and a penalty for Wales – it was only the lack of a confident place-kicker that cost Ireland the match. For every penalty that was scored, two others went whistling carelessly down the wind.

By preference or necessity, Wales played four new caps – Clive Rees and Finlayson in the threequarter line, Williams at prop and Wheel at lock – and scored one good try. Bennett began it, feinting to the open side then rounding to the blind, and the Williamses completed it, JPR rushing it to send JJ over. To Ireland's chagrin, Bennett's fine conversion from the touchline bounced on the crossbar and toppled safely over. This left the game drawn 6–6 at the interval and for Wales, who had been playing into the teeth of the gale, it looked as though the good times were ahead.

The Irish pack ensured that they were not. Edwards found himself taking the ball on the retreat from the scrums, and moreover was worried by Moloney as he did so. Bennett, who must have hoped to float deep kicks to feed his wings with JPR in support, found himself starved of the ball. The Williamses, in action again, almost swung the game for Wales; Moloney almost did the same for Ireland, but passed to JPR by mistake. Enosr and Bennett instead swopped penalties and left matters where they were.

Wales had not been impressive, but they had broken a run of fifteen home wins in the championship, and they had scored the only try in this game. And on that slim evidence they were now judged favourites for the title.

Scorers IRELAND – penalty goals: Ensor 3. WALES – try: J. J. Williams; conversion: Bennett: penalty goal: Bennett.

Ireland A. H. Ensor (Wanderers); V. A. Becker (Lansdowne), C. M. H. Gibson (North of Ireland F.C.), R. A. Milliken (Bangor), P. Lavery (London Irish); M. A. M. Quinn (Lansdowne), J. J. Moloney (St Mary's College); J. F. Lynch (St Mary's College), K. W. Kennedy (London Irish), R. J. McLoughlin (Blackrock College), M. I. Keane (Lansdowne), W. J. McBride (Ballymena, capt.), J. F. Slattery (Blackrock College), S. M. Deering (Garryowen), T. A. P. Moore (Highfield).

Wales J. P. R. Williams (London Welsh); C. F. W. Rees (London Welsh), I. Hall (Aberavon), A. A. J. Finlayson (Cardiff), J. J. Williams (Llanelli); P. Bennett (Llanelli), G. O. Edwards (Cardiff, capt.); G. Shaw (Neath), R. W. Windsor (Pontypool), W. P. J. Williams (Neath), G. Wheel (Swansea), A. J. Martin (Aberavon), W. D. Morris (Neath), T. J. Cobner (Pontypool), T. M. Davies (Swansea).

Referee K. A. Pattinson (England).

On the same afternoon Scotland beat England 16–14 at Murrayfield.

Wales 16 pts France 16 *Cardiff, 16 February 1974*

Whatever the forecast after the Dublin game, this second draw – a symmetrical try, dropped goal and three penalties to either side – left the championship wide open. It also left the impression of a Welsh side on the decline, still immensely strong at full-back, on the wing, at scrum-half and in the back row, but carrying little conviction in the mid-field (where admittedly Bennett, who had 'flu, was playing with a temperature) or in the tight.

The French, too, had their threequarter problems and relied heavily on Romeu to contribute the points. They were a side with more competence than flair, and contributed no more than the Welsh in breadth or fluency of play.

Excitement compensated a little, with the lead changing five times before the interval when it settled at 13–13. For France Romeu scored twelve points and also made the other four with a long pass which missed out the inside centre. This left Lux with a three-two advantage which he exploited by using his back-up men as a foil and himself sliding past Hall for the try.

The Welsh try came from their only genuine threequarter movement of the afternoon. At its conclusion J. J. Williams grub-kicked past Bertranne, fly-kicked over the full-back and, grabbing the ball head-high, dived over the line. Otherwise the Welsh scores came from the halves: a fine thirty-five-yard dropped goal by Bennett from the back of the lineout and Bennett's reliable penalties. Bennett's third, ten minutes from the end, looked to be the winner. But in the fortieth minute Romeu dropped a difficult, angled goal, and for the first time ever, Wales had played in two consecutive draws.

Scorers WALES – try: J. J. Williams; dropped goal: Edwards; penalty goals: Bennett 3. FRANCE – try: Lux; dropped goal: Romeu; penalty goals: Romeu 3.

Wales J. P. R. Williams (London Welsh); T. G. R. Davies (London Welsh), I. Hall (Aberavon), A. A. J. Finlayson

(Cardiff), J. J. Williams (Llanelli); P. Bennett (Llanelli), G. O. Edwards (Cardiff, capt.); W. P. J. Williams (Neath), R. W. Windsor (Pontypool), G. Shaw (Neath), D. L. Quinnell (Llanelli), I. R. Robinson (Cardiff), W. D. Morris (Neath), T. J. Cobner (Pontypool), T. M. Davies (Swansea).

France J–M. Aguirre (Bagnères); R. Bertranne (Bagnères), J. Pecune (Tarbes), J–P. Lux (Dax), A. Dubertrand (Montferrand); J–P. Romeu (Montferrand), J. Fouroux (La Voulte); A. Vaquerin (Béziers), R. Bénésis (Agen), J. Iraçabal (Bayonne), A. Extève (Bèziers), E. Cester (Valence Sp., capt.), J–C. Skréla (Toulouse), V. Boffelli (Aurillac), C. Spanghero, (Narbonne).

Referee N. R. Sanson (Scotland).

On the same afternoon Ireland beat England 26–21 at Twickenham. A fortnight later (2 March), when Wales had a bye, France and England drew 12–12 at Parc des Princes and Ireland beat Scotland 9–6 at Lansdowne Road.

England 16 pts Wales 12 *Twickenham, 16 March 1974*

For the first time in eleven years, and for the first time at Twickenham for fourteen, England beat Wales, mainly by forward power, to deny them the championship. Each side scored a goal and two penalties, but England also got the crucial second try.

Oddly enough, Wales played with more attacking spirit than they had all season, making good use of Roger Blyth who had come in as J. P. R. Williams's deputy. But England employed their forwards even more effectively, regularly using a mid-field scissors move to carry the ball back to them, and it was by this means that they scored the opening try. Burton, Uttley and Ralston all handled the ball before giving Duckham his head for the final break. Though Old missed the conversion, he put England further ahead with a penalty.

Then England made a mistake in tapping back from the lineout, presenting Mervyn Davies with the chance to drive over their line. Bennett converted from the touchline and followed up with a penalty to give Wales an interval lead of 9–7. It was brief. Ripley picked up at the back of the scrum to hurtle over for a try, and the rest was near-misses, place-kicks and controversy. Two apparent tries, one on either side, were disallowed, and Wales were particularly aggrieved when J. J. Williams, having beaten Duckham and Squires to the dive, was judged not to have touched the ball down. The Welshman most entitled to feel some contentment was Phil Bennett. He had played his best rugby of the season, and even if that season had been unmemorable for the others, it had brought Bennett a Welsh record of thirty-six points in its five internationals.

Scorers ENGLAND – tries: Duckham, Ripley; conversion: Old; penalty goals: Old 2. WALES – try: T. M. Davies; conversion: Bennett; penalty goals: Bennett 2.

England W. H. Hare (Nottingham); P. J. Squires (Harrogate), G. W. Evans (Coventry), K. Smith (Roundhay), D. J. Duckham (Coventry); A. G. B. Old (Leicester), J. G. Webster (Moseley); M. A. Burton (Gloucester), J. V. Pullin (Bristol, capt.), C. B. Stevens (Penzance & Newlyn), C. W. Ralston (Richmond), R. M. Uttley (Gosforth), P. J. Dixon (Gosforth), A. Neary (Broughton Park), A. G. Ripley (Rosslyn Park).

Wales W. R. Blyth (Swansea); T. G. R. Davies (London Welsh), R. T. E. Bergiers (Llanelli), A. A. J. Finlayson (Cardiff), J. J. Williams (Llanelli); P. Bennett (Llanelli), G. O. Edwards (Cardiff, capt.); P. D. Llewellyn (Swansea), R. W. Windsor (Pontypool), G. Shaw (Neath); I. R. Robinson (Cardiff), W. D. Thomas (Llanelli), W. D. Morris (Neath), T. J. Cobner (Pontypool), T. M. Davies (Swansea).

Referee J. R. West (Ireland).

On the same afternoon France, the only other country which might have overtaken Ireland, lost 19–6 to Scotland at Muurayfield.

Championship Table 1974

	P	W	D	L	For	Ag	Pts
Ireland	4	2	1	1	50	45	5
Scotland	4	2	0	2	41	35	4
Wales	4	1	2	1	43	41	4
France	4	1	2	1	43	53	4
England	4	1	1	2	63	66	3

British Lions in South Africa

The twenty-two-match tour, lasting from mid-May to the end of July, was the most successful since the four home unions combined to form the first British Isles party in 1924. The team won twenty-one matches and drew one – the final test. Their 729 points and 107 tries, their 79 points in four tests and 28–9 win in the second test all broke records. There were nine Welshmen in the party of thirty, of whom six played in all four tests: J. P. R. Williams, J. J. Williams, T. G. R. Davies, Bennett, Edwards and Windsor. Andy Irvine (Scotland), who played at wing and full-back, was top scorer with 156 points followed by Bennett with 103. Bennett's twenty-six points was the highest individual total in the tests, and J. J. Williams's sixteen points from a record-breaking four tries, the next highest. The first three tests were won 12–3, 28–9 and 26–9, the last drawn 13–13.

13
Second Half: 1974–75

Another season, another game of musical chairs around the championship table. And for Wales the start of their second and even greater spell of success in the seventies. Two figures dominated the scene by their presence. One was John Dawes who, only three years after captaining the Lions on their splendid 1971 tour of New Zealand, took over from Clive Rowlands as national coach. It was rare even at club level for a coach to take charge of a team when so many of his contemporaries were still playing an active part in it. For this to happen at national level was even more remarkable.

The second figure was Mervyn Davies, another London Welshman – though back now with Swansea – and one of Dawes's former team-mates, who succeeded Gareth Edwards in the Welsh captaincy. There was little doubt that the pack needed revitalizing, and that the back row, with its foot in both camps, was an appropriate position from which to lead the side. Davies did so by the authority of his example, as much as by his tactical discretion, until the dreadful misfortune of a brain haemorrhage, which occurred during a cup match, cut short his rugby career at the end of the following season.

The man whose absence was just as much a talking point during the winter was Phil Bennett. After playing in the 'friendly' international against the All Blacks in January, he was dropped for the early championship matches in favour of John Bevan, the Aberavon stand-off. Bevan was not as rich a player as Bennett at his best, but he filled the role of strong-man in the Welsh mid-field and gave it the thrust it had lacked.

With Bevan playing alongside Edwards, Wales won their

CIS

Cardiff's natural heirs to the half-back heroes of the seventies: *(previous page)* the strong, combative Terry Holmes at scrum-half and *(above)* the coolly elegant stand-off, Gareth Davies.

(Opposite) Brian Price head and shoulders above the lineout in a match for Newport against Newbridge.

The long arms of Alan Martin reach for the ball.

first two matches, against France and England, by fifteen and sixteen points. But at Murrayfield Bevan was injured after twenty-six minutes; Bennett, who replaced him, had a nightmare game; and Wales, although they scored the only try, lost by a couple of points. Bevan had not recovered in time for the final match against Ireland at Cardiff, and Wales had little option but to reselect Bennett. And this time he made a triumphant return, providing an unfaultable service to his centres, kicking twelve points and contributing handsomely to a 32–4 win which brought Wales their first championship in three years.

The Tongans in Wales

During September and October a party of twenty-seven players from Tonga, the Friendly Islands, arrived in Britain, another sign that while the international community of rugby was rapidly growing larger, it was also growing closer together. The Tongans played ten games, six of them in Wales, which is where they got their only win, 18–13 against East Wales in their opening fixture. The other nine games they lost, including an unofficial international with Scotland, 44–8, and their Twickenham engagement with England Under-23, by the identical margin, 40–4.

Like the Japanese the autumn before, the Tongans lost their games in the set-pieces, although in their case it was less from lack of height and weight than from underdeveloped technique. Scrummaging, rucking and lineout work simply didn't figure very largely in their game at home; running and passing were the thing. But by the time they reached their final game against Wales they had been through a week's intensive coaching by Carwyn James – acting as devil's advocate against his own country – and had tightened up their play considerably.

Like the Scots, Wales did not award caps for this match (Cardiff, 19 October) and rested all the players who had spent that summer with the Lions in South Africa. What they fielded was a combination of old lags who hadn't made the trip and also some fresh faces from the shadow team:

C. Bolderson (Pontypridd); T. G. R. Davies (Cardiff, capt.), S. P. Fenwick (Bridgend), R. W. R. Gravell (Llanelli), A. A. J. Finlayson (Cardiff); J. D. Bevan (Aberavon), D. B. Williams (Cardiff); D. B. Llewelyn (Llanelli), E. R. Thomas (Llanelli), G. B. Wallace (Cardiff), A. J. Martin (Aberavon), M. G. Roberts (London Welsh), T. J. Cobner (Pontypool), T. P. Evans (Swansea), D. L. Quinnell (Llanelli). Replacement: I. Hall (Aberavon) for R. W. R. Gravell, 36 min.

The Tongans had been such vital and exuberant visitors that – again like the Japanese – they drew a crowd of thirty-thousand to their final appearance. Most expected a slaughter of these innocents, but although Wales won without great difficulty they achieved no more than the modest margin of 26–7 – five tries and two penalties to a try and a penalty. Indeed the Tongans' try was the most enjoyable, drawn-out moment of the afternoon: a powerful run of forty-five yards by their right wing, Talilotu.

As a Welsh pre-trial it created more problems than it solved. Two men made their mark and were to be rewarded for it during the championship. They were Bevan, cool and decisive at stand-off, and the untiring Trevor Evans at flank forward. But there was a general lack of urgency in the pack and an ominous fragility in the defence of the threequarters which offered little promise for the coming internationals.

All Blacks in Ireland, Wales and England

As it happened Wales had the opportunity for a second unofficial dress rehearsal that autumn. New Zealand were on a short tour of Ireland to celebrate the IRUFC centenary (during which they won all their matches, beating Ireland 15–6), and rounded off their visit with fixtures at Cardiff and Twickenham.

Wales were not prepared to treat the match as a full test, and awarded no caps to what was pointedly entitled A Welsh XV – although it was as strong a side as they could muster:

J. P. R. Williams (London Welsh); T. G. R. Davies (Cardiff), R. T. E. Bergiers (Llanelli), I. Hall (Aberavon), J. J. Williams (Llanelli); P. Bennett (Llanelli), G. O. Edwards (Cardiff, capt.); D. B. Llewelyn (Llanelli), R. W. Windsor (Pontypool), A. G. Faulkner (Pontypool), D. L. Quinnell (Llanelli), G. A. D. Wheel (Swansea), T. J. Cobner (Pontypool), T. P. Evans (Swansea), T. M. Davies (Swansea). Replacements: W. R. Blyth (Swansea) for I. Hall, 39 min; J. D. Bevan (Aberavon) for R. T. E. Bergiers, 75 min.

Even on a Wednesday afternoon (27 November), however, a capacity crowd of fifty-thousand treated it as the real thing and saw the Welsh defeated by a goal and two penalty goals to a penalty. The home pack couldn't control the shove of the tourists in the scrum – leaving Gareth Edwards to scramble for the ball on the retreat – or counter their onward drive in the loose. Bennett had the chance to keep the Welsh in the game but missed five of his six penalty attempts, a failure which was costly to the Welsh and to his own immediate prospects as an international.

The match was won by Ian Kirkpatrick's try to which Joe Karam added a conversion and his second penalty. It was left to the Barbarians at Twickenham on the Saturday to end the All Blacks' victorious run for forcing a 13–13 draw, and to Mervyn Davies to save Wales's good name by scoring the crucial try in the closing minutes.

The International Championship

France 10 pts Wales 25 *Parc des Princes, 18 January 1975*

Few teams so radically altered have enjoyed such immediate success as Wales did this day. There were nine changes from the side which had lost to England at the end of the previous season, and although some of these reflected injuries or temporary switches in favour, six new caps contributed to Wales's biggest victory in Paris since 1911. The changes brought a reconstruction of the mid-field and the pack. One Llanelli centre, Ray Gravell, was preferred to another, Bergiers, and was also partnered by a newcomer, Steve Fenwick of Bridgend. Bevan won his No 10 jersey at Bennett's expense. In the pack, Faulkner and Price joined Windsor to complete a Pontypool front row which was to endure for Wales to the end of the decade. And Trevor Evans came in at flank-forward.

It helped that France gave an uncharacteristically inept display in the open field, but there was no denying that Wales had rediscovered their confidence and commitment. Their forwards won rucks and set-pieces as if by right. Gareth Edwards, with the ball-and-chain of captaincy removed, was playing with all his old self-assurance, kicking creatively and running with a ferocity which had Frenchmen cannoning off him like billiard balls.

Wales scored within four minutes, Edwards putting in a diagonal kick, Lux misreading the bounce, and Fenwick stealing in for a try. The French came back with Taffary's first penalty and then a try which Lux made for Gourdon. But once Fenwick had evened things up with a penalty, the French never caught a glimpse of victory again.

The best try came in the thirty-second minute. Gravell burst through a tackle; Fenwick, Mervyn Davies and Gerald Davies carried on the movement; Cobner completed it in the corner and Fenwick converted. With Gerald Davies touching down his own kick ahead, Wales changed ends with a 17–7 lead. They were now bursting with a determination which Taffary's second penalty did nothing to puncture. Edwards, plunging around from a short lineout, got their fourth try, and Price their fifth by following up for seventy-five yards to grab the loose ball and crash over. So two of the new men had scored tries in their memorable first international.

Scorers FRANCE – try: Gourdon; penalty goals: Taffary 2. WALES – tries: Fenwick, Cobner, T. G. R. Davies, Edwards, Price; conversion: Fenwick; penalty goal: Fenwick.

France M. Taffary (Racing Club de France); J. F. Gourdon (Racing Club de France), C. Dourthe (Dax), R. Bertranne (Bagnères), J–P. Lux (Dax); J–P. Romeu (Montferrand), J. Fouroux (La Voulte, capt.); J–L. Azarete (St-Jean-de-Luz), A. Paco (Béziers), A. Vaquerin (Béziers), A. Estève (Béziers), G. Senal (Béziers), V. Boffelli (Aurillac), O. Saiset (Béziers), J–P. Bastiat (Dax). Replacements: J. Cantoni (Béziers) for J–F. Gourdon, 40 min.; J–C. Skréla (Toulouse) for O. Saisset, 40 min.

Wales J. P. R. Williams (London Welsh); T. G. R. Davies (Cardiff), S. P. Fenwick (Bridgend), R. W. R. Gravell (Llanelli), J. J. Williams (Llanelli); J. D. Bevan (Aberavon), G. O. Edwards (Cardiff); G. Price (Pontypool), R. W. Windsor (Pontypool), A. G. Faulkner (Pontypool), G. A. D. Wheel (Swansea), A. J. Martin (Aberavon), T. P. Evans (Swansea), T. J. Cobner (Pontypool), T. M. Davies (Swansea, capt.).

Referee K. A. Pattinson (England).

On the same afternoon Ireland beat England 12–9 at Lansdowne Road. A fortnight later (1 February), when Wales had no game, France beat England 27–20 at Twickenham, and Scotland beat Ireland 20–13 at Murrayfield.

Wales 20 pts England 4 *Cardiff, 15 February 1975*

After their win in Paris, Wales very naturally kept the same side for their first home game, and duly beat England by a goal, two tries and two penalties to a try. But it was a curiously inert performance which left no-one satisfied. The English were good ball-winners – taking the lineouts 13–12 though conceding the rucks 16–11 – and efficient smotherers of Welsh opportunities. But they offered little positive challenge while Wales, over-casual in their approach, leaned heavily on Edwards's tactical kicking, the individual thrust of Gravell and J. P. R. Williams, and the industry of their back-row.

Within three minutes Martin had put Wales ahead with a monstrous fifty-yard penalty which was followed by a highly competent try. Bevan sent Gravell through on an old-fashioned scissors move; Gravell cut to the outside to link up with the other centre, Fenwick; and a final overhead pass put J. J. Williams over in the corner.

Then a short lull while the Welsh built up pressure again, and they repeated the process. A forty-yard penalty from Martin this time, and a try from Gerald Davies on the other wing – Gravell again making the initial break – which Martin converted from the touchline.

The only serious check to Wales's progress was the loss of Wheel with a dislocated shoulder, but in the second half they did little to press home their advantage. It was not until the final ten minutes, when Horton scored for England, toppling over like a felled sapling directly from the lineout, that they were stung to reply. Quinnell, Wheel's replacement, charged down a kick, and after the ball had passed through several hands, Fenwick went over for the final try.

Scorers WALES – tries: J. J. Williams, T. G. R. Davies, Fenwick; conversion: Martin; penalty goals: Martin 2. ENGLAND – try: Horton.

Wales J. P. R. Williams (London Welsh); T. G. R. Davies (Cardiff), S. P. Fenwick (Bridgend), R. W. R. Gravell (Llanelli), J. J. Williams (Llanelli); J. D. Bevan (Aberavon), G. O. Edwards (Cardiff); G. Price (Pontypool), R. W. Windsor (Pontypool), A. G. Faulkner (Pontypool), G. A. D. Wheel (Swansea), A. J. Martin (Aberavon), T. P. Evans (Swansea), T. J. Cobner (Pontypool), T. M. Davies (Swansea, capt.). Replacement: D. L. Quinnell (Llanelli) for G. A. D. Wheel, 25 min.

England A. M. Jorden (Bedford); P. J. Squires (Harrogate), K. Smith (Roundhay), P. S. Preece (Coventry), D. J. Duckham

(Coventry); M. J. Cooper (Moseley), J. G. Webster (Moseley); F. E. Cotton (Coventry, capt.), P. J. Wheeler (Leicester), C. B. Stevens (Penzance & Newlyn), N. E. Horton (Moseley), C. W. Ralston (Richmond), J. A. Watkins (Gloucester), A. Neary (Broughton Park), R. M. Uttley (Gosforth). Replacements: S. J. Smith (Sale) for Webster, 20 min; J. V. Pullin (Bristol) for P. J. Wheeler, 44 min.

Referee A. M. Hosie (Scotland).

On the same afternoon France beat Scotland 10–9 at Parc des Princes.

Scotland 12 pts Wales 10 *Murrayfield, 1 March 1975*

A record crowd of more than eighty-thousand saw Scotland dismiss any Welsh pretensions to the triple crown with a brutally efficient performance by their pack – their tight forwards in particular. It was not that they won more of the ball, but they consistently disrupted Welsh efforts at clean possession. The Scottish back row completed the damage by keeping Edwards under constant pressure, and for once he found himself giving best to an opposing scrum-half. This was Douglas Morgan whose tactical and place-kicking not only prevented Wales from developing any pattern in their play but also put the onus upon them to work their way back into the game when they were trailing on points.

A tit-for-tat run of penalties provided the only scores of the first half. Morgan's initial shots were from fifty-three and forty-eight yards, Fenwick's from closer range, and crucially Morgan had the last word to make it 9–6 in Scotland's favour at half-time. By then, too, the hard, physical nature of the match had cost Wales two key players: Bevan with a dislocated shoulder and Fenwick with a fractured cheekbone. It was a difficult game to enter cold, and their replacements, Bennett and Blyth, did not distinguish themselves.

After thirty-five minutes of the second half, McGeechan, at a scrum in front of the Welsh posts, dropped a perfect goal with his left foot to put Scotland further ahead. By successful goal-kicking Wales might still have won, but Bennett missed a thirty-five yard penalty and Martin a conversion when finally they broke through for a try. This came from a short penalty, Edwards and Gravell working the ball across to Gerald Davies, and the wing, having danced inside the defence, put Trevor Evans over.

A touchline conversion, which Martin had kicked with such self-assurance against England, would still have drawn the match. But this time, although he kicked the ball truly, he and a deafeningly silent crowd, saw the ball fade outside the posts with the last hopes of the Welsh.

Scorers SCOTLAND – dropped goal: McGeechan; penalty goals: Morgan 3. WALES – try: Edwards; penalty goals: Fenwick 2.

Scotland A. R. Irvine (Heriot's F.P.); W. C. C. Steele (London Scottish), J. M. Renwick (Hawick), D. L. Bell (Watsonians), L. G. Dick (Jordanhill); I. R. McGeechan (Headingley), D. W. Morgan (Stewart's-Melville F.P.); A. B. Carmichael (West of Scotland), D. F. Madsen (Gosforth), J. McLauchlan (Jordanhill, capt.), A. F. McHarg (London Scottish), G. L. Brown (West of Scotland), M. A. Biggar (London Scottish), N. A. MacEwan (Highland), D. G. Leslie (Dundee H.S.F.P.).

Wales J. P. R. Williams (London Welsh); T. G. R. Davies (Cardiff), S. P. Fenwick (Bridgend), R. W. R. Gravell (Llanelli), J. J. Williams (Llanelli); J. D. Bevan (Aberavon), G. O. Edwards (Cardiff); G. Price (Pontypool), R. W. Windsor (Pontypool), A. G. Faulkner (Pontypool), A. J. Martin (Aberavon), M. G. Roberts (London Welsh), T. P. Evans (Swansea), T. J. Cobner (Pontypool), T. M. Davies (Swansea, capt.). Replacements: P. Bennett (Llanelli) for J. D. Bevan, 26 min; W. R. Blyth (Swansea) for S. P. Fenwick, 37 min.

Referee J. R. West (Ireland).

On the same afternoon Ireland beat France 25–6 at Lansdowne Road.

Wales 32 pts Ireland 4 *Cardiff, 15 March 1975*

Their harassed behaviour at Murrayfield had done nothing to suggest that Wales would close the season with their biggest win over Ireland since 1907 (when it was 29–0). They didn't collect their points frugally either. They gave a definitive exhibition of attacking rugby, keeping up momentum by the quality and energy of their supporting play to score five tries to one, plus three conversions and two penalties.

Three countries started this final day of the championship on equal terms: Wales, Ireland, and Scotland who were competing at Twickenham for the Calcutta Cup. Depending on the various options of wins and draws, any of the three could win the title outright, and any two or all three could share it. In the event Scotland's narrow defeat and Wales's sumptuous victory made all that speculation academic.

This was the last international of such Irish heroes as McBride, McLoughlin and Kennedy, and their experience was not enough to balance the vigour of a Welsh pack restored to full strength and led superbly by Mervyn Davies. Behind them Bennett returned for the injured Bevan to play his most accomplished game for Wales so far, giving his Llanelli team-mates, Gravell and Bergiers (Fenwick, too, was convalescing) a service precisely timed to devastate the Irish centre.

For nearly half an hour, apart from conceding an early penalty, the Irish held their ground. But such intense pressure was building up that they were bound to crack. Typically it was Edwards who wielded the hammer, brushing away a couple of strong tackles to cross the Irish line.

The rest of the Welsh tries came regularly through the second half: from Gerald Davies after a second-phase move created by Bergiers; from Faulkner in the wake of J. J. Williams and his hooker, Windsor; from J. J. Williams when JPR made the extra man in the line; and from Bergiers going on his own. The Irish by now were overwhelmed, which did not stop Duggan intercepting from Edwards and racing over gratefully for the last try. As a reply to the force of the Welsh argument, however, it was scarcely audible amid the general relief and rejoicing at Cardiff.

Scorers WALES – tries: Edwards, T. G. R. Davies, Faulkner, J. J. Williams, Bergiers; conversions: Bennett 3; penalty goals: Bennett 2. IRELAND – try: Duggan.

Wales J. P. R. Williams (London Welsh); T. G. R. Davies (Cardiff), R. T. E. Bergiers (Llanelli), R. W. R. Gravell (Llanelli), J. J. Williams (Llanelli); P. Bennett (Llanelli), G. O. Edwards (Cardiff); G. Price (Pontypool), R. W. R. Windsor (Pontypool), A. G. Faulkner (Pontypool), A. J. Martin (Aberavon), G. A. D. Wheel (Swansea), T. P. Evans (Swansea), T. J. Cobner (Pontypool), T. M. Davies (Swansea, capt.).

Ireland A. H. Ensor (Wanderers); T. O. Grace (St Mary's College), R. A. Milliken (Bangor), C. M. H. Gibson (North of Ireland F.C.), A. W. McMaster (Ballymena); W. McCombe (Bangor), J. J. Moloney (St Mary's College); R. J. Clegg (Bangor), K. W. Kennedy (London Irish), R. J. McLoughlin (Blackrock College), M. I. Keane (Lansdowne), W. J. McBride (Ballymena, capt.), M. J. A. Sherry (Lansdowne), J. F. Slattery (Blackrock College), W. P. Duggan (Blackrock College).

Referee G. Guilhem (France).

On the same afternoon England beat Scotland, who might otherwise have shared the championship with Wales, 7–6 at Twickenham.

Championship Table 1975

	P	W	D	L	For	Ag	Pts
Wales	4	3	0	1	87	30	6
France	4	2	0	2	53	79	4
Ireland	4	2	0	2	54	67	4
Scotland	4	2	0	2	47	40	4
England	4	1	0	3	40	65	2

14
Year of the Century: 1975–76

Wales picked up where they had left off against Ireland the previous season. After an autumn trip to Japan – where the main danger was of contracting a severe case of complacency – they returned home to inflict a heavy defeat on the Wallabies before Christmas. So to the championship which opened with a win over England by twelve points – the widest margin they had ever achieved at Twickenham. Next they beat Scotland at Cardiff by twenty-two points. In both games, however, the critics felt that Wales had been no better than they ought to have been. And it was only when the side went on to win their thirteenth triple crown, to equal England's record, by scoring more points at Lansdowne Road than ever before (34–9 was the result), that they were generally allowed to have acquitted themselves pretty remarkably.

Their final game against France, when a 19–13 victory brought them their nineteenth championship and seventh grand slam (again putting them level with England) was another matter. Wales were battle-weary and acknowledged it, although as Mervyn Davies, their captain, pointed out afterwards, it said something about the Welsh that even when playing poorly by their own high standards, they had still won. Perhaps that is one definition of maturity and quality in a side. Another, surely, is that Wales for the first time broke the century in the championship, scoring a record 102 points while conceding only 37.

Inevitably these successes carried individuals on to new levels of achievement. For J. J. Williams, the first hat trick of tries against a visiting Australian side, and for J. P. R. Williams, in the

England game, the first pair of tries by any full-back in an international. JPR, with thirty-seven caps by the end of the season, beat Billy Bancroft's Welsh record of thirty-three appearances in that position. Gareth Edwards became the country's most-capped player, making his forty-fifth consecutive appearance to beat Ken Jones's total of forty-four caps. He also took over as its top try-scorer, with his eighteenth try going one better than a brace of wings – Ken Jones and J. L. Williams – and R. A. Gibbs who had played variously at wing, stand-off and 'extra back'.

Considering the vagaries of his career, however, perhaps the most astonishing records were those set by Phil Bennett. On the strength of his performance against Ireland in 1975 and in Japan during the autumn, he was preferred to Bevan for the Wallabies game, But injury prevented him playing; Bevan stood in successfully; and when it came to the trials before the championship, Bennett found himself apparently relegated to *fourth* choice. Bevan was picked at stand-off for the Probables, and the Swansea man, David Richards, for the Possibles. And even when Richards was switched to the Probables after twelve minutes, it was the Cardiff stand-off, Gareth Davies, who took over from him.

Only subsequent injuries to Bevan and Richards brought Bennett back into the Wales side. But the selectors' lack of faith in his abilities seemed to act as a spur not a snaffle. During the season he found his form as a kicker and his confidence as a runner and distributor. By the end of it, he had become Wales's highest and first century scorer with 117 points from twenty-one games (Barry John's total had been 90). He had scored the greatest number of points in a single championship season: thirty-eight. And by scoring nineteen points in a single match – at Dublin – he had equalled the record of Jack Bancroft and Keith Jarrett.

The one great sadness of the season was the loss to active rugby of Mervyn Davies, who had also set a new mark with an unbroken run of thirty-eight appearances at No 8. During a Challenge Cup semi-final between Swansea and Pontypool on

28 March he suffered a brain haemorrhage. Thankfully it was not directly the result of any rugby injury and he made a full recovery. But although he has continued in the game as a rugby journalist, he was unable ever to play again.

Wales in Hong Kong and Japan

During September Wales made a five-match tour of the Far East, returning Japan's 1973 visit. They took their full championship side, with strong reserves, and outclassed their opposition even more exaggeratedly than they had the Canadians two summers before. They might have been better advised to send a team of young aspirants, but the standing of the members of their party was a kind of compliment to their hosts, and the trip had useful side-effects in bringing the Welsh side closer together. They won all their matches, scoring 261 points to 31, and in the two unofficial tests (21 and 24 September), they beat Japan 56–12 and 82–6. In the second of these Bennett scored thirty-four points from two tries, ten conversions and two penalty goals; he was also the tour's top scorer with sixty-three points in three matches.

The Sixth Wallabies

Although they scored more points than any previous tourists from their country – the balance was 427–337 – and won eighteen of their twenty-five matches, drawing one, the Australians left the British Isles with only one international scalp: Ireland's. They lost to Scotland 10–3, to Wales 28–3 and to England 23–6; it was in their final test at Lansdowne Road that they won 20–10. In their other matches in Wales they lost to Cardiff 14–9, drew with Llanelli 28–28, but beat Swansea, Glamorgan, Newport and Gwent. The Barbarians, captained by Mervyn Davies, defeated them at Cardiff 19–7. Paul McLean at stand-off broke the Australian touring record with 154 points which included two tries.

Wales 28 pts Australia 3 *Cardiff, 20 December 1975*

Wales announced their return to serious rugby with a fully-orchestrated fanfare, beating Australia by the greatest margin in seven encounters: three goals, a try, a dropped goal and a penalty to a penalty. And as usual when Wales are on top form, the performance was conducted with impassioned flair by Gareth Edwards.

Before him the pack won eighty per cent of the usable line-out ball and fiercely wheeled the scrum to upset Australia's possession. In the loose Mervyn Davies and Evans met little competition. To the rear Bevan was supremely sound, and Gravell and Fenwick so belligerently effective in attack and defence that the Australian wings were not given a single run.

After twenty minutes' gladiatorial battle between the forwards, which brought a referee's warning to the captains, Fenwick put Wales ahead with a penalty and Edwards presented him with a try to convert. It was characteristic: a burst on the open side which probably no other scrum-half would have the strength to carry to the line. So at half-time Wales were nine points up, and Australia had lost not only their wing-forward, Lambie but, disastrously, their scrum-half, captain and finest player, Hipwell.

The devastation continued into the second half. Wales sent J. J. Williams through for three tries, assisted first by Gravell and Bevan, then by Mervyn Davies and Evans, and finally by Evans and Gravell, back row and threequarters expertly combining. Bevan also dropped a goal after being coolly fed from the loose by Martin whose pass would have looked well coming from a scrum-half. And in the circumstances McLean's penalty for the Wallabies had all the lethal qualities of a rubber dagger.

Scorers WALES – tries: Edwards, J. J. Williams 3; conversions: Fenwick 2, Martin; dropped goal: Bevan; penalty goal: Fenwick. AUSTRALIA – penalty goal: McLean.

Wales J. P. R. Williams (London Welsh); J. J. Williams

(Llanelli), R. W. R. Gravell (Llanelli), S. P. Fenwick (Bridgend), C. F. W. Rees (London Welsh); J. D. Bevan (Aberavon), G. O. Edwards (Cardiff); G. Price (Pontypool), R. W. Windsor (Pontypool), A. G. Faulkner (Pontypool), A. J. Martin (Aberavon), G. A. D. Wheel (Swansea), T. P. Evans (Swansea), T. J. Cobner (Pontypool), T. M. Davies (Swansea, capt.).

Australia P. E. McLean (Queensland); P. G. Batch (Queensland), R. D. L'Estrange (Queensland), G. A. Shaw (New South Wales), L. E. Monaghan (NSW); J. C. Hindmarsh (NSW), J. N. B. Hipwell (NSW, capt.); R. Graham (NSW), P. A. Horton (NSW), J. E. C. Meadows (Victoria), R. A. Smith (NSW), G. Fay (NSW), A. A. Shaw (Queensland), J. K. Lambie (NSW), G. Cornelsen (NSW). Replacements: G. K. Pearse (NSW) for J. K. Lambie, 14 min; R. G. Hauser (Queensland) for J. N. B. Hipwell, 39 min.

Referee D. P. d'Arcy (Ireland).

The International Championship

England 9 pts Wales 21 *Twickenham, 17 January 1976*

This may have been the biggest Welsh victory at Twickenham, but in only one respect was it the greatest: the phenomenal performance of J. P. R. Williams, whose two tries from full-back, both of them converted, accounted exactly for the difference in score between the sides. In fact the English played with more spirit than for many years, and although their only points came from Hignell's three penalty kicks, they stayed in touch to the end. To illustrate the near-equality of opportunity, the scrums were level; the lineouts went 13–12 in England's favour; seven penalties were conceded by England against thirteen by Wales; and it was only in the rucks that Wales won a critical 12–7 advantage.

Yet there was a great difference in the two sides' use of the ball. Every kick from Edwards was telling as he turned the English back upon themselves to create a new base for attack.

England, in contrast, were working to no discernible plan, and while for long stretches they effectively blanketed the Welsh moves they seemed incapable of striking back.

After seventeen minutes Wales scored when they savagely wheeled a scrum to the open side near the English line. Lampkowski was unable to gather the ball as his forwards heeled, and Edwards snatched at it to hustle over for a try which Fenwick converted. Next, Martin's penalty was cancelled out by Hignell's first, but once again Edwards put England under pressure with a chip to the corner. From there the ball reached Fenwick who, instead of playing it out towards the wing, flicked it back over his head to JPR who ran through majestically to the line.

Again Fenwick converted, and even if their ardour was cooling, Wales looked safe enough. But just before the interval and again four minutes from the end, Hignell added two penalties, and a late England revival could still achieve a draw. It was JPR once more who saved the situation, running through on a scissors with Bennett to score between the posts. He had been playing in some discomfort with seven stitches in his left cheek. And afterwards, when these were removed, another seven stitches were needed to close a gash on the right. He had played innumerable brave games for Wales, but this was surely his finest hour and a half.

Scorers ENGLAND – penalty goals: Hignell 3. WALES – tries: Edwards, J. P. R. Williams 2; conversions: Fenwick 3; penalty goal: Martin.

England A. J. Hignell (Cambridge University); P. J. Squires (Harrogate), A. W. Maxwell (Headingley), D. A. Cooke (Harlequins), D. J. Duckham (Coventry); M. J. Cooper (Moseley), M. S. Lampkowski (Headingley); M. A. Burton (Gloucester), P. J. Wheeler (Leicester), F. E. Cotton (Sale), W. B. Beaumont (Fylde), R. M. Wilkinson (Bedford), M. Keyworth (Swansea), A. Neary (Broughton Park, capt.), A. G. Ripley (Rosslyn Park). Replacement: P. S. Preece (Coventry) for P. J. Squires, 30 min.

Wales J. P. R. Williams (London Welsh); T. G. R. Davies (Cardiff), R. W. R. Gravell (Llanelli), S. P. Fenwick (Bridgend), J. J. Williams (Llanelli); P. Bennett (Llanelli), G. O. Edwards (Cardiff); G. Price (Pontypool), R. W. Windsor (Pontypool), A. G. Faulkner (Pontypool), A. J. Martin (Aberavon), G. A. D. Wheel (Swansea), T. P. Evans (Swansea), T. J. Cobner (Pontypool), T. M. Davies (Swansea, capt.).

Referee G. Domercq (France).

On the same afternoon France beat Scotland 13–6 at Murrayfield.

Wales 28 pts Scotland 6 *Cardiff, 7 February 1976*

Here again was a comprehensive victory for Wales which still left their supporters slightly dissatisfied. A legacy of resentment from the previous year's extremely physical encounter was partly to blame. So was poor refereeing which allowed illegal activities, especially in the ruck, to go unpunished – a problem which was compounded in the second half when, after pulling a muscle, Dr Cluny declined to go off even though he couldn't keep up with the play. The result was a ragged, incoherent game with sporadic bursts of energy and excitement, which brought Bennett his record ninety-two points, but even the home crowd little satisfaction.

Bennett had a thoroughly good afternoon with the boot, not only scoring thirteen points but largely taking over the tactical kicking from Edwards. It was his chip to the corner, followed up by J. J. Williams, which gave Wales their opening try in the second minute. And it was his conversion and the first two of his penalties which brought Wales a 12–6 lead at half-time – Irvine having meanwhile completed an intricate scoring move for Scotland.

Other memorable players in an easily forgotten match were J. P. R. Williams and Fenwick, both implacable in defence and attack. JPR not only set up the ruck from which Fenwick dropped a goal but had a hand in the move which sent Trevor

Evans racing over in the corner for the second Welsh try. Edwards, however, had saved the best for last, twice turning Steele the wrong way with a prodigious dummy before crossing for his seventeenth Welsh try. The trio of record-holders was now a quartet.

Scorers WALES – tries: J. J. Williams, Evans, Edwards; conversions: Bennett 2; dropped goal: Fenwick; penalty goals: Bennett 3. SCOTLAND – try: Irvine; conversion: Morgan.

Wales J. P. R. Williams (London Welsh); T. G. R. Davies (Cardiff), R. W. R. Gravell (Llanelli), S. P. Fenwick (Bridgend), J. J. Williams (Llanelli); P. Bennett (Llanelli), G. O. Edwards (Cardiff); G. Price (Pontypool), R. W. Windsor (Pontypool), A. G. Faulkner (Pontypool), A. J. Martin (Averavon), G. A. D. Wheel (Swansea), T. P. Evans (Swansea), T. J. Cobner (Pontypool), T. M. Davies (Swansea, capt.).

Scotland A. R. Irvine (Heriot's F.P.); W. C. C. Steele (London Scottish), J. M. Renwick (Hawick), A. G. Cranston (Hawick), D. Shedden (West of Scotland); I. R. McGeechan (Headingley), D. W. Morgan (Stewart's-Melville F.P.); A. B. Carmichael (West of Scotland), C. D. Fisher (Waterloo), J. McLauchlan (Jordanhill, capt.), A. F. McHarg (London Scottish), G. L. Brown (West of Scotland), D. G. Leslie (West of Scotland), M. A. Biggar (London Scottish), G. Y. Mackie (Highland).

Referee Dr A. Cluny (France).

On the same afternoon France beat Ireland 26–3 at Parc des Princes.

Ireland 9 pts Wales 34 *Lansdowne Road, 21 February 1976*

This match for the triple crown suddenly changed character in the final quarter of an hour. The most persistent impression for the first sixty minutes or so was of the extraordinary composure and grim efficiency of the Welsh side in breaking the stubborn will of their opponents. The Irish had thrown themselves into the match with a furious zeal, and it took all the experience and character of Mervyn Davies to hold his forwards together. But he found sufficient steel in Evans, Wheel and Price especially – to shore up the occasional rift in the pack, while Bennett and Fenwick held steady under fire to protect the mid-field.

Bennett and Martin kicked penalties, and Gerald Davies got the opening try after charging down a kick; but even a ten-point lead brought little relief. McGann responded with three successive penalties to reduce the Welsh lead to a single point at half-time. And although Bennett followed up with two more penalties it was still desperately hard going. The Welsh lead remained 16–9 after an hour, and there was no knowing which, if either, side would crack.

Then with very little warning Wales scored three tries and eighteen points within the space of six minutes. The turning point came when Ensor failed to mark Bennett's kick ahead. He was nailed by Gravell and Fenwick; Wheel won the ruck; Edwards switched the ball from open to blind; and JPR came in to make the overlap for Gerald Davies's second try.

Immediately Edwards tried a speculative chip into the blind-side corner and, while three or four others might have done the same, determinedly gathered to score his surpassing eighteenth try for Wales. Having converted both tries, Bennett now converted himself into a running stand-off to score his first try in twenty international appearances. And he did so with a verve which Llanelli might have recognized but which, until now, had largely been suppressed on the great occasions. Dummying, feinting, side-stepping he reached the line, and with the kick that followed he completed another milestone, his record-equalling nineteen points for the match.

Scorers IRELAND – penalty goals: McGann 3. WALES – tries: T. G. R. Davies 2, Edwards, Bennett; conversions: Bennett 3; penalty goals: Bennett 3, Martin.

Ireland A. H. Ensor (Wanderers); T. O. Grace (St Mary's

College, capt.); P. J. Lavery (London Irish); C. M. H. Gibson (North of Ireland F.C.); A. W. McMaster (Ballymena); B. J. McGann (Cork Constitution); D. M. Canniffe (Lansdowne); P. O'Callahan (Dolphin), J. L. Cantrell (University College, Dublin), P. A. Orr (Old Wesley), R. F. Hakin (CIYMS), M. I. Keane (Lansdowne), S. A. McKinney (Dungannon), S. M. Deering (Garryowen), W. P. Duggan (Blackrock College).

Wales J. P. R. Williams (London Welsh); T. G. R. Davies (Cardiff), R. W. R. Gravell (Llanelli), S. P. Fenwick (Bridgend), J. J. Williams (Llanelli); P. Bennett (Llanelli), G. O. Edwards (Cardiff); G. Price (Pontypool), R. W. Windsor (Pontypool), A. G. Faulkner (Pontypool), G. A. D. Wheel (Swansea), A. J. Martin (Aberavon), T. P. Evans (Swansea), T. P. David (Pontypridd), T. M. Davies (Swansea, capt.).

Referee N. R. Sanson (Scotland).

On the same afternoon Scotland beat England 22–12 at Murrayfield.

Wales 19 pts France 13 *Cardiff, 6 March 1976*

Gareth Edwards led the side out on to the field to mark his forty-fifth appearance for Wales. And for his tactical appreciation of the pressure his side was under, his tight kicking into the box and to the diagonal which stopped the French gathering momentum, Edwards also deserved to be carried from it after Wales had won their seventh grand slam. And perhaps equally J. P. R. Williams for a tackle on Gourdon which prevented an apparently certain French try late in the game.

Either way, a hard season, in which Wales had been everyone's target, culminated in their hardest match against a young, ambitious and energetic French team. The Welsh made more mistakes and suffered greater loss of concentration than they had all winter. Their forwards looked ponderous. Their mid-field fell far below their usual level. What did not desert them was their essential character, and it saved them from destruction in the final quarter.

Wales were ill at ease from the start, and six points down within five minutes. Fenwick, with unusual carelessness, gave a badly-directed pass when he was tackled as he ran the ball out of defence. Romeu and the ball found each other, and Gourdon was on the flank to score a try which Romeu then converted.

This might have been a numbing blow, but Edwards immediately began to get the situation under control by turning the French back into the corners. Bennett eased it, too, with the first of the five Welsh penalties. By the end of the first quarter Wales sufficiently recovered their poise to overhaul the French with a try. Price peeled from a lineout to set up a ruck. Wales won it, tried the blind side then open, and Fenwick created just sufficient room to send J. J. Williams over in the corner.

The lead lengthened when Bennett and Martin kicked further penalties (Martin's was one of his mortar shots from fifty yards), and now France would have to score twice to get ahead. They did so once, a Romeu penalty, to make it 13–9 at half-time.

It was still touch and go. Even when Wales began to carry the game to France early in the second half their only reward was yet another penalty – this time by Fenwick since Bennett had slightly injured his leg. Fenwick was to land one more, though only after a kick-ahead by the French replacement, Aguirre, had sent Averous scampering over for a try, and for the final twenty minutes nearly all the attacking came from France. If Wales had shown some elegance earlier in the season, they won their grand slam more grittily than prettily.

Scorers WALES – try: J. J. Williams; penalty goals: Bennett 2, Fenwick 2, Martin. FRANCE – tries: Gourdon, Averous; conversion: Romeu; penalty goal: Romeu.

Wales J. P. R. Williams (London Welsh); T. G. R. Davies (Cardiff), R. W. R. Gravell (Llanelli), S. P. Fenwick (Bridgend), J. J. Williams (Llanelli); P. Bennett (Llanelli), G. O. Edwards (Cardiff); G. Price (Pontypool), R. W. Windsor

(Pontypool), A. G. Faulkner (Pontypool), A. J. Martin (Aberavon), G. A. D. Wheel (Swansea), T. P. Evans (Swansea), T. P. David (Pontypridd), T. M. Davies (Swansea, capt.). Replacement: F. M. D. Knill (Cardiff) for Price, 35 min.

France M. Droitecourt (Montferrand); J–F. Gourdon (Racing Club de France), R. Bertranne (Bagnères), J. Pecune (Tarbles), J–L. Averous (La Voulte); J–P Romeu (Montferrand), J. Fouroux (La Voulte, capt.); R. Paparemborde (Pau), A. Paco (Béziers), G. Cholley (Castres), J–F. Imbernon (Perpignan), M. Palmié (Béziers), J–C. Skréla (Toulouse), J–P. Rives (Toulouse), J–P. Bastiat (Dax). Replacement: J–M. Aguirre (Bagnères) for M. Droitecourt, 40 min.

Referee J. R. West (Ireland).

On the same afternoon Ireland beat England 13–12 at Twickenham. Although the championship had been decided, there were still two matches to play on 20 March when France beat England 30–9 at Parc des Princes and Scotland beat Ireland 15–6 at Lansdowne Road.

Championship Table 1976

	P	W	D	L	For	Ag	Pts
Wales	4	4	0	0	102	37	8
France	4	3	0	1	82	37	6
Scotland	4	2	0	2	49	59	4
Ireland	4	1	0	3	31	87	2
England	4	0	0	4	42	86	0

15
Le Grand Slam: 1976–77

Ever since they had reluctantly accepted the wooden spoon in 1969, the best the French had done was to share the title with Wales in the following year. But equally the worst was to share second place in the championship. They were always the unknowable factor, the side that the others were relieved to find themselves playing at home – preferably on a wet and miserable January afternoon. Springtime in Paris might be appealing, but not to the other four nations.

The French have been known to claim that they possess enough first-class players to field three international sides; the Welsh, they say, could field two; the other home countries only one. But whether from an embarrassment of talent – or simply because of the contentious politics of their domestic game – the French have often found it uncommonly difficult to put their fifteen most effective players into action at any one time.

Still, they did so this season, producing a pack of massive proportions and fierce dedication, backed by a kicking stand-off, Romeu, who kept them to their task and reaped the points from their efforts. Occasionally their backs would flare irrepressibly into life and play for the hell of it, but basically the French played to win, not to express any native talent for running and passing. They were a comparatively low-scoring side, putting together 58 points compared with Wales's 102 the season before. But at the same time they conceded only twenty-one in four matches, and by their heavy-handed method won the second grand slam in their history.

Playing their key match in Paris against a side of such

imposing physical presence, Wales badly missed the steadying influence of Mervyn Davies in the pack, and lost 16–9. But their remaining matches they won with varying degrees of comfort to earn their second successive triple crown, which they had not done since 1909. The captaincy passed to Terry Cobner for the autumn match against Argentina, but it shows how rapidly international players rise and fall and sometimes rise again in the favour of selectors that Phil Bennett, who had almost lost his place in the national side in the previous season, was appointed captain of Wales throughout the championship and then of the British Lions in New Zealand.

Argentina in Wales and England

A year before, Argentina had made their first short tour of France, losing both tests by fairly wide, but not humiliating, margins, and winning three of their five provincial games. Like Romania, their closest equivalent in Europe, they gave the impression of being almost up to the general level of member-countries of the International Board. Not a match for the All Blacks, perhaps, but capable, on a good day, of giving some of the home countries or Australia an anxious time.

This view was confirmed when they visited Wales, and briefly England, in September–October 1976, and in their closing game led the Welsh grand slam side 19–17 in the fifth minute of injury time. They lost even then, but in terms of international competence they had little more to prove.

Their play on the tour was crisp and exciting in the best (if not the current) French manner, and they possessed some players of undeniable world class: the deceptively frail-looking Sansot at full-back; the powerful centre, Travaglini, an indefatigable lock-forward, Fernandez; and above all Hugo Porta, as gifted a runner and kicker of the ball as any stand-off of his day. Their record was remarkably even; they won their first three games against East Wales, Cardiff and Aberavon, lost their last three to North and Midlands (England), West Wales and Wales, scoring 112 points – just one more than they conceded.

Wales 20 pts Argentina 19 *Cardiff, 16 October 1976*

Although they awarded no caps for this match, Wales paid the Pumas of Argentina the compliment of fielding their best available side – which their visitors repaid by nearly beating them. Two minutes into injury time Wales found themselves 17–19 down, and Argentina were on the brink of making rugby history. Instead they threw the chance away. Travaglini, desperately trying to stop the final Welsh attack, was penalized for a short-arm tackle, and with the match already overrunning by five minutes, Bennett kicked the saving goal.

Wales, who could only plead that the season was still young, gave a patchy, wan performance. Their forward play was sluggish, particularly in the lineout where the ball was won twice as often by the Argentinians. The back row was failing to stem the Pumas' counter-attacks, while Porta was keeping Wales back and J. P. R. Williams quiet by some finely-placed tactical kicks.

It was Porta's penalty which gave Argentina their early lead and his subtle running out of defence which relieved much of the Welsh territorial pressure. Yet with the first half drawn 6–6 on penalty points, Wales seemed to be getting the measure of the Pumas, and it was no great surprise when they built a 17–6 lead from Bennett's third penalty, a Gerald Davies try, created by Evans and Cobner, and another from Edwards which was typically all his own work.

But no sooner had the crowd come to accept that Wales had simply been slow starters and were finally on top, than the Pumas struck two very elegant blows: a try for Gauweloose after Sansot had come gliding in from full-back, and one for G. B. Varela following a sophisticated mid-field move. Varela's one conversion put Argentina back in the game, his penalty in injury time gave them the lead – and only Travaglini's indiscretion brought Wales some embarrassed relief.

Scorers WALES – tries: T. G. R. Davies, Edwards; penalty goals: Bennett 4. ARGENTINA – tries: Gauweloose, G. B. Varela; conversion: Porta; penalty goals: G. B. Varela 2, Porta.

Wales J. P. R. Williams (Bridgend); T. G. R. Davies (Cardiff), R. W. R. Gravell (Llanelli), R. T. E. Bergiers (Llanelli), J. J. Williams (Llanelli); P. Bennett (Llanelli), G. O. Edwards (Cardiff); A. G. Faulkner (Pontypool), R. W. Windsor (Pontypool), G. Price (Pontypool), B. Clegg (Swansea), G. A. D. Wheel (Swansea), T. J. Cobner (Pontypool, capt.), T. P. Evans (Swansea), D. L. Quinnell (Llanelli). Replacement: J. Squire (Newport) for B. Clegg, 56 min.

Argentina M. Sansot; D. B. Varela, A. A. Travaglini, G. B. Varela, J. M. Gauweloose; H. Porta, A. M. Etchegaray (capt.); R. L. Irantea, J. D. Constante, F. Insua, E. N. Branca, J–M. Fernandez, J. Carracedo, C. M. Neyra, R. Mastai. Replacement: J. G. Braceras for J. D. Constante, 23 min.

Referee N. R. Sanson (Scotland).

The International Championship

Wales 25 pts Ireland 9 *Cardiff, 15 January 1977*

The score suggests an emphatic Welsh win – which indeed it was in the end – but does not reflect the extent of the Irish challenge, the fluctuating fortunes of the play, or the incidental dramas which accompanied Wales home by two goals, a try, a dropped goal and two penalties to three penalties.

The moment that overshadowed the whole game, and affected its course, came late in the first half when a series of punches brought Geoff Wheel and Willie Duggan the unhappy distinction of becoming the first players ever sent off in an international at Cardiff (which is not to say that others hadn't deserved to be). The loss of Duggan, and then of the injured Hakin at half-time hit Ireland severely, for it deprived them of the ability to win the ball just when they had Wales in trouble and, by the grace of Gibson's boot, were deservedly leading 6–0.

The first half had belonged entirely to the Irish forwards and half-backs – in particular Gibson, their thirty-four-year-old virtuoso – and at the interval nobody would have bet on Wales's survival, let alone their capacity to score twenty-five points from scratch. Even when Bennett brought them level with two penalties, Gibson pegged them back again with his third.

Yet there was a new sense of urgency as Wales set out to spring their trap. Fenwick, on second thoughts, moved to the blind side; Bennett made a half-break; and Burcher rounding in support sent out a pass which Gerald Davies picked brilliantly from the ground to score in the corner. That made it 10–9, and then in an eight-minute spell came fifteen points to mock the crowd's lack of faith. Fenwick, missing out Burcher, gave J. P. R. Williams the ball to carry to the posts; Bennett converted. Fenwick then dropped a goal from a ruck set up by the substitute, Quinnell. And finally a scissors with Bennett sent Gerald Davies off again on a side-stepping run which presented the dogged Burgess with a try by the posts and Bennett with a simple last conversion. Twice Wales had pulled the fat from the fire this season.

Scorers WALES – tries: T. G. R. Davies, J. P. R. Williams, Burgess; conversions: Bennett 2; dropped goal: Fenwick; penalty goals: Bennett 2. IRELAND – penalty goals: Gibson 3.

Wales J. P. R. Williams (Bridgend); T. G. R. Davies (Cardiff), S. P. Fenwick (Bridgend), D. H. Burcher (Newport), J. J. Williams (Llanelli); P. Bennett (Llanelli, capt.), G. O. Edwards (Cardiff); G. Shaw (Neath), R. W. Windsor (Pontypool), G. Price (Pontypool), A. J. Martin (Aberavon), G. A. D. Wheel (Swansea), T. P. Evans (Swansea), J. Squire (Newport), R. C. Burgess (Ebbw Vale). Replacement. D. L. Quinnell (Llanelli) for T. P. Evans, 68 min. Sent off: G. A. D. Wheel, 38 min.

Ireland F. Wilson (CIYMS); T. O. Grace (St Mary's College, capt.), A. R. McKibbin (Instonians), J. A. McIlrath (Ballymena), D. St J. Bowen (Cork Constitution); C. M. H. Gibson

(North of Ireland F.C.), R. J. N. McGrath (Wanderers); P. A. Orr (Old Wesley), P. C. Whelan (Garryowen), T. A. O. Feighery (St Mary's College), M. Keane (Lansdowne), R. F. Hakin (CIYMS), S. A. McKinney (Dungannon), W. P. Duggan (Blackrock College), S. M. Deering (Garryowen). Replacement: B. O. Foley (Shannon) for R. F. Hakin, 40 min. Sent off: W. P. Duggan, 38 min.

Referee N. R. Sanson (Scotland).

On the same afternoon England beat Scotland 26–6 at Twickenham.

France 16 pts Wales 9 *Parc des Princes, 5 February 1977*

Not since the late fifties had the French so physically dominated a Welsh side as they did throughout this match. Wales were forced to feed on scraps, and though the French themselves didn't lay on much of a feast from their ample means, their victory – by a goal, a try and two penalties to three penalties – could only be accepted uncomplainingly as one of the less palatable facts of life.

It had been clear all the season that, without Mervyn Davies there to hold it together, the Welsh pack was vulnerable, and today the animal power of the massive French forwards found it out. The possession was nearly all French. Wales won only one of the first twelve lineouts, and only seven of the thirty-five in the first half. In the scrums the French struck twice against the head.

That Wales kept an active interest in the game for so long was due to the defensive qualities of the backs, and their willingness to counter-attack from the most unpromising situations. And in this they found unexpected co-operation from the French backs who squandered most of their chances and, except for flashes of inspiration, were the least effective that lively nation had fielded for perhaps twenty years.

By the break it was all-square at 3–3 – with penalties first from Fenwick then Romeu – and promisingly Fenwick put

Wales back in the lead with another kick at goal early in the second half. The Welsh were notoriously better players in the second forty minutes than the first. But then their hopes subsided as Gerald Davies was injured and left the field, and the French wheeled a scrum across the Welsh line – Skréla was credited with the try which Romeu converted – to take the lead for the first time. That inspired them to a long-drawn-out move which recalled better days, Aguirre beginning it with a thrust on the left, and Harize completing it with a try on the right. Fenwick's last penalty and a gutsy rearguard action stopped the French running away with the match, but it could not stave off Wales's first defeat in the championship since Murrayfield 1975.

Scorers FRANCE – tries: Skréla, Harize; conversion: Romeu; penalty goals: Romeu 2. WALES – penalty goals: Fenwick 3.

France J–M. Aguirre (Bagnères); D. Harize (Toulouse), R. Bertranne (Bagnères), F. Sangalli (Narbonne), J–L. Averous (La Voulte); J–P. Romeu (Montferrand), J. Fouroux (Auch, capt.); R. Paparemborde (Pau), A. Paco (Béziers), G. Cholley (Castres), M. Palmié (Béziers), J–F. Imbernon (Perpignan), J–C. Skréla (Toulouse), J–P. Rives (Toulouse), J–P. Bastiat (Dax).

Wales J. P. R. Williams (Bridgend); T. G. R. Davies (Cardiff), S. P. Fenwick (Bridgend), D. H. Burcher (Newport), J. J. Williams (Llanelli); P. Bennett (Llanelli, capt.), G. O. Edwards (Cardiff); G. Shaw (Neath), R. W. Windsor (Pontypool), G. Price (Pontypool), A. J. Martin (Aberavon), D. L. Quinnell (Llanelli), T. J. Cobner (Pontypool), J. Squire (Newport), R. C. Burgess (Ebbw Vale). Replacement: G. L. Evans (Newport) for T. G. R. Davies, 49 min.

Referee A. M. Hosie (Scotland).

On the same afternoon England beat Ireland 4–0 at Lansdowne Road. A fortnight later (19 February), when Wales had a bye,

England went on to beat France 4–3 at Twickenham, and Scotland defeated Ireland 21–18 at Murrayfield.

Wales 14 pts England 9 *Cardiff, 5 March 1977*

England had been having a revival this season, and they came to Cardiff with wins over Scotland and Ireland behind them and their eyes fixed ahead to the triple crown. But Wales were also due for something of a renaissance. Their pack had been shuffled with a new man, Clive Williams, at prop, Wheel restored to his partnership with Martin at lock, and Quinnell moved from the second row to his more effective position at the rear. These small adjustments made an enormous difference, and by the end the Welsh pack had torn the heart out of the optimistic England forwards. Clean possession from the lineout went their way 22–15, the mauls 10–5; the rucks were equally divided and in the scrum England won the only strike against the head.

This gave Wales an enormous advantage, allowing Edwards to control the rest of the game with his tactical kicking and Bennett to general the mid-field with impressive calm. The result may have been a narrower win over England than many of that period – two tries and two penalty goals to three penalties – but for all their opponents' stubborn resistance it was unequivocal.

One simple and one difficult penalty from forty-seven yards by Hignell let Wales know that victory wouldn't come easily. But Edwards steadily kicked his side back into tactically sound positions, and then with a typical burst from a five-yard scrum scored the opening try. It was his nineteenth for Wales and for the time being gave him a one-try advantage over Gerald Davies in their private duel for the national record (they were eventually to tie on twenty).

Fenwick gave them the lead with a penalty shortly before the interval. Hignell snatched it back with another, and again Fenwick replied in kind. But the game deserved something grander in the way of a finale, and reliably the old hands behind the scrum provided it. Edwards made a gymnastic reverse pass to Bennett which exposed the England centre. Bennett and Burcher delicately opened it up. And J. P. R. Williams came through on the ball, feinting to the outside then turning in unstoppably. The prospect of the triple crown had disappeared for England and opened up for Wales.

Scorers WALES – tries: Edwards, J. P. R. Williams; penalty goals: Fenwick 2. ENGLAND – penalty goals: Hignell 3.

Wales J. P. R. Williams (Bridgend); T. G. R. Davies (Cardiff), S. P. Fenwick (Bridgend), D. H. Burcher (Newport), J. J. Williams (Llanelli); P. Bennett (Llanelli, capt.), G. O. Edwards (Cardiff); C. Williams (Aberavon), R. W. Windsor (Pontypool), G. Price (Pontypool), A. J. Martin (Aberavon), G. A. D. Wheel (Swansea), R. C. Burgess (Ebbw Vale), T. J. Cobner (Pontypool), D. L. Quinnell (Llanelli).

England A. J. Hignell (Cambridge University); P. J. Squires (Harrogate), C. P. Kent (Rosslyn Park), B. J. Corless (Moseley), M. A. C. Slemen (Liverpool); M. J. Cooper (Moseley), M. Young (Gosforth); F. E. Cotton (Sale), P. J. Wheeler (Leicester), R. Cowling (Leicester), W. B. Beaumont (Fylde), N. E. Horton (Moseley), P. J. Dixon (Gosforth), M. J. Rafter (Bristol), R. M. Uttley (Gosforth, capt.).

Referee D. Burnett (Ireland).

On the same afternoon France beat Scotland 23–3 at Parc des Princes.

Scotland 9 pts Wales 18 — *Murrayfield, 19 March 1977*

Wales came to Edinburgh for the triple crown, and found themselves treated as though they were trying to run off with the Crown jewels. This was the staunchest Scottish performance for two seasons. They out-scrummaged the Welsh to the extent of taking three strikes against the head, and poured

The strong men of the Welsh lineout in the late seventies: Graham Price, Geoff Wheel and Alan Martin opposed to England's Barry Nelmes, Billy Beaumont, Robin Cowling and Nigel Horton.

(Overleaf) Nigel Horton, the England lock, holds back the Welsh in the lineout to leave Barry Nelmes free to feed out the ball.

Geoff Wheel tries to wrest the ball from French hands while Alan Martin looks down on the struggle.

9

The daunting sight that faced opposing packs: the Pontypool front-row of (*l–r*) Graham Price, Bobby Windsor and Charlie Faulkner.

into the rucks with suicidal abandon. And far from simply playing the negative spoiling game which had been predicted of them, they ran and constructed their attacks with more imagination than even the Welsh mid-field could muster.

That Wales won – by two goals and two penalties to a goal and a dropped goal – was due to their experience and coolness, and to their ability to counter-attack. Both their tries came from running out of defence on their twenty-five, and that not only expressed the spirit of their play, but also their great indebtedness to that supremely combative full-back, J. P. R. Williams.

Scotland, as they surged repeatedly at Wales, were unlucky not to score at least one try in the first half. Instead they had to be content with a neatly dropped goal from McGeechan in the opening minute to which Bennett replied with a forty-five-yard penalty. In the last ten minutes it looked as if the Scots had spent themselves, but their best period was to come early in the second half. Irvine, having missed two penalties, scored a superb try from the build-up of Morgan and Renwick, and having cut around behind the posts, made the simple conversion.

Wales took immediate reprisals. Edwards, feinting to the right of the scrum, sent a long pass out to Bennett who, inevitably, found JPR outside him to give J. J. Williams the scoring pass. That try, Bennett's conversion and his subsequent penalty gave Wales the lead for the first time. But there was no comfort in three clear points. That only came when Gerald Davies emerged from his own twenty-five to sway and switch through two determined tackles and open up the most attractive movement of the game. He put Burcher away on the right, and Burcher, seeing the defensive cover gathering, timed the most perfect lob across to Fenwick. A quick pass and Bennett was cruising away for the final try and crowning conversion.

Scorers SCOTLAND – try: Irvine; conversion: Irvine; dropped goal: McGeechan. WALES – tries: J. J. Williams, Bennett; conversions: Bennett 2; penalty goals: Bennett 2.

Scotland A. R. Irvine (Heriot's F.P.); W. B. B. Gammell (Edinburgh Wanderers), J. M. Renwick (Hawick), A. G. Cranston (Hawick), D. Shedden (West of Scotland); J. R. McGeechan (Headingley, capt.), D. W. Morgan (Stewart's-Melville); J. McLauchlan (Jordanhill), D. F. Madsen (Gosforth), A. B. Carmichael (West of Scotland), I. A. Barnes (Hawick), A. F. McHarg (London Scottish), M. A. Biggar (London Scottish), D. S. M. MacDonald (London Scottish), W. S. Watson (Boroughmuir).

Wales J. P. R. Williams (Bridgend); T. G. R. Davies (Cardiff), S. P. Fenwick (Bridgend), D. H. Burcher (Newport), J. J. Williams (Llanelli); P. Bennett (Llanelli, capt.), G. O. Edwards (Cardiff); C. Williams (Aberavon), R. W. Windsor (Pontypool), G. Price (Pontypool), A. J. Martin (Aberavon), G. A. D. Wheel (Swansea), R. C. Burgess (Ebbw Vale), T. J. Cobner (Pontypool), D. L. Quinnell (Llanelli).

Referee G. Domercq (France).

On the same afternoon France beat Ireland 15–6 at Lansdowne Road.

Championship Table 1977

	P	W	D	L	For	Ag	Pts
France	4	4	0	0	58	21	8
Wales	4	3	0	1	66	43	6
England	4	2	0	2	42	24	4
Scotland	4	1	0	3	39	85	2
Ireland	4	0	0	4	33	65	0

British Lions in New Zealand

In May the British Lions left for New Zealand and Fiji with John Dawes returning to the scene of his 1971 triumph as assistant manager and coach to George Burrell of Scotland, and Phil Bennett as captain of the party. They did not repeat that earlier success, however, losing the test series 3–1 (L 16–12 at Wellington, 18 June; W 13–9 at Christchurch, 9 July; L 19–7 at Dunedin, 30 July; L 10–9 at Auckland, 13 August). They also lost one of their secondary matches, 21–9, to New Zealand Universities, and on the way home were defeated 25–21 by Fiji.

The original party contained sixteen Welshmen, and in addition A. D. Lewis (Cambridge University and London Welsh) and Faulkner were flown out as replacements. It probably made a considerable difference to the success of the tour that J. P. R. Williams, Gerald Davies and Gareth Edwards were all unable to accompany it, although the Welsh influence remained strong. Phil Bennett was top scorer with 112 points, eighteen of them from six penalties in the tests (but the more remarkable performance came from the Scot, Andy Irvine, with eleven tries from full-back). J. J. Williams scored ten tries and Elgan Rees seven. Terry Cobner also made a good impression as pack leader on the latter section of the tour.

16
Treble Top: 1977–78

This season was not the end of the second Golden Era but was certainly its climax. A year later the Welsh team began to disband as some of its older members decided to retire while they still had an unequivocal right to their places in it, or were forced to acknowledge that recurring injury owed as much to age as to accident. But during February and March 1978 the Welsh were in their high prime with a small fortune in experience underwriting their natural gifts. Anyone who had the opportunity to watch them might never see their equal again.

Throughout the decade Welsh success had been built on continuity, and by the end of the 1978 home season the basic XV for the championship had collected a phenomenal 352 caps between them. In fact if the selectors could have had their wish, the team would have been unchanged from the first to last. Unfortunately hamstring trouble prevented Gerald Davies playing in the final match against France with the result that Gareth Evans, the Newport wing, became (since no replacements were needed during play) only the sixteenth player capped that winter. As it proved, the Welsh crowds had seen the last of the incomparable Davies with his slightly Edwardian elegance and the capacity of a Raffles to keep out of his opponents' clutches. But he was to reappear twice for Wales in Australia during June and so become, with forty-six appearances, Wales's most-capped threequarter.

For all that, Wales did not have things entirely their own way during the championship. They beat England only by scoring the odd penalty goal in five, and to overcome Ireland in Dublin they needed depths of character as much as craft.

But by mid-March their singular stature as a team had been happily commemorated by a series of records.

They became the first country ever to win three successive triple crowns (to the relief of the manufacturers who had begun to sell a souvenir tie even before the deciding match at Lansdowne Road). The new crown was their fifteenth to England's fourteenth, and the grand slam which followed, their eighth to England's seventh. They were also outright champions for the twentieth time, although in this case England's record of seventeen wins had already fallen in 1975.

There were no visiting tourists this season, but in the early summer of 1978 Wales paid their own visit to Australia. After the thrilling success of the home season, the trip was a sad if salutary anti-climax. Several key players were missing from the party, others were injured at crucial times during the tour, and both test matches were lost. However Wales had to reconcile themselves to change some day, and in defeat at least they discovered a new half-back partnership (new, that is, to Wales, though not to Cardiff): Terry Holmes and Gareth Davies. These two would go a long way to ease the impending loss of the seemingly indispensable Edwards and Bennett.

The International Championship

Wales had a bye on 21 January 1978, the first Saturday of the championship, when France beat England 15–6 at Parc des Princes and Ireland beat Scotland 12–9 at Lansdowne Road.

England 6 pts Wales 9 — *Twickenham, 4 February 1978*

In its headline *The Observer* described this match as 'A Welsh elegy in an English graveyard'. Yet on a dismally cold, wet afternoon, it might equally have been the Welsh who caught their death. They owed their victory solely to penalty goals, and even these came from fewer chances. Three of Bennett's four kicks at goal went home compared with two of Hignell's six.

If only Hignell had achieved Bennett's ratio of success – and he had several near-misses – the critics might have justified an England victory on the strength of their pack. The English forwards had the Welsh struggling in the first half, and even though they lost ground in the second, they still emerged overall winners. The rucks went 14–9 and the mauls 11–6 in their favour while the Welsh advantage in the lineouts was a slender 24–23. But as so often during this period, the performance of the England backs came well below that of their forwards.

So, as things turned out, the critics were able to explain the Welsh win largely in terms of a collective recovery based on one man's skill. And that man, inevitably, was Gareth Edwards. To honour his fiftieth cap, the rest of the team held back so that he could lead them on to the field, and once there he repaid the courtesy by saving the day. If Bennett was the captain, Edwards was very much the general, shaping the game by the power, exactness and ingenuity of his kicking.

Having played with the wind at their backs, the English were deservedly 6–3 up at half-time. After seven minutes Hignell had put them in the lead when the Welsh front row were penalized at a scrum. Only two minutes later Edwards lured Young off-side to give Bennett the chance to equalize, but for the next half-hour England spent more time in the Welsh half than in their own. It was harsh luck that Hignell's second penalty, for Welsh barging at the lineout, was their only reward.

The change of ends brought a change in control, but not in the dour nature of the game. Three minutes into the second half, Wales drew level again when Bennett kicked a forty-three-yard penalty, the longest of the afternoon. But it was an even longer touch-kick by Edwards which gave Wales the moral ascendancy. From only two feet inside the touchline he put the ball out of play seventy yards upfield, and from that point in time and place England were fighting against the odds.

Repeatedly Edwards turned them wearily on their heels with his deep diagonal kicks into the far corner while Bennett harried them with high punts in all directions. It was rarely that Wales attempted to pass the ball beyond the stand-off, though Bennett once sent JPR through on a scissors move to within six yards of the English line.

Defending sturdily, England countered that threat and every other until, five minutes from no-side, one of their forwards was judged to have handled in the ruck. Bennett kicked his easiest penalty from the England twenty-five, and since Hignell narrowly failed with another kick just before the whistle, that remained the final score.

Scorers ENGLAND – penalty goals: Hignell 2. WALES – penalty goals: Bennett 3.

England A. J. Hignell (Cambridg University); P. J. Squires (Harrogate), B. J. Corless (Moseley), P. W. Dodge (Leicester), M. A. C. Slemen (Liverpool); J. P. Horton (Bath), M. Young (Gosforth); M. A. Burton (Gloucester), P. J. Wheeler (Leicester), B. G. Nelmes (Cardiff), W. B. Beaumont (Fylde, capt.), N. E. Horton (Toulouse), R. J. Mordell (Rosslyn Park), M. Rafter (Bristol), J. P. Scott (Rosslyn Park).

Wales J. P. R. Williams (Bridgend); T. G. R. Davies (Cardiff), R. W. R. Gravell (Llanelli), S. P. Fenwick (Bridgend), J. J. Williams (Llanelli); P. Bennett (Llanelli, capt.), G. O. Edwards (Cardiff); G. Price (Pontypool), R. W. Windsor (Pontypool), A. G. Faulkner (Pontypool), A. J. Martin (Aberavon), G. A. D. Wheel (Swansea), J. Squire (Newport), T. J. Cobner (Pontypool), D. L. Quinnell (Llanelli).

Referee N. R. Sanson (Scotland).

On the same day France beat Scotland 19–16 at Murrayfield.

Wales 22 pts Scotland 14 *Cardiff, 18 February 1978*

In the past fifty years Scotland had beaten Wales only once at Cardiff (though they had managed a couple of victories at Swansea) and now the Welsh were too experienced and composed a side to repeat the lapse of 1962. They controlled the game for as long as was required to score four tries, a penalty and a dropped goal, but at 22–7 lost a little of their concentration. The Scots, who played with great panache, came back at them, doubled their own score to two tries and two penalties and, without ever threatening to overturn the game, ran up more points than they had ever done before on Welsh soil.

The game was played on a day of steely cold when most sport in the country had been cancelled. Indeed shortly after the finish a blizzard cut West Wales off from Cardiff, marooning many of the players and spectators. And although the pitch at the national stadium was in fine condition, a stiff breeze blew from end to end. Winning the toss, Wales gave their opponents first advantage of it, hoping to hold them in the first half and then run the ball at them.

They did better than that. In reply to an opening penalty by Morgan, the Scottish scrum-half, Gareth Edwards dummied away from a ten-yard scrum, then used his remarkable strength to break a tackle and cross for a typical blind-side try – his twentieth for Wales. Then again when Renwick cut through on an inside pass to put Scotland ahead once more, Gravell restored the position by barging bravely through from a tapped penalty.

So at the interval Wales were 8–7 up, with the wind now at their backs and every prospect of winning handsomely. Their pack had exerted far greater pressure in the tight that they had against England a fortnight before; in all they won four scrums against the head. Their back row, dashingly led by Quinnell, had dominated the loose. The midfield players had performed with clinical efficiency. Having held Scotland, now they could let themselves go.

This they did to such effect that they scored ten points in the opening seven minutes of the second half, fourteen points in the first quarter-of-an-hour. First Bennett dropped a goal after Morgan had kicked the ball into his hands from a lineout. This was followed by a try from Fenwick who picked up the loose ball jerked from J. J. Williams's hand in a tackle. Then a Bennett penalty when Scotland collapsed a scrum. And finally, after a decent interval, a try by Quinnell running up in support of a clever blind-side move by Edwards and J. J. Williams. Wales were now fifteen points in the clear and the game was as good as won.

Unfortunately Wales believed this themselves, and letting their minds wander they allowed the Scots to produce a spell of counter-pressure during which Morgan first kicked a penalty and then, rocketing away from a short penalty, sent Tomes crashing over for a try. This concentrated the Welsh minds wonderfully, and they were back on the attack when the final whistle blew.

Scorers WALES – tries: Edwards, Gravell, Fenwick, Quinnell; dropped goal: Bennett; penalty goal: Bennett. SCOTLAND – tries: Renwick, Tomes; penalty goals: Morgan 2.

Wales J. P. R. Williams (Bridgend); T. G. R. Davies (Cardiff), R. W. R. Gravell (Llanelli), S. P. Fenwick (Bridgend), J. J. Williams (Llanelli); P. Bennett (Llanelli, capt.), G. O. Edwards (Cardiff); G. Price (Pontypool), R. W. Windsor (Pontypool), A. G. Faulkner (Pontypool), A.. J. Martin (Aberavon), G. A. D. Wheel (Swansea), J. Squire (Newport), T. J. Cobner (Pontypool), D. L. Quinnell (Llanelli).

Scotland B. H. Hay (Boroughmuir); W. B. B. Gammell (West of Scotland), J. M. Renwick (Harwick), A. G. Cranston (Hawick), D. Shedden (West of Scotland); I. R. McGeechan (Headingley), D. W. Morgan (Stewart's-Melville F.P.); N. E. K. Pender (Hawick), C. T. Deans (Hawick), J. McLauchlan (Jordanhill), A. F. McHarg (London Scottish), A. J. Tomes (Hawick), M. A. Biggar (London Scottish), C. B. Hegarty (Hawick), D. S. M. MacDonald (West of Scotland). Replacement: C. G. Hogg (Boroughmuir) for D. Shedden, 8 min.

Referee J. R. West (Ireland).

On the same day France beat Ireland 10–9 at Parc des Princes.

Ireland 16 pts Wales 20 *Lansdowne Road, 4 March 1978*

Memories of the rancorous battle at Cardiff the year before, when two players were sent off for fighting, left its mark on this return match – and on many players. This time nobody left early for the dressing-room, even for injury, though that seemed a matter of good fortune. There were constant penalties, and the struggle for possession in mauls and rucks was so ferocious that afterwards Welsh players complained that if internationals were to continue at this pitch of intensity, someone would surely be killed.

There was no suggestion that the passion was confined to Ireland, but they certainly responded to the occasion as though they had been specially chosen to foil Welsh hopes of a third triple crown. Keane and Slattery played with devouring energy in the pack, and while they and Mike Gibson (setting a world record with his sixty-fourth international cap) brought the benefits of great maturity to the side, Ireland had also been rejuvenated by several young players, notably the gifted Tony Ward at stand-off. If they failed to win it was not from want of endeavour, and they ran Wales to a desperately close decision by two tries and four penalty goals to a try, a dropped goal and three penalties.

In the circumstances the discipline of the Welsh team counted for everything: the unrelenting pressure of the Pontypool front row, the controlled feeding of the ball at the back of the scrum; the unshakeable poise of Edwards; JPR's general coolness under fire; Fenwick's steadiness in scoring sixteen points from four penalties and a try.

In fact Fenwick's first remarkable penalty, a thumping kick from inside the Welsh half, brought Wales a gasp of relief in the tenth minute when they were coping with Ireland's initial onslaught. And since his try, after Price had fed him from the ruck, was sandwiched between two further penalties, he accounted for all the Welsh points in their 13–6 half-time lead – Ward having kicked both Ireland penalties.

It was Ward again who, in effect, levelled the scores in the second half, first dropping a goal from a tapped penalty and then sending down a high punt which forced JPR into a rare error. Harassed by the pursuing Irish – and also booed by the crowd ever since he had made a late tackle on Gibson – the Welsh full-back sliced his clearance. It was a gift which Moloney pounced upon for a try.

The crown seemed to be slipping away from Wales as the Irish heightened their resistance, but Edwards, as ever, broke the deadlock with a high lobbed pass to Fenwick over the defence. Repeating the ploy, Fenwick put J. J. Williams over in the corner. A fourth penalty by Fenwick and a third from Ward left Wales with the trophy – an imaginary one, but what the Celts don't suffer from is lack of imagination.

Scorers IRELAND – try: Moloney; dropped goal: Ward; penalty goals: Ward 3. WALES – tries: Fenwick, J. J. Williams; penalty goals: Fenwick 4.

Ireland A. H. Ensor (Wanderers); C. M. H. Gibson (North of Ireland F.C.), A. R. McKibbin (London Irish), P. P. McNaughton (Greystones), A. C. McLennan (Wanderers); A. J. P. Ward (Garryowen), J. J. Moloney (St Mary's College, capt.); E. M. J. Byrne (Blackrock College), P. C. Whelan (Garryowen), P. A. Orr (Old Wesley), M. J. Keane (Lansdowne), H. W. Steele (Ballymena), S. A. McKinney (Dungannon), J. F. Slattery (Blackrock College), W. P. Duggan (Blackrock College).

Wales J. P. R. Williams (Bridgend), T. G. R. Davies (Cardiff), R. W. R. Gravell (Llanelli), S. P. Fenwick (Bridgend), J. J. Williams (Llanelli); P. Bennett (Llanelli, capt.), G. O. Edwards (Cardiff); G. Price (Pontypool), R. W. Windsor (Pontypool), A. G. Faulkner (Pontypool), A. J. Martin (Aberavon), G. A. D. Wheel (Swansea), J. Squire (Newport), T. J. Cobner (Pontypool), D. L. Quinnell (Llanelli).

Referee G. Domercq (France).

On the same day England beat Scotland 15–0 at Murrayfield

Wales 16 pts France 7 *Cardiff, 18 March 1978*

After the emotional and physical turmoil of Dublin, Wales still had the title and the grand slam to go for when they met France, the only other country with maximum points, on the last cold, sunny afternoon of the championship. In these conditions, and in the absence of the injured Gerald Davies from the Welsh threequarter line, France started favourites. They were a brilliant side, their forwards led by the energetic Rives, their backs served by a sharp young scrum-half, Gallion. And within twenty-four minutes they were seven points clear. But Wales, if rocked back on their heels, were not thrown off balance. It was a measure of their own talents that against opponents of this quality, and after such a reverse, they still won emphatically by a goal, a try and two dropped goals to a try and a dropped goal.

The Welsh tactics were to tie down the French back row before taking the campaign into the enemy camp, and in this they eventually succeeded, with Martin adding the bonus of clean possession from the lineout in his best performance for Wales so far. Meanwhile, making their twenty-fourth appearance together, an international record, the Edwards-Bennett partnership waited to exert an influence both calming and electifying.

Often this winter it was Edwards who stole the game, but on this day he had to give way to his stand-off. Bennett scored two tries, the first Welshman in his position to do so in an international since Raymond Ralph (Newport) twice cut through the French defence in 1931. In addition a conversion brought his total for the afternoon to ten points, and for Wales, in twenty-nine internationals, to 166, comfortably passing the European record of 158 points set by Tom Kiernan of Ireland. Add the forty-four points which Bennett had scored for the British Lions, and his 210 edged past Don Clarke's world record of 207 for New Zealand. Not that he had much time to think about that.

The first blow to the Welsh came after eighteen minutes

when they were living from hand to mouth to keep the French out and a forward, in desperation, tried to fly-kick clear. The ball ricocheted into the hands of Skréla who was bundled over for a try, and within six minutes France went further ahead as Viviès dropped a goal from an indirect penalty.

An immediate and positive counter-attack was required from the Welsh, and they provided it, practically clawing their way back to the French twenty-five. But once there they abruptly reversed the course of the game by scoring thirteen points in eight minutes.

At a French put-in the Welsh wheeled the scrum, Quinnell picked up to feed Edwards, and a quick pass put the ball into the hands of Bennett who jinked his way through for a try – which he converted. Wales were back in the game, and with a vengeance when next Edwards raced away from the lineout to drop a goal and snatch the lead. Finally Martin won yet another lineout to send Gravell crashing through the centre. From the ruck Edwards broke and put out a difficult pass which J. J. Williams had to take stud-high from the ground before lobbing inside to give Bennett his second try. So this brief, unscheduled spell of activity left Wales with a half-time lead of 13–7.

The second half couldn't be expected to continue at that pace, but the scores were still close, the struggle still intense enough to sustain the excitement. It was only in injury time, after 40 minutes' stalemate, that Wales broke through again. Bennett hoisted a high kick which brought a scrum in front of the French posts, and as the ball emerged the ubiquitous Fenwick pounced upon it to drop a goal. At which success was complete and the Welsh were left with only their own championship record to beat.

Scorers WALES – tries: Bennett 2; conversion: Bennett; dropped goals: Edwards, Fenwick. FRANCE – try: Skréla; dropped goal: Viviès.

Wales J. P. R. Williams (Bridgend); J. J. Williams (Llanelli),

R. W. R. Gravell (Llanelli), S. P. Fenwick (Bridgend), G. L. Evans (Newport); P. Bennett (Llanelli, capt.), G. O. Edwards (Cardiff); G. Price (Pontypool), R. W. Windsor (Pontypool), A. G. Faulkner (Pontypool), A. J. Martin (Aberavon), G. A. D. Wheel (Swansea), J. Squire (Newport), T. J. Cobner (Pontypool), D. L. Quinnell (Llanelli).

France J–M. Aguirre (Bagnères); D. Bustaffa (Carcassonne), R. Bertranne (Bagnères), C. Belescain (Bayonne), G. Novès (Toulouse); B. Viviès (Agen), J. Gallion (Toulouse); R. Paparemborde (Pau), A. Paco (Béziers), G. Cholley (Castres), F. Haget (Biarritz), M. Palmié (Béziers), J–C. Skréla (Toulouse), J–P. Rives (Toulouse), J–P. Bastiat (Dax, capt.).

Referee A. Welsby (England).

On the same day England beat Ireland 15–9 at Twickenham.

Championship Table 1978

	P	W	D	L	For	Ag	Pts
Wales	4	4	0	0	67	43	8
France	4	3	0	1	51	47	6
England	4	2	0	2	42	33	4
Ireland	4	1	0	3	46	54	2
Scotland	4	0	0	4	39	68	0

Welsh Tour of Australia

In mid-May Wales, captained by Terry Cobner, went to Australia as European champions for a month-long nine-match visit – the first they had ever paid to that country alone. It proved even more disastrous than the 1969 tour on which they twice lost to New Zealand but at least managed to beat Australia. This time, against restricted opposition, they lost four matches including both tests.

True, Edwards and Bennett felt unable to make the trip, but once the selectors had finally sorted out their preferences,

Wales were able to go into the second test with Holmes and Gareth Davies, the very half-backs who enabled them to win a fourth triple crown the following season. And at full strength they could field their complete championship back division and pack. But as injuries accumulated, one problem was to achieve anything like representative strength.

All the same that alone did not explain the poor results. Another factor was that the players had been through a particularly exacting season at home: their success had been bought at a high price in physical effort and concentration. And for those who were also British Lions there had been eighteen months of near-continuous rugby. They found it hard to respond whole-heartedly when they were called upon once more to raise their game.

Added to which the Australians were ruthlessly intent on success, and there were no neutral referees to give the Welsh the protection they felt they deserved. Or, for that matter, some benefit of the doubt when interpretation of the laws differed so widely. It was frustrating to return home with such a poor record to show for thirty-four tries scored and only seven conceded, and to lose both tests when in either match they scored two tries to one.

A favourite story from the tour was of the referee who said unguardedly to the Welsh scrum-half, 'It's not *your* ball, it's *our* ball.' Even the scrupulously fair-minded Gerald Davies later described one test in his autobiography as 'very much like one of the home countries playing in Pontypool, Llanelli or Aberavon with ten local players in the Welsh team and a local referee. And the visitors having no say whatsoever in this choice.

Australia 18 pts Wales 8 — *Brisbane, 11 June 1978*

Before the match Welsh objections to the Queensland referee, R. T. Burnett, had been overruled by the Australian Rugby Union, and not only was the spirit of the game soured by the dispute but the tourists were rattled by Burnett's rulings, particularly his judgement of off-side. They failed to play with any fluency, and although they scored two good tries they went down by a goal and four penalties. It was the widest margin by which Australia had ever beaten Wales.

The man of the match was undoubtedly the Australian stand-off, Paul McLean, who not only scored fourteen points with his goals but kicked from the hand with great variety and accuracy. The Australian forwards, too, performed with unexpected authority.

Except at half-back (where the veteran Brynmor Williams was preferred to Holmes as Gareth Davies's partner) Wales played their championship side. And had they concentrated on their game instead of allowing themselves to be distracted by the referee's inconsistencies they might have scored sufficient points to withstand the McLean barrage.

As it was they got a try in either half, Gerald Davies running on to a diagonal kick from Gareth Davies to cross near the corner, and Brynmor Williams reappearing to take Gravell's inside pass and dive over. From being 8–4 down at half-time they close to 9–8 towards the end of the third quarter. But from a ruck near the Welsh line Australia passed quickly to the left and Crowe was able to circle to the posts before he put down. McLean's place kicking settled the matter.

Scorers AUSTRALIA – try: Crowe, conversion: McLean; penalties: McLean 4. WALES – tries: T. G. R. Davies, D. B. Williams.

Australia L. E. Monaghan (New South Wales); P. G. Batch (Queensland), A. G. Slack (Queensland), M. Knight (NSW), P. J. Crowe (NSW); P. E. McLean (Queensland), R. G. Hauser (Queensland); S. J. Pilecki (Queensland), P. A. Horton (Queensland), S. C. Finnane (NSW), G. Fay (NSW), D. W. Hillhouse (Queensland), G. Cornelsen (Queensland), A. A. Shaw (Queensland, capt.), M. E. Loane (Queensland).

Wales J. P. R. Williams (Bridgend); T. G. R. Davies (Cardiff), S. P. Fenwick (Bridgend), R. W. R. Gravell (Llanelli), J. J. Williams (Llanelli); W. G. Davies (Cardiff), D. B. Williams (Newport); G. Price (Pontypool), R. W. Windsor

(Pontypool), A. G. Faulkner (Pontypool), G. A. D. Wheel (Swansea), A. J. Martin (Aberavon), J. Squire (Newport), T. J. Cobner (Pontypool, capt.), D. L. Quinnell (Llanelli).

Referee R. T. Burnett (Queensland).

Australia 19 pts Wales 17 *Sydney Cricket Ground, 17 June 1978*

Against the identical side in the second test, Wales rallied their forces despite even greater problems. Their entire back row of Cobner, Squire and Quinnell had to cry off through injury, and as a seemingly desperate measure (although it worked out well in practice) the versatile JPR was converted into a flank-forward to replace Cobner. This left Alun Donovan to play at full-back and Gerald Davies to captain Wales for the first time in his forty-sixth and final international. Stuart Lane and Clive Davies won their first caps on the flank and at No 8 while Terry Holmes won his as Gareth Davies's scrum-half.

These, however, were only the teething troubles. Within three minutes of the start a fight broke out in which Price, apparently struck from behind, went down with a double fracture of the jaw; although the assailant was identified from the stands and on the field, he went unpunished. After thirty-six minutes Donovan, too, went off with a damaged knee, and Gareth Evans, who substituted for him, fractured his cheekbone in the first tackle. Since Wales had used up both their replacements, Evans stayed on the field, as did J. J. Williams when he twisted an ankle, but J. P. R. Williams was forced to drop back in reinforcement leaving the pack with only seven men.

All the same, Wales did most of the attacking and might well have won if they hadn't left Loane unmarked to score a try from the lineout. Otherwise it was McLean who again won the day for Australia, kicking twelve points to bring his total to twenty-six out of thirty-seven in the two internationals, with Monaghan adding an excellent dropped goal from forty yards.

The two Welsh tries came from Holmes who barged over from a five-yard scrum, and from Gerald Davies in a late ten-yard burst to the line. It was Davies's twentieth try for Wales, so equalling Gareth Edwards's record. Had it been converted the Welsh would have drawn. Instead they left happier with their own performance but still dismayed by Australian refereeing and convinced that McLean's decisive dropped goal had in fact passed wide of the posts.

Scorers AUSTRALIA – try: Loane; dropped goals: Monaghan, McLean; penalty goals: McLean 3. WALES – tries: Holmes, T. G. R. Davies; dropped goal: W. G. Davies; penalty goals: W. G. Davies 2.

Australia L. E. Monaghan (New South Wales); P. G. Batch (Queensland), A. G. Slack (Queensland), M. Knight (NSW), P. J. Crowe (NSW); P. E. McLean (Queensland), R. G. Hauser (Queensland); S. J. Pilecki (Queensland), P. A. Horton (Queensland), S. C. Finnane (NSW), G. Fay (NSW), D. W. Hillhouse (Queensland), G. Cornelsen (Queensland), A. A. Shaw (Queensland, capt.), M. E. Loane (Queensland).

Wales A. J. Donovan (Swansea); T. G. R. Davies (Cardiff, capt.), R. W. R. Gravell (Llanelli), S. P. Fenwick (Bridgend), J. J. Williams (Llanelli); W. G. Davies (Cardiff), T. D. Holmes (Cardiff); G. Price (Pontypool), R. W. Windsor (Pontypool), A. G. Faulkner (Pontypool), G. A. D. Wheel (Swansea), A. J. Martin (Aberavon); J. P. R. Williams (Bridgend); S. M. Lane (Cardiff), C. Davies (Newbridge). Replacements: S. J. Richardson (Aberavon) for A. Price, 5 min; G. L. Evans (Newport) for A. J. Donovan, 36 min.

Referee R. G. Byres (NSW).

17

The Unexpected Encore: 1978–79

Rarely happier than when they are predicting disaster, the Welsh had a lot to be cheerfully gloomy about that autumn. Now that the third consecutive jewel had been set in the crown, what was there to look forward to? The Australian tour had been a flop. Phil Bennett and Gerald Davies were following Gareth Edwards into retirement, leaving JPR as the sole survivor of the old guard among the backs. The country's most recent captain, Terry Cobner, was also on his way out. It had been a marvellous decade, but surely it must now be someone else's turn?

Reserves of talent also seemed to be running low. Argentina, on a mainly English tour, paid a single visit to Wales on 17 October and, led by the stylish architect, Hugo Porta, beat the 'B' team 17–14 at Stradey Park. Worse still, in the 'B' international at Aberavon on 2 December, Wales went down 18–31 to France. In between the senior side, though putting up a heartening performance, had lost by a single, dubious point to New Zealand. The prospects for the international championship were unappealing.

Yet, as it proved, Wales's second-best was still good enough. They played only one really convincing game, eventually making tinder of their perpetual chopping-block, England. But equally they lost only one match – again by a single point – in Paris. And since France, having drawn in Dublin, went on to commit tactical suicide at Twickenham, that defeat cost the Welsh only the grand slam. By mid-March they had seized their fourth triple crown in four years, their fourth championship in five. When would it end?

There were no major law changes during the season, but there was growing concern at two particular developments in the game. One was the anarchic and potentially dangerous 'pile-up' which occurred when a player, not having been tackled, kept possession of the ball at the bottom of a heap of bodies. The other – linked to this perhaps by a feeling of frustration – was an increase in violence on the field of play.

Two particularly gory incidents made headlines. John Ashworth, the New Zealand prop, raking away at the ashes of a ruck, drove a stud through JPR's cheek in the All Blacks' match against Bridgend. And Chris Ralston similarly received a horrifying gash on the side of the head from Anon. of Llanelli in a club match at Richmond. No individual was punished for either assault, nor was any acceptable answer found to the basic problem.

The Ninth All Blacks

They may have lacked the élan of their forerunners, but spurred on by the industrious Graham Mourie and as disciplined as ever in their close support play, the ninth All Blacks proved extremely hard to beat. Only Munster brought them down, 12–0 at Limerick, fiercely knocking over a side which had set out to move the ball freely and seemed unable to switch its tactics. The All Blacks didn't make that mistake again. They won all seventeen of their other matches, scoring 364 points to 147, and bringing off the first grand slam against the home countries in the history of New Zealand tours.

Wales 12 pts New Zealand 13 — *Cardiff, 11 November 1978*

It was twenty-five years since Wales had beaten the All Blacks, but until the final moments it seemed as though the record had at last played itself out. In a ferocious struggle Wales took a 9–0 lead, kept 12–4 ahead until just before the interval, and with only two minutes to go looked like winning 12–10. Then came an incident as rich in controversy as the disallowed

Deans 'try' of 1905 – but this time deciding the match in the All Blacks' favour.

A lineout was formed near the Welsh twenty-five, and out of the confusion which followed only two incontrovertible facts emerged: a Welsh forward was penalized for lifting himself on an opponent's shoulder; and McKechnie, who had come on as a substitute in the fifth minute when Currie's jaw was broken, with great composure kicked his third and the winning goal.

If it had all been that simple the Welsh could only have blamed themselves for pushing their luck at a lineout so close to their goal-line and to the final whistle. But over the next few days that lineout was repeatedly shown in slow motion and endlessly analysed on television in Wales. It became clear that Haden, the New Zealand lock, had taken a dive from the lineout to give the impression that he had been shoved. At the same time it appeared that Oliver had backed into Wheel (the apparent lifting culprit, although Mr Quittenton, the referee, didn't name him) before himself running out of the line. There was a general feeling that the All Blacks, far from deserving a penalty, had earned an Oscar for their acting.

At times it had been a fractious game, with a couple of bouts of fighting and a warning to Bush. But it had also been stirring and vigorous, with Wales the more successful ball-winners and ball-users. Their veteran pack showed no hint of declining power, the Pontypool front row continuing to live their legend. And the new half-backs – the Cardiff club partnership of Terry Holmes and Gareth Davies – launched themselves before the Welsh public with astonishing confidence, keeping the All Blacks under pressure with their kicking. All the same they hadn't the experience to split their opponents' defence, and the Welsh kept ahead solely on penalties: three from Davies and a typical forty-five-yarder from Fenwick.

New Zealand, hard-pressed, did manage to construct a try, Osborne kicking diagonally to the right and Stuart Wilson running and pouncing on the ball as it rolled across near the corner. Perhaps that try and the tenacity of the All Blacks in fighting back from the cliff-edge might have reconciled Welsh supporters to the result. But by the time they had watched the action replays of that final lineout they found it hard to believe that they had really seen justice done.

Scorers WALES – penalty goals: Davies 3, Fenwick. NEW ZEALAND – try: Wilson; penalty goals: McKechnie 3.

Wales J. P. R. Williams (Bridgend, capt.); J. J. Williams (Llanelli), R. W. R. Gravell (Llanelli), S. P. Fenwick (Bridgend), C. F. W. Rees (London Welsh); W. G. Davies (Cardiff), T. D. Holmes (Cardiff); A. G. Faulkner (Pontypool), R. W. Windsor (Pontypool), G. Price (Pontypool), A. J. Martin (Aberavon), G. A. D. Wheel (Swansea), R. Ringer (Ebbw Vale), J. Squire (Pontypool), D. L. Quinnell (Llanelli).

New Zealand C. J. Currie (Canterbury); S. S. Wilson (Wellington), B. J. Robertson (Counties), W. M. Osborne (Wanganui), B. G. Williams (Auckland); O. D. Bruce (Auckland), D. S. Loveridge (Taranaki); B. R. Johnstone (Auckland), A. G. Dalton (Counties), W. K. Bush (Canterbury), A. M. Haden (Auckland), F. J. Oliver (Otago), L. N. Rutledge (Southland), G. N. K. Mourie (Taranaki, capt.), G. A. Seear (Otago). Replacement: B. J. McKechnie (Southland) for C. J. Currie, 5 min.

Referee R. C. Quittenton (England).

The International Championship

Scotland 13 pts Wales 19 *Murrayfield, 20 January 1979*

Wales made only one change – indeed only a change of initials – from the team that played the All Blacks, bringing in Elgan Rees of Neath for a first cap in place of the London Welsh wing-threequarter, Clive Rees. And at half-time, when they were trailing 13–6, they must have wondered whether their confidence in some others hadn't been misplaced.

So far only two men had scored – Fenwick kicking two penalties and Irvine landing three as well as crossing for the only try. But while Fenwick's first penalty had put Wales ahead in the opening minute, the Scots were unshaken. With the wind behind them they kept up the pressure, charging up, cavalry-fashion, on Lawson's deep, diagonal kicks. And from the attacking position they earned they were never afraid to run the ball.

After twenty-four minutes their reward came as Gareth Davies failed to find touch. Irvine, fielding the ball, began a handling movement – involving McGeechan, Rutherford and Tomes – which he completed by popping up again to dive over in the corner.

Against the wind in the second half, however, Scotland failed to score at all. Magnificently led by Quinnell, the Welsh pack used the greater weight of their bodies and their experience to subdue the Scots. Their front five bent and broke them in the tight, and a series of forceful surges by Jeff Squire completed the destruction.

Fenwick promptly opened the second half, as he had the first, with a penalty goal, and within eight minutes the scores were level. JPR came into the line, as ever, to smash through a tackle and put in the perfect chip-kick to the corner where Rees followed up to score his inaugural try for Wales.

It went unconverted, and for nearly half an hour the game was deadlocked. But the increasing dominance of the Welsh pack, the mature steadiness of Holmes and Davies in their first championship match, and the crushing defence of Fenwick in mid-field denied the Scots all but one scoring chance: a long-range penalty which Irvine missed. At the same time the constant wear and tear was beginning to undermine the Scottish resistance.

In the end the Welsh forwards stormed back into the Scottish twenty-five after a high kick by Fenwick had put Irvine in trouble. Twice Quinnell got to within a foot of the line from successive pick-ups at the back of the scrum. And then, five minutes from no-side, the Scots lost a scrum against the head on their line, the Welsh wheeled the ball over, and Holmes was there to drop on the ball. Fenwick's conversion brought the final points of the match.

Even so soon the Welsh could think about another triple crown. They had survived what was potentially their hardest match; they would be playing Ireland and England on home ground. The championship was another matter, with France to be faced in Paris. But the news from Dublin was heartening. The French had already compromised themselves by only drawing with Ireland.

Scorers SCOTLAND – try: Irvine; penalty goals: Irvine 3. WALES – tries: Rees, Holmes; conversion: Fenwick; penalty goals: Fenwick 3.

Scotland A. R. Irvine (Heriot's F.P.); K. W. Robertson (Melrose), J. M. Renwick (Hawick), I. R. McGeechan (Headingley, capt.), B. H. Hay (Boroughmuir); J. Y. Rutherford (Selkirk), A. J. M. Lawson (London Scottish); J. McLauchlan (Jordanhill), C. T. Deans (Hawick), R. F. Cunningham (Gala), A. J. Tomes (Hawick), A. H. McHarg (London Scottish), M. A. Biggar (London Scottish), G. Dickson (Gala), I. K. Lambie (Watsonians).

Wales J. P. R. Williams (Bridgend, capt.); H. E. Rees (Neath), S. P. Fenwick (Bridgend), R. W. R. Gravell (Llanelli), J. J. Williams (Llanelli); W. G. Davies (Cardiff), T. D. Holmes (Cardiff); A. G. Faulkner (Pontypool), R. W. Windsor (Pontypool), G. Price (Pontypool), A. J. Martin (Aberavon), G. A. D. Wheel (Swansea), P. Ringer (Llanelli), J. Squire (Pontypool), D. J. Quinnell (Llanelli).

Referee F. Palmade (France).

On the same day Ireland and France drew 9–9 at Lansdowne Road.

Wales 24 pts Ireland 21 *Cardiff, 3 February 1979*

This was almost Murrayfield in reverse. After leading 21–9

a quarter of an hour from the finish, the unchanged Welsh side managed to win by only three points. And in the mounting tension of the final quarter Ireland put together their highest score in all their eighteen games with Wales – and in Cardiff at that.

Yet the match was not as exciting as the result on the page makes it seem. In the end it resolved into a duel between two remarkable place-kickers: the Welsh centre, Fenwick, and the Irish stand-off, Ward. Both had only one failure, but crucially Fenwick had the extra chance. So while Ward totted up thirteen points from two conversions and three penalties, Fenwick went one better with four penalties to score sixteen and pass his century for Wales – a feat previously accomplished only by Phil Bennett.

Apart from the fact that goal-kicking is the least thrilling way of scoring points, there was a lack of real suspense. That may seem strange to say since one more score could have settled the game in Ireland's favour. But the Irish narrowed the gap only in the thirty-eighth minute of the second half. They had left themselves too much to do in too little time, and Wales always seemed to have something in hand.

Just the same it was an unconvincing Welsh performance. They played carelessly. Davies, although he kicked superbly and made the occasional clean break, received an indifferent service from Holmes. The centres, Fenwick and Gravell, showed up well only in defence. And in general the team displayed less aggression than Ireland, whose pack was continually erupting away from rucks and mauls.

The Irish were six points up before Davies found their weak point with a massive kick up-field. Spring let the ball bounce, and Martin galloped on to it for their opening try. Their second came after half-time (at which point Wales led 12–9) when Holmes worried Patterson at the scrum, and a wild pass back to nobody in particular was gratefully snapped by up Ringer.

Ireland's two tries came during their late revival when McLennan brilliantly picked up a Ward chip ahead, snatching the ball up on the half-volley, and later Patterson broke brilliantly from a ruck. But by the time Ward converted, the opportunity to produce any further shocks had run out.

Scorers WALES – tries: Martin, Ringer; conversions: Fenwick 2; penalty goals: Fenwick 4. IRELAND – tries: McLennan, Patterson; conversions: Ward 2; penalty goals: Ward 3.

Wales J. P. R. Williams (Bridgend, capt.); H. E. Rees (Neath), R. W. R. Gravell (Llanelli), S. P. Fenwick (Bridgend), J. J. Williams (Llanelli); W. G. Davies (Cardiff), T. D. Holmes (Cardiff); A. G. Faulkner (Pontypool), R. W. Windsor (Pontypool), G. Price (Pontypool), A. J. Martin (Aberavon), G. A. D. Wheel (Swansea), P. Ringer (Llanelli), J. Squire (Pontypool), D. L. Quinnell (Llanelli). Replacement: S. M. Lane (Cardiff) for G. A. D. Wheel, 48 min.

Ireland R. M. Spring (Lansdowne); T. J. Kennedy (St Mary's College), A. R. McKibbin (London Irish), P. P. McNaughton (Greystones), A. C. McLennan (Wanderers); A. J. P. Ward (Garryowen), C. S. Patterson (Instonians); P. A. Orr (Old Wesley), P. C. Whelan (Garryowen), G. A. J. McLoughlin (Shannon), M. I. Keane (Lansdowne), H. W. Steele (Ballymena), C. C. Tucker (Shannon), J. F. Slattery (Blackrock College, capt.), M. E. Gibson (Lansdowne).

Referee A. M. Hosie (Scotland).

On the same day England and Scotland drew 7–7 at Twickenham.

France 14 pts Wales 13 *Parc de Princes, 17 February 1979*

For the match which Wales was always least likely to win they made two changes. Wheel, injured against the Irish, had to make way for his Swansea second row partner, Clegg. And to bring more pace and variety into the centre, the selectors dropped Gravell in favour of David Richards, normally the Swansea stand-off.

In the event the reshuffle made no significant difference. On a Siberian afternoon the French went into the attack with wolfish appetites, led by Rives who played his greatest game for his country. Rives constructed and he demolished, and his foraging for the loose ball had a fanatical intensity. The French mid-field was faster and more incisive – though Richards, forced into a mainly defensive role, had little real chance to show his talents. And Gourdon proved his title to the right wing with subtlety and power and two fine tries.

The Welsh forwards were comparatively slow and uncertain particularly in the back row, and it was largely due to Holmes that Wales kept defeat to a single point. He came of age here. His harassing of Gallion disrupted the French attack, and his tackling prevented at least three or four French tries. With limited opportunities he cleverly varied his game, kicking skilfully into the box and, for the first time during the season, providing an unfaultable service.

All the same Wales twice took the lead in the first half, and at the interval the match was drawn at 7–7. Fenwick opened the scoring with a penalty, and, after Gourdon, with ominous ease, had cut inside Williams for a try, Wales came back with another. They called a four-man lineout in a strong attacking position; the French won the ball but let it run loose, and Holmes crashed through a débris of bodies to touch down. An Aguirre penalty completed the half.

The second half brought two more penalties for Fenwick and one for Aguirre, but the critical one-point difference in the final score came from a try. It was beautifully constructed: a surge by Novès, two successively won rucks, a quick pass from Gallion, and Bertranne put Gourdon over once more in the corner.

France kept the best of a patchy season for this match, which they described as 'the roof of the championship', and Wales could only acknowledge them masters. France were now favourites for the title, for who would have bet that a fortnight later poor tactics and even poorer place-kicking would bring their defeat at Twickenham?

Scorers FRANCE – tries: Gourdon 2; penalty goals: Aguirre 2. WALES – try: Holmes; penalty goals: Fenwick 3.

France J–M. Aguirre (Bagnères); J–F. Gourdon (Bagnères), R. Bertranne (Bagnères), B. Belescain (Bayonne), G. Novès (Toulouse); A. Caussade (Lourdes), G. Gallion (Toulon); A. Vaquerin (Béziers), A. Paco (Béziers), R. Paparemborde (Pau), F. Haget (Biarritz), A. Maleig (Oloron), J–L Joinel (Brive), J–P. Rives (Toulouse, capt.), A Guilbert (Toulon).

Wales J. P. R. Williams (Bridgend, capt.); H. E. Rees (Neath), D. S. Richards (Swansea), S. P. Fenwick (Bridgend), J. J. Williams (Llanelli); W. G. Davies (Cardiff), T. D. Holmes (Cardiff); A. G. Faulkner (Pontypool), R. W. Windsor (Pontypool), G. Price (Pontypool), A. J. Martin (Aberavon), B. G. Clegg (Swansea), P. Ringer (Llanelli), J. Squire (Pontypool), D. L. Quinnell (Llanelli).

Referee D. Burnett (Ireland).

On the same day Ireland beat England 12–7 at Lansdowne Road. On 3 March England beat France 7–6 at Twickenham; Scotland and Ireland drew 11–11 at Murrayfield.

Wales 27 pts England 3 *Cardiff, 17 March 1979*

Looking at that scoreline it's hard to credit that before this match England had perfectly respectable hopes of winning the championship. Like France they had three points to Wales's four. So victory over Wales would give them the title outright if France, on the same afternoon, lost to Scotland in Paris, and at least a half-share in the title if France won.

Nor was it simply a matter of mathematics. England had just beaten France, the only side to have beaten Wales, and were full of new-found confidence. Meanwhile Wales were in some trouble. Wheel was still on the injured list, and was replaced this time by the veteran Mike Roberts, uncapped for four seasons. And of the Pontypool front row only Price was fit to play. Phillips, the Cardiff hooker, and Richardson, the Aberavon prop, had to fill the considerable gaps.

Yet all these hopes and doubts proved groundless. Except for a short period in the second half, England never summoned up the spirit of their victory over France. Wales, on the other hand, played their finest rugby of the season: disciplined and efficient in the pack; fluent, skilful and varied among the backs. Holmes with his strength and ability, and Davies with his whipcord elegance, looked as though they had reserved the Welsh half-back positions for the next decade. Persistence with Richards at centre was repaid: he scored the first try and brought a long-absent cutting edge to the threequarter play. And alongside him Fenwick, although missing five penalties, compensated with a hand in three tries.

Even so there was little early suggestion of England's ultimate collapse. After an hour Wales led only 7–3. England were on the counter-attack and seemed to have the perfect opportunity to break back into the game when, at that point, JPR received a bad gash on the calf. Like a wounded general leaving the battle, he redeployed his troops, gave his final orders and hobbled off to have eight stitches sewn in his wound.

But far from benefiting England the reverse served to rally Wales. After Ringer and Fenwick had nailed Hignell to clear their line and raise the siege, Mike Roberts, responding to the critics with undiminished energy, seized a loose ball at the lineout to score a critical try. And as England realized that their opportunity had slipped away, Ringer from Fenwick's pass, and J. J. Williams from Richards's, scored two quick tries to put the game beyond argument. Finally Clive Griffiths, who had come on as substitute to JPR showed that no-one is irreplaceable by confidently picking up the ball and running thirty-five yards before punting ahead for Rees to score. Abruptly England had foundered without trace.

For Wales, an unprecedented fourth triple crown as well as the championship. For England, their greatest defeat at Welsh hands since 1905. For J. P. R. Williams, a triumphant end to his eleven-year international career (or so it seemed at the time). And for Fenwick, despite his misses, a total of thirty-eight championship points to equal Phil Bennett's record.

Scorers WALES – tries: Richards, Roberts, Ringer, J. J. Williams; conversions: Martin, Fenwick; dropped goal: Davies. ENGLAND – penalty goal: Bennett.

Wales J. P. R. Williams (Bridgend, capt.); H. E. Rees (Neath), D. S. Richards (Swansea), S. P. Fenwick (Bridgend), J. J. Williams (Llanelli); W. G. Davies (Cardiff), T. D. Holmes (Cardiff); S. J. Richardson (Aberavon), A. Phillips (Cardiff), G. Price (Pontypool), M. G. Roberts (London Welsh), A. J. Martin (Aberavon), P. Ringer (Llanelli), J. Squire (Pontypool), D. L. Quinnell (Llanelli). Replacement: C. Griffiths (Llanelli) for J. P. R. Williams, 60 min.

England A. J. Hignell (Bristol); P. J. Squires (Harrogate), R. M. Cardus (Roundav), P. W. Dodge (Leicester), M. A. C. Slemen (Liverpool); W. N. Bennett (London Welsh); P. Kingston (Gloucester); C. E. Smart (Newport), P. J. Wheeler (Leicester), G. S. Pearce (Northampton), N. E. Horton (Toulouse), W. B. Beaumont (Fylde, capt.), M. Rafter (Bristol), A. Neary (Broughton Park), J. P. Scott (Cardiff).

Referee J–P. Bonnet (France).

On the same day France beat Scotland 21–17 at Parc des Princes.

Championship Table 1979

	P	W	D	L	For	Ag	Pts
Wales	4	3	0	1	83	51	6
France	4	2	1	1	50	46	5
Ireland	4	1	2	1	53	51	4
England	4	1	1	2	24	52	3
Scotland	4	0	2	2	48	48	2

18
Unacceptable Phase of Rugby: 1979–80

'It was war on the field and like *M*A*S*H* in the medical room,' said Leon Walkden, the RFU honorary doctor, after the England–Wales game. And those who watched it at Twickenham or on television found little to quarrel with in the description. It was a match of much courage, some craft and great drama and excitement; but it was played in such a mean-spirited mood that its final effect was chilling. After a quarter of an hour, during which the forwards had set about each other as though they would only be satisfied by total physical submission, Paul Ringer, the Llanelli flanker, was sent from the field for a late and dangerous tackle on John Horton, the England stand-off. That expulsion overshadowed the match; reduced to fourteen men for more than an hour's play, Wales lost 9–8. And the match overshadowed the rest of the season for Wales.

They had begun the championship with considerable promise. On the opening Saturday at Cardiff, in what was generally considered the season's summit meeting, Wales decisively beat France 18–9 – stopping dead in its tracks the side which had returned in triumph from beating the All Blacks at Auckland on Bastille Day.

It was a comprehensive victory, but already there were warning signs which Wales should have heeded. Analysis of the television film of the game revealed a number of acts of foul play which cast doubts on the self-control of various players. Similarly, when England won in Paris a fortnight later, the cameras picked up misdemeanours by two England forwards in particular. But both selection panels declined to have anything to do with 'trial by television' and no players were dropped. Wales, too, missed the opportunity to recall Derek Quinnell who, by experience and temperament, was probably the man best qualified to defuse a potentially explosive situation.

So two unchanged and unbeaten teams, both with credible ambitions to bring off the grand slam, came together in circumstances of heightened tension. And the sending off of Ringer at Twickenham didn't stop the series of kicking, knee-ing and punching incidents which disfigured the game. English players afterwards required twenty-two stitches in their wounds, the Welsh six, and there was an immediate public protest at the spectacle. Many former internationals claimed that they had known times as hard or even harder in their day; and no doubt there was some over-reaction, especially outside the game. But there was also a genuine and well-found concern at rugby's inability to legislate against danger areas in the game and to control its unrulier players.

Throughout the rest of the championship the Welsh never completely lost their sense of embarrassment and bewilderment. They played the Scots at Cardiff a fortnight later as though in kid gloves, winning 17–6 more by innate skill than by force. But the Irish were lying in wait at Lansdowne Road in the final match, ready to destroy any opponents with less than complete self-confidence.

Had Wales won there and England lost their Calcutta Cup match at Murrayfield on the same afternoon, the title would have been shared. But England were keyed-up to seize the day splendidly 30–18, while Wales let it slip through their fingers 21–7. Only the announcement that weekend of the Lions team for South Africa brought a little balm for their wounded pride. Wales, with twelve players, contributed the largest national segment. Others hadn't lost faith in Welsh rugby even if, for the moment, the Welsh had lost a little faith in themselves. It was a fresh beginning.

Mervyn Davies, the finest No. 8 of his time, rising for the ball at the back of the lineout.

(Far left) Mervyn Davies meeting head-on the tackle of Alistair McHarg in an exiles' match between the Welsh and Scottish.

(Left) Derek Quinnell making off with the ball in one of his too-few appearances for Wales.

England v. Wales at Twickenham, 1980. *(Left)* Geoff Wheel and Billy Beaumont get to grips in one of the opening passages of arms, fists and feet.

(Overleaf) The Irish referee, DIN Burnett, sends off the Welsh flanker, Paul Ringer, for a late and dangerous tackle on John Horton.

The Romanians in Wales

When can an emerging rugby nation be said to have emerged? The Romanians, like the Argentinians of 1976, proved to be scarcely distinguishable in either talent or technique from their supposed seniors on the International Board. On the five-match tour of Wales in the autumn of 1979 they beat Ebbw Vale, Pontypridd, North Wales and West Wales before losing by a single point – as the Pumas had done – to the national side. Their total score over the tour was 86–42.

Again only an unofficial Test was offered. Yet while the Wales XV – which turned out before an almost packed house at Cardiff on 6 October and won 13–12 – was in part experimental, it was not rashly chosen:

P. Morgan (Llanelli); R. W. R. Gravell (Llanelli), S. P. Fenwick (Bridgend), D. S. Richards (Swansea), J. Griffiths (Llanelli); W. G. Davies (Cardiff), T. D. Holmes (Cardiff); C. Williams (Swansea), R. W. Windsor (Pontypool), G. Price (Pontypool), R. Norster (Cardiff), A. J. Martin (Aberavon), P. Ringer (Llanelli), D. L. Quinnell (Llanelli, capt.), J. Squire (Pontypool).

The Welsh found themselves up against a highly-organized side, in defence particularly, with good lineout jumpers, a mobile back row and an eager scrum-half in Paraschiv. They needed all their character to assert themselves over Romania, and only fairly late in the game found their touch and their verve in attack.

Scores were finely balanced. Fenwick's opening penalty was matched by Constantin to make it 3–3 at the break, and Constantin's second penalty by a calm dropped goal from Gareth Davies. But when Romania got their try – Ionescu smashing across from a maul, and Bucos converting to make it 12–6 – it did provoke a new urgency of effort from the Welsh. Davies, Fenwick, Morgan and Davies again combined to put Jeff Griffiths over on the wing. And Davies finally tilted the game in Wales's favour with his second dropped goal. When Wales were lagging, Quinnell's steady captaincy had proved decisive. It was a shame that, first because of injury and then from neglect, he was not to play any part in the championship.

The International Championship

Wales 18 pts France 9 *Cardiff, 19 January 1980*

In almost every respect this was a magnificent start for Wales. With only five men left of the side which had won the grand slam two seasons before – Fenwick in the threequarter line and Price, Martin, Wheel and Squire in the pack – the Welsh seemed to have found another combination capable of doing the same again. They virtually destroyed the momentum of the confident French side – which had anticipated their first win at Cardiff since 1968 – in scoring a goal and three tries to a goal and a dropped goal.

Their forwards overwhelmed the French in the scrums – helped by the dubious choice of Salas to prop opposite the mighty Price. And rarely have they arrived so quickly and effectively at every situation where they were needed. Holmes and Davies were getting surer and more authoritative with every game they played at half-back. And remarkably even the threequarter line, with Fenwick and Richards running incisively, outpaced the French.

The really serious French challenge petered out in the first quarter, although by that time they had taken the lead when Wales allowed them a three-to-one overlap in the line. Costes cut through for Paco to set up a ruck from which Caussade dropped an untroubled goal. Eventually, however, their pressure was relieved by a seventy-yard kick by Davies, and from that point Wales cut loose.

After thirty-four minutes and several near-misses with runs and kicks, Holmes, Squire, Phillips and Fenwick, working the ball away from a ruck, put Rees over for a try and a 4–3 half-time advantage. This Wales increased with a burrowing try from Holmes in the Gareth Edwards manner when the ball went loose at a wheeled scrum. And since Davies made the conversion, they were able to keep ahead even when some clever running in the French mid-field brought a try by Marchal which Caussade, too, converted.

Immediately Wales replied with a move in which Davies handled twice before giving out to Richards for a try. And six minutes from the end, with Wales now in complete control as they carried the play to the French or forced them back with the precision of their half-backs' kicks, they delivered the *coup de grâce*. Martin stole the ball from a French palm eight yards out and Price, the people's hero, stormed over for the final try. There was a month to go before the next game, at Twickenham, but Wales seemed to have laid an immovable foundation for the season.

Scorers WALES – tries: Rees, Holmes, Richards, Price; conversion: Davies. FRANCE – try: Marchal; conversion: Caussade; dropped goal: Caussade.

Wales W. R. Blyth (Swansea); H. E. Rees (Neath), S. D. Richards (Swansea), S. P. Fenwick (Bridgend), L. Keen (Aberavon); W. G. Davies (Cardiff), T. D. Holmes (Cardiff); C. Williams (Swansea), A. J. Phillips (Cardiff), G. Price (Pontypool), A. J. Martin (Aberavon), G. A. D. Wheel (Swansea), P. Ringer (Llanelli), J. Squire (Pontypool, capt.), E. T. Butler (Pontypool).

France J–M. Aguirre (Bagnères); D. Bustaffa (Carcassonne), R. Bertranne (Bagnères), D. Codorniou (Narbonne), F. Costes (Montferrand); A. Caussade (Lourdes), J. Gallion (Toulon); P. Salas (Narbonne), A. Paco (Béziers), R. Paparemborde (Pau), F. Haget (Biarritz), J–F. Marchal (Lourdes), J–P. Rives (Toulouse, capt.), J–L. Joinel (Brive), A. Maleig (Oloron).

Referee A. M. Hosie (Scotland).

On the same afternoon England beat Ireland 24–9 at Twickenham, and a fortnight later (2 February), when Wales had a bye, beat France 17–3 at Parc des Princes. On that afternoon, too, Ireland beat Scotland 22–15 at Lansdowne Road.

England 9 pts Wales 8 *Twickenham, 16 February 1980*

The English, with two victories behind them – including their first in Paris for sixteen years – felt that at last it was to be their year. Wales, with no less passionate certainty, were convinced that their new generation of players was capable of outdoing the old. So with unwise accusations from the English camp that Price deliberately collapsed scrummages, and with general predictions that this would be the match, if not the blood match, of the season, the two sides met in an unhealthy atmosphere of emotion. Even when Paul Ringer, after fifteen minutes, became only the third player ever sent off in the championship, his expulsion did little to reduce the temperature. Although both sides were upset by the incident, the ill-will simmered on. The Englishmen Colclough, Beaumont, Smith and Scott, and the Welsh hooker, Phillips, all needed stitches after the affray, while Uttley had to leave the field at half-time.

In a sense it was as much a hollow victory for England as it was an embarrassing defeat for the Welsh. Between the ugly incidents and stoppages, Wales had played the cooler, more creative rugby. But since they were cast as the villains and did little to repudiate it, Wales were in no position to maintain that, having scored the only two tries of the match, they were unfairly beaten by Hare's three penalties for England.

Setting aside what the French would aptly describe as 'the brutalities', this was a thoroughly engrossing and – especially in the second half – exciting match. There was no score while the sides were still at full strength, only a narrow miss at a long-range penalty by Fenwick. The Ringer incident, however, was further punished by Hare's first penalty, and Wales, with an hour to play with fourteen men, looked in a desperate position. Yet within two minutes they were ahead. The ball eluded Smith behind a scrum close to the England line, and Squire dived on and over for a try. That one point separated the sides not only to the end of a tense first half but to the end of the first hour.

Wales, too, had their penalty chances, and four men – Fenwick, Davies, Martin and Blyth – failed in turn to take them. Eventually, in the sixty-fifth minute, Hare succeeded with what might well have been the conclusive kick. But again Wales came back as Phillips charged down a clearance kick by Smith, turned adroitly inwards and drew the defence to give a scoring pass outside to Rees who put down in the corner. Only two minutes to go, and Wales looked to have saved the game. But there was still time for England's last attack and Hare's third penalty from near the right touchline. Wales saw their prospects of a grand slam and a fifth consecutive triple crown disappear between the posts.

Scorers ENGLAND – penalty goals: Hare 3. WALES – tries: Squire, Rees.

England W. H. Hare (Leicester); J. Carleton (Orrell), C. R. Woodward (Leicester), P. W. Dodge (Leicester), M. A. C. Slemen (Liverpool); J. P. Horton (Bath), S. J. Smith (Sale); F. E. Cotton (Sale), P. J. Wheeler (Leicester), P. Blakeway (Gloucester), W. B. Beaumont (Fylde, capt.), M. J. Colclough (Angoulême), A. Neary (Broughton Park), R. M. Uttley (Wasps), J. P. Scott (Cardiff). Substitute: M. Rafter (Bristol) for R. M. Uttley, 40 min.

Wales W. R. Blyth (Swansea); H. E. Rees (Neath), D. S. Richards (Swansea), S. P. Fenwick (Bridgend), L. Keen (Aberavon); W. G. Davies (Cardiff), T. D. Holmes (Cardiff); C. Williams (Swansea), A. J. Phillips (Cardiff), G. Price (Pontypool), A. J. Martin (Aberavon), G. A. D. Wheel (Swansea), P. Ringer (Llanelli), J. Squire (Pontypool, capt.), E. T. Butler (Pontypool). Sent off: P. Ringer, 15 min.

Referee D. Burnett (Ireland).

On the same afternoon Scotland beat France 22–14 at Murrayfield.

Wales 17 pts Scotland 6 *Cardiff, 1 March 1980*

Wales still appeared to be suffering from a kind of moral hangover when they met Scotland on St. David's Day and in front of the Prince of Wales. It was as if they had sworn off the hard stuff, and they leant so far backwards not to offend that they toppled into a slough of conformity. Their win was substantial – a goal, two tries and a penalty to a goal – but it all added up to a bloodless and unreal afternoon's rugby.

Scotland, as it turned out, were not the least threatening either, and without difficulty Wales maintained an unbeaten championship record at Cardiff which stretched back through twenty-five games to the winter of 1968.

The Scots later said that they were almost unnerved by the Welsh lack of aggression in the lineouts, and they were able to win these 24–18. Another Welsh problem was their feed at the base of the scrum, where Holmes rarely got the ball quickly or cleanly enough to set up attacks with any real urgency. In fact if Scotland had developed more drive, the Welsh were there to be taken. But the Scots, too, had their handicaps, which included three team changes, the loss of Laidlaw through injury during the game, and Irvine's erratic failure with his place-kicks until the very end.

If there was one man who came out of the game with a totally enhanced reputation it was David Richards. In the second half he moved from centre to stand-off in place of Gareth Davies, who had damaged a hamstring, with Peter Morgan coming on at centre to win his first cap. There Richards played with marvellous self-assurance, rounding off the display with the last and best Welsh try. He took Holmes's pass from the ruck, bolted back to the blind side, and ripped through the defence to give Blyth his one conversion.

By then Wales were out of any conceivable danger. After only ten minutes Fenwick had put them ahead with a thirty-five-yard penalty goal, and again before the interval, Holmes ran in after chipping ahead for Rees who returned the ball to its donor. In the second half the ball was spun left to bring a try for Keen, and after Richards's effort Wales were a clear seventeen points up. Only then Renwick's try and Irvine's death-bed conversion filled the blank space against Scotland's name.

Scorers WALES – tries: Holmes, Keen, Richards; conversion: Blyth; penalty goal: Fenwick. SCOTLAND – try: Renwick; conversion: Irvine.

Wales W. R. Blyth (Swansea); H. E. Rees (Neath), D. S. Richards (Swansea), S. P. Fenwick (Bridgend), L. Keen (Aberavon); W. G. Davies (Cardiff), T. D. Holmes (Cardiff); C. Williams (Swansea), A. J. Phillips (Cardiff), G. Price (Pontypool), A. J. Martin (Aberavon), G. A. D. Wheel (Swansea), S. M. Lane (Cardiff), J. Squire (Pontypool, capt.), E. T. Butcher (Pontypool). Replacement: P. Morgan (Llanelli) for W. G. Davies, 36 min.

Scotland A. R. Irvine (Heriot's F.P.); K. Robertson (Melrose), J. M. Renwick (Hawick), D. L. Johnston (Watsonians), B. H. Hay (Boroughmuir); B. M. Gossman (West of Scotland), R. J. Laidlaw (Jedforest); J. N. Burnett (Heriot's F.P.), K. G. Lawrie (Gala), N. A. Rowan (Boroughmuir), A. J. Tomes (Hawick), D. Gray (West of Scotland), M. A. Biggar (London Scottish, capt.), J. R. Beattie (Glasgow Academicals), G. Dickson (Gala). Replacement: A. J. M. Lawson (Heriot's F.P.) for R. J. Laidlaw, 28 min.

Referee L. M. Prideaux (England).

On the same afternoon France beat Ireland 19–18 at Parc des Princes.

Ireland 21 pts Wales 7 *Lansdowne Road, 15 March 1980*

If Wales had managed to pull the fat from the fire against Scotland, they were engulfed by the flames when they went to Dublin for their final match. This was not only Ireland's first win over Wales for a decade, it was a thorough destruction of their favourite enemies. They scored three goals and a penalty goal to a try and a penalty, and it might, even then, have been worse for Wales if McNaughton hadn't once knocked on as he reached the Welsh line.

Until late in the game Keane and Foley outplayed Martin and Wheel in the middle of the lineout. In the scrums the Irish wheeled on the Welsh strike so that, at best, Holmes could only scramble the ball away. From lineout and loose, Keane, Orr, Spring and O'Driscoll, with Slattery always in attendance, came charging through to give Morgan, selected for the first time at stand-off, a painful afternoon of defence. And behind the scrum, the excellent Irish halves, Patterson and Campbell, ensured that by playing the ball for their forwards to move on to, the Irish pressure never relaxed.

If ever Quinnell had been needed it was at this hour, to snap Wales out of their mourning, if that's what it was, and to stiffen and direct their resistance. But this was something that the Lions selectors seemed to appreciate better than the Welsh. As it was, the pack lacked all fire and the Welsh were reduced to attacking from poor possession, which only compounded their problems.

Fenwick gave them a good start with a magnificent penalty from near the half-way line, but those three points were soon overwhelmed as, from surging Irish forward play and forced errors by the Welsh, Irwin, O'Driscoll and Fitzgerald made their way across the line.

It was not until the last few minutes that Wales scored once again, Blyth coming in on the burst to take Morgan's pass behind the scrum and career over for a try. To a side with such high expectations of success, it was about as much consolation as a cup of tea. And as a final sign that times had changed so drastically in only eight weeks, it was an Irishman who was making the record today. Ollie Campbell, by scoring nine points, had brought his championship total to forty-six, eight more than another Irishman, Tony Ward, the Englishman, Roger Hosen, and, of course, two Welsh stars of the past twelve years, Phil Bennett and Steve Fenwick.

Scorers IRELAND – tries: Irwin, O'Driscoll, Fitzgerald; conversions: Campbell 3; penalty goal: Campbell. WALES – try: Blyth; penalty goal: Fenwick.

Ireland R. C. O'Donnell (St Mary's College); T. J. Kennedy (St Mary's College), D. Irwin (Queen's University), P. P. McNaughton (Greystones), J. J. Moloney (St Mary's College); S. O. Campbell (Old Belvedere), C. S. Patterson (Instonians); P. A. Orr (Old Wesley), C. F. Fitzgerald (St Mary's College), M. P. Fitzpatrick (Wanderers), M. I. Keane (Lansdowne), B. O. Foley (Shannon), J. B. O'Driscoll (London Irish), J. F. Slattery (Blackrock College, capt.), D. E. Spring (Dublin University).

Wales W. R. Blyth (Swansea); H. E. Rees (Neath), D. S. Richards (Swansea), S. P. Fenwick (Bridgend), L. Keen (Aberavon); P. Morgan (Llanelli), T. D. Holmes (Cardiff); C. Williams (Swansea), A. J. Phillips (Cardiff), G. Price (Pontypool), A. J. Martin (Aberavon), G. A. D. Wheel (Swansea), S. M. Lane (Cardiff), J. Squire (Pontypool, capt.), E. T. Butler (Pontypool).

Referee L. M. Prideaux (England).

On the same afternoon England beat Scotland 30–18 at Murrayfield to complete their eighth grand slam.

Championship Table 1980

	P	W	D	L	For	Ag	Pts
England	4	4	0	0	80	48	8
Ireland	4	2	0	2	70	65	4
Wales	4	2	0	2	50	45	4
France	4	1	0	3	55	75	2
Scotland	4	1	0	3	61	83	2

Lions party to South Africa

In Edinburgh on the weekend after the final championship match, the players for the British Lions' summer tour of South Africa were selected. Fairly, and almost inevitably, Billy Beaumont, who had led the England grand slam side, was picked as captain. But to some surprise twelve Welsh players were numbered among the party compared with eight English, five Irish and five Scots. Two of the Welshmen, Derek Quinnell and Ray Gravell, had not even played during the season's championship. Another of them – Peter Morgan, a utility back – had been selected only once, as stand-off against Ireland, although he had also played in the centre as a replacement, and at full-back in the unofficial test with Romania. The remaining Welshmen chosen were Price, Williams, Phillips, Martin, Squire and Lane in the pack, Holmes and Davies at half-back, and Richards at stand-off or centre. A two-month tour, and after that scarcely a six-weeks' break before the Welsh centenary season began. The international pressure was building up once again.

Indexes

General Index

Index

of Internationals, Test Matches, and other matches